AF386452

TRAILBLAZING
MEDIEVAL
WOMEN

TRAILBLAZING MEDIEVAL WOMEN

ASHLEY SARAH FIRTH

PEN & SWORD HISTORY

AN IMPRINT OF PEN & SWORD BOOKS LTD.
YORKSHIRE - PHILADELPHIA

First published in Great Britain in 2026 by
PEN AND SWORD HISTORY
An imprint of
Pen & Sword Books Ltd
Yorkshire – Philadelphia

Typeset in Times New Roman 10/13 by
SJmagic DESIGN SERVICES, India.
Printed and bound in the UK by CPI Group (UK) Ltd.

The Publisher's authorised representative in the EU for product safety is
Authorised Rep Compliance Ltd., Ground Floor, 71 Lower Baggot Street,
Dublin D02 P593, Ireland.
www.arccompliance.com

For a complete list of Pen & Sword titles please contact
PEN & SWORD BOOKS LIMITED
George House, Units 12 & 13, Beevor Street, Off Pontefract Road,
Barnsley, South Yorkshire, S71 1HN, England
E-mail: enquiries@pen-and-sword.co.uk
Website: www.pen-and-sword.co.uk

or

PEN AND SWORD BOOKS
1950 Lawrence Rd, Havertown, PA 19083, USA
E-mail: uspen-and-sword@casematepublishers.com
Website: www.penandswordbooks.com

Contents

List of Illustrations

1. Statue of King Alfred the Great, Winchester (1901). (*Photograph: Ashley Firth*)

2. Æthelflæd Monument in Tamworth Castle Grounds (1913). (*Photograph: Ashley Firth*)

3. Statue of Æthelflæd, near Tamworth Railway Station (2018). (*Photograph: Ashley Firth*)

4. The ruins of St Oswald's Priory, Gloucester. (*Photograph: Ashley Firth*)

5. A page from the *Anglo-Saxon Chronicle*. (*Public domain via Wikimedia Commons*)

6. Queen Emma and her sons being received by Duke Richard II of Normandy. (*Cambridge University Library, Ee.3.59: fol. 4v; public domain via Wikimedia Commons*)

7. *The Ordeal of Queen Emma*, by William Blake. (*Public domain via Wikimedia Commons*)

8. 'God Begot House', reportedly the former home of Emma of Normandy. (*Photograph: Ashley Firth*)

9. Emma receiving the *Encomium* – illumination from *Encomium Emmae Reginae*. (*Public domain via Wikimedia Commons*)

10. Winchester Cathedral, burial place of Emma of Normandy. (*Photograph: Ashley Firth*)

11. Empress Matilda, depicted at the crowning of her granddaughter as Duchess of Saxony. (*Public domain via Wikimedia Commons*)

12. Wedding of Louis VII and Eleanor of Aquitaine. (*Chantilly, Bibliothèque du château, 0867 (0324), f. 121r; public domain via Wikimedia Commons*)

13. The ruins of Old Sarum. (*Photograph: Ashley Firth*)

14. Isabella of France and her son, Prince Edward paying homage to Charles IV. (*Public domain via Wikimedia Commons*)

15. Isabella of France. (*Public domain via Wikimedia Commons*)

16. Signature of Matilda of Tuscany. (*Public domain via Wikimedia Commons*)

17. Matilda and Hugh of Cluny interceding for Henry IV. (*Public domain via Wikimedia Commons*)

Acknowledgements

My first thanks must go to my publisher, Pen & Sword, and in particular to Sarah-Beth Watkins for affording me the opportunity to create this book.

I would also like to thank my 'History Mother', Professor Katherine Lewis, for her inspiration and mentoring over the years. I am extremely lucky to have so many wonderful historians in my life who have helped to make me into the historian I am today. A special thanks must go to my many long-suffering friends who have little or no interest in History yet have endured my ceaseless conversations about the women in this book. In particular, Claire (my cheerleader), Sam, Deb, Francesca, and Jo, who unknowingly provided much-welcomed distractions from mounds of papers on several occasions.

As always, my ultimate thanks go to my wonderful family. 'For we put the thought of all that we love into all that we make.' To my Great-Auntie Sheila, Maria, Morgan, Adele, Kenzie, Teddy, Sam, my brother, Michael and especially to my Mum, Teresa, the best mother in the world, for her unwavering support and love. And to my deceased grandparents, Pat and Bernard, for their care and devotion. My husband, Brian, as always, has encouraged me throughout this journey, and I thank him for his exemplary listening skills in innumerable one-way conversations. My daughters, Kerri and Aurelia, remain my motivation in life, and my greatest thanks go to them for their patience and love.

Thank you to the women featured in this book for the examples they left to us, those who have gone before us and those yet to come. May those yet to come continue to preserve the memory of these most remarkable women.

Introduction

As portrayed in *SIX The Musical*, Catherine Parr asks if anyone knows the names of the wives of Henry VI or Henry VII. The other five of Henry VIII's wives are unable to name them. In a conversation that followed, I asked my companions to the theatre if they knew the names of these women, or indeed any other English consorts aside from those married to Henry VIII. The silence that followed revealed a broader historical amnesia: many medieval queens and consorts remain overshadowed by the more widely known women of the early modern period. This is indicative of a general unfamiliarity with medieval women, whose stories are often left untold in favour of the male experience. Yet in recent years, we have witnessed the introduction of some women who feature in this book into popular culture. Æthelflæd became a central figure in the book and TV series *The Last Kingdom*. Although many elements of her story are largely fictional, Æthelflæd has been introduced to a much broader audience beyond the pages of academia. More recently, Emma of Normandy appeared as a strong, formidable queen in the TV series *Vikings: Valhalla,* prompting interest in her story. Elizabeth Woodville has been an object of fascination for decades, but her counterparts in the Wars of the Roses, Margaret of Anjou and Elizabeth of York, Elizabeth Woodville's daughter, are the unnamed wives of Henry VI and Henry VII alluded to above.

This book explores the lives of both familiar and lesser-known medieval women, each one of whom shaped history through their extraordinary deeds. There is a focus on royal and aristocratic women, with the exception of Margery Kempe and Joan of Arc. This emphasis reflects the greater availability of surviving source material for elite women, particularly queens, compared to other groups of women in the Middle Ages. The book is organised into four sections: *Women Who Ruled, Women Who Fought, Women Who Wrote,* and *Women of the Wars of the Roses*. These categories are not intended to reduce their lives to a single function, for some women could be assigned to multiple categories. First, it is necessary to establish ideologies surrounding women and expectations of female behaviour in the Middle Ages.

Ideas regarding medieval attitudes towards women originated in the Bible and were developed by Classical and later authors. When we speak of authors or chroniclers, almost all of them were men, and most of them were monks.

They often portrayed women as temptresses whose sexuality threatened male celibacy, undoubtedly a reflection of their own anxieties. And so overall, medieval women were categorised as lustful, irrational creatures who posed a dangerous threat to men and their masculinity. Due to perceived insatiable lust, women were deemed incapable of rational thought and were thus to be placed under the control of men. However, theory does not necessarily equate to practice, and there were exceptions to this rule.

Women were considered to be weak, motivated by lust and therefore unsuitable for rulership, but there was an acknowledgement that on occasion, women could abandon the weakness of their sex and take on manly characteristics that rendered them capable of ruling. But such women were understood to be exceptions to the rule. Even among women, the consensus in the Middle Ages upheld male authority in both governance and domestic life. Although we have no way of knowing an individual's thoughts and feelings, there is little evidence of widespread calls for women's emancipation from the patriarchal structures. Though some women did, indeed, act outside of the gender hierarchy.

Most (although not all) medieval queens became queens by marriage rather than succession. As historian Theresa Earenfight notes, queens usually require a qualifying adjective: 'She was a queen-consort when she married a king, a queen-mother when she bore his children, a queen-regent when she governed for or with her husband'.[1] Queen consorts were confined to a genealogical vocation. In theory, they were passive yet indispensable. Although their legal status was second to that of the king, a queen consort was an essential part of the monarchy because, without her, the dynasty could not continue.[2] Although their public office was limited, confined by the limitations of their gender, a queen could exercise indirect public power by interceding with the king on important political matters and tempering the king's wrath, ensuring he enforced justice, providing him with counsel, and helping the oppressed. This was a widely accepted queenly role in the Middle Ages.[3] As the king's bed mate, the queen had a proximity to her husband which could render her the most frequent and effective of intercessors. Through her access to the king, the queen acquired political authority and influence within the kingdom. If a queen's access to her husband in this regard was limited and a king refused to share his wife's bed, this was considered problematic and a limit on her royal authority. The queen consort had to strike the correct balance when exerting this indirect power; if she was deemed to be too assertive, or if the king appeared to be weak, criticism could be levelled at the queen for disturbing the gender and political order and thus endangering the kingdom. Yet despite misogynistic attitudes in the Middle Ages, the queen's political role was necessary and significant. She was conceived as the feminine aspect of rulership, the complement of her husband's masculine qualities, and therefore an integral component of monarchy.[4]

x

Being a mother was politically advantageous for queens, as they could often wield more authority as widows and mothers to the succeeding king than as wives to the king.[5] We see several women exerting considerable political influence in this conventional capacity, indicating why it was advantageous for consorts to further the interests of their sons at all costs. Often, this required a woman to defy gender boundaries and expectations and take on masculine traits.

Engagement in the military sphere offered women a further means of challenging conventional gender ideologies. As warfare was considered an inherently masculine domain, women who took up arms had to be portrayed as adopting masculine virtues such as strength and courage. This tactic became a way of explaining how women, supposedly inferior to men in every respect, could possibly come to play an active and effective part in military activities in exceptional circumstances.[6] Women who participated in warfare were sometimes referred to by contemporaries as a *virago*. This term had positive and negative associations; consequently, the author could use the term *virago* to praise a woman whom he considered to have acted in a just cause, for example, in defence of the Church, or to criticise her for stepping out of bounds.

All of the women featured in this book challenged conventional medieval notions of gender and are noted for their impact on the history of women. Æthelflæd's contribution to the establishment of England cannot be overstated. Successfully ruling, firstly on behalf of her husband and then in her own right, she made a significant contribution to pushing back the Vikings and enabling the creation of a unified English kingdom. Emma of Normandy, the only woman to have been a queen consort of England on two separate occasions, was an astute politician and survivor. Her second husband and her sons benefited from her political experience. The first succession of a female ruler in post-conquest England proved to be unsuccessful, but Empress Matilda was nevertheless a force to be reckoned with, and her pivotal position within the English monarchy ultimately secured her father's dynasty. Her daughter-in-law, Eleanor of Aquitaine, was one of the richest medieval women, and her political intrigues saw her imprisoned by her second husband. Isabella of France was the first woman in English history to have successfully overthrown an anointed king, and despite her efforts to further the interests of her son, she has been tarnished as a tyrant and a 'She-wolf'.

We find women such as Joan of Arc, Matilda of Tuscany and Sikelgaita publicly rejecting perceived feminine attributes, such as fragility and fear, performing the roles of generals or captains, and directly participating in military activities. Although it is debatable whether or not they actually engaged in hand-to-hand combat, these women nonetheless undertook military responsibilities and exercised influence in a domain traditionally monopolised by men.

There is a popular perception that few women could read and/or write in the Middle Ages. This book hopes to dispel that myth by illustrating how it was permissible for women with access to education to be taught literary skills and often encouraged in their literary pursuits. Some women were successful and renowned authors. Anna Comnena has earned praise as one of the first female historians of the medieval period, and her epic biography of her father gives us a rare insight into Byzantine politics from the perspective of a woman. Christine de Pizan is recognised to be the first woman to make a career as an author, and like Anna Comnena, Christine is a political commentator offering a contemporary account of events in fourteenth and fifteenth-century France. Margery Kempe has attracted significant attention as an outspoken woman who was questioned by the Church on several occasions for her unconventional piety and had her life committed to paper.

The women of the Wars of the Roses furthered the interests of their husbands and/or children during one of the most tumultuous times in English history. Refusing to abandon her husband and then her son's claims to the throne, Margaret of Anjou was given the epithet 'She-wolf of France' by Shakespeare, and her chapter within this book aims to challenge some of the enduring negative portrayals of Margaret that have prevailed throughout the centuries. Elizabeth Woodville was likewise a devoted mother, but her familial background provided the pretext for criticism of her as the consort of King Edward IV. The establishment of the Tudor dynasty would not have been possible without the energetic efforts of Margaret Beaufort, whose relentless pursuit of her son's interests marks her as one of the most remarkable women in history. Margaret's plans for a Tudor dynasty could only be realised with the assistance of Elizabeth of York, who lent legitimacy to Henry Tudor's kingship, and the children she bore helped stabilise the kingdom.

Many of these women have been overshadowed by the deeds of their male counterparts, or their narratives have been unfairly shaped by the prejudices of those who told their stories. Their stories can only be analysed with an appreciation of the complexities of medieval attitudes to women. Their individual contributions to the history of women and broader historical narratives cannot be overstated.

Women Who Ruled

Chapter 1

Æthelflæd (*c*.870–918)

> O mighty Æthelflæd! O virgin, the dread of men, conqueror of nature,
> worthy of a man's name! Nature made you a girl, so you would be
> more illustrious; your prowess made you acquire the name of man.
> For you alone it is right to change the name of your sex: you were a
> mighty queen and a king who won victories. Even Caesar's triumphs
> did not bring such great rewards. Virgin heroine, more illustrious
> than Caesar, farewell.[1]

So, Henry of Huntingdon, writing in the twelfth century, some two centuries after her death, described Æthelflæd, Lady of the Mercians. Henry depicted Æthelflæd as not only a queen, but also a king whose victories were equal to those of the mighty Caesar. The author adds an interesting detail – that God created her as a woman to make her achievements all the more remarkable. Æthelflæd abandoned the limitations of her sex and embraced and performed roles traditionally reserved for men. Æthelflæd's sex did not hinder her success; rather, it enhanced it and rendered her more praiseworthy. Æthelflæd holds a special status as the first example we have in English history of a woman ruling in her own right, and following her death, she is the first example to be found of a woman handing power to another woman (her daughter).

Æthelflæd's exceptional position within Anglo-Saxon politics made her noteworthy among her contemporaries, and she appears as a prominent character in a set of annals called the *Mercian Register.* Indeed, Æthelflæd may have been the impetus behind their composition, and as such, they are often called the *Annals of Æthelflæd,* written contemporaneously with her life and reign, and completed shortly after her death (902–924). The *Mercian Register* was later inserted into a collection of annals, known as the *Anglo-Saxon Chronicle,* which began at the behest of Æthelflæd's father, Alfred the Great (*c*.849–899) at his court of Wessex. Despite the *Anglo-Saxon Chronicle's* efforts to portray the rulers of Wessex, namely Alfred and his son, Edward the Elder, as the only rulers to present a substantial and successful challenge to the Vikings in what would become England, historical evidence substantiates the significant contributions of Æthelflæd and the Mercians to this resistance. Æthelflæd was instrumental in not only pushing back the Vikings but also furthering urbanisation and organising the Anglo-Saxon defence through the creation of burhs (fortified towns).

Æthelflæd was born around 870, the eldest child of an illustrious marriage between Alfred the Great and Ælswith (d. 902). Asser, Alfred's biographer, from whom we have much of our information regarding Alfred, the man, fails to name Ælswith, although interestingly, he names her mother, Eadburh 'a notable woman' and identifies her as born of the royal Mercian line.[2] Ælswith's father, Æthelred, was likewise named in the account as the Earl of the Gaini.[3] Perhaps the omission of Ælswith's name reflected her lack of standing within Alfred's court and perhaps for Asser, she as a person was irrelevant; what mattered was her genealogy.[4] The marriage between Alfred and Ælswith, celebrated in 868, was a prestigious one aimed at uniting the West Saxon kingdom of Alfred with Mercia, that of his bride. Æthelflæd was joined by two brothers, Edward the Elder (d. 924) and Æthelweard (d. 922) and two sisters Æthelgifu, Abbess of Shaftesbury (d. *c.*899), Ælfthryth, Countess of Flanders (d. 929).

The youngest of five sons, Alfred was not destined for kingship, but following the deaths of his elder brothers, the throne passed to him in 871 and he became King of the West Saxons, or King of Wessex. In 866, the Great Viking army arrived in England, and by the end of the ninth century, the only remaining Anglo-Saxon kingdom to have survived decades of Viking attacks intact was Wessex. The eastern part of Mercia fell to the Vikings in 877, and the Vikings held the southern part of Northumbria. East Anglia was completely absorbed into the Viking-held territory known as the Danelaw. Turning their attention to Wessex, Alfred faced this formidable foe with incredible courage and resilience and refused to entertain the notion of the very real possibility that he might, in fact, be the last ruler of his kingdom.[5]

Æthelflæd may have experienced first-hand the intense pressure her father was under when she was a child in 878, aged around 8 or 9. Since Alfred was said to have taken his wife and household with him, Æthelflæd may have been with her father when he found himself surrounded by the Vikings at Athelney, in the Somerset marches.[6] From there, he escaped in disguise and was offered shelter by a peasant woman. Pondering his next move against the relentless Viking foe, the woman chastised Alfred for failing to mind her cakes left on the fire, before he earned the epithet 'Great' in defeating the Vikings at Edington and halting their expansion. Alfred was able to expand his own borders beyond Wessex at the expense of the Vikings, and a significant victory came in 886 when he captured London, an important Viking stronghold. From this time on, Alfred styled himself *King of the Anglo-Saxons,* thereby claiming jurisdiction over all Anglo-Saxons in England, even those living under Viking rule. Alfred envisaged a united Anglo-Saxon people presenting a united front to the Vikings under one king, and he sought to realise his vision not just through military victories but also through Church and legal reform, the compiling of a shared history and town planning.[7]

Little is known about Æthelflæd's early years, as is true for her male counterparts in this period. The date of her birth, and details regarding her childhood and eventual marriage negotiations are left for historians to speculate.[8] Asser arrived at Alfred's court after her marriage, and so his silence on her upbringing may be due to his lack of knowledge rather than a lack of interest. Alfred placed great emphasis on the importance of education and even initiated educational reform within his kingdom. Indeed, education was part of Alfred's ambition to create a unified England based upon the development of the English language and providing access to literary texts in the vernacular. Understanding the significance of the written word, Alfred translated several texts himself from Latin into Old English, thus making them more accessible to his subjects. It is inconceivable to assume that this emphasis on learning and the written word did not extend to his children and, in particular, to his eldest daughter, Æthelflæd. We know that Alfred did not prohibit his daughters from gaining an education, for Asser tells us: 'Edward and Ælfthryth were at all times fostered at the royal court under the solicitous care of tutors and nurses'.[9] This may then suggest that Æthelflæd and her remaining siblings were raised and educated elsewhere. It is plausible then that Æthelflæd may have been raised or at least spent a substantial portion of her childhood in Mercia, in her mother's homeland and her paternal aunt's court, in preparation for her eventual role at the Mercian court.[10]

Alfred's vision of a united Anglo-Saxon kingdom informed his decision in selecting a groom for Æthelflæd. Consequently, in around 887, Æthelflæd married the Mercian ealdorman and ruler, Æthelred, probably around the age of 16, while he was probably significantly older.[11] The Mercian king, Ceowulf, disappears from the historical record in 879 and is presumed to have died or been removed from power. Mercia then passed into the hands of Ealdorman Æthelred, and from around 883, Æthelred had ruled Mercia under the overlordship of Alfred.[12] The Latin sources refer to Æthelred as *Dux,* which had military overtones, whereas the *Anglo-Saxon Chronicle* and other Wessex sources described him as an ealdorman. Whatever term is used to define him, we are discussing the same role, essentially the ruler of Mercia.[13] Evidently a trusted ally of Alfred, he was responsible for the fortification of London in 886 and to demonstrate their friendship, Alfred presented Æthelred with an incredibly expensive sword.[14] Indeed, the marriage may have taken place within the context of a strengthened alliance between Wessex and Mercia, an element of which was Alfred's grant of control of London to his new son-in-law.[15]

This marriage drew these two Anglo-Saxon kingdoms closer and continued a pattern of royal marriages between Wessex and Mercia spanning throughout the ninth century, which included the union of Æthelflæd's parents.[16] The unity of Wessex and Mercia was evidently considered an essential component of

Anglo-Saxon survival, and as a Wessex princess with a blood claim to Mercia through her mother, Alfred must have imagined his daughter enjoying a special status and the key to the unification of both kingdoms. Her offspring, preferably sons (should she have them), would play crucial roles in uniting the Anglo-Saxon kingdoms into one unified conglomerate against the Vikings. However, Æthelflæd and Æthelred did not bear sons, but a daughter, named Ælfwynn, born probably shortly after their marriage. It remains unknown whether the couple bore any additional children who did not survive into adulthood, and nothing is known of the personal relationship the couple shared. The couple gave generous religious grants throughout Mercia and jointly founded the abbey of St Oswald (a warrior saint) in Gloucester in 909. Indeed, Gloucester appears to have held special significance for the couple, perhaps indicative of Æthelred's roots.[17]

William of Malmesbury, writing some century and a half after her death, suggested that following the birth of Ælfwynn, Æthelflæd became extremely sick. This illness, combined with her youth, may account for her absence in the Mercian charters in the late 880s. However, in the 890s, Æthelflæd becomes more visible, likely due to her maturity, and as she grew into a political role she could enjoy as a woman in Mercia, which had been barred to her as a Wessex princess.[18] Indeed, marrying into Mercia did much for Æthelflæd's political career; royal women in Wessex had little political power, whereas Wessex women who married into Mercia and other Anglo-Saxon kingdoms had the opportunity to be politically active.[19] Æthelflæd's paternal aunt, Æthelswith, the wife of Burgred of Mercia can be found as a prominent witness in her husband's charters and was referred to as 'queen' by the *Anglo-Saxon Chronicle*.[20]

In comparison, as noted above, Æthelflæd's mother, Ælswith, a Mercian woman who married into the kingdom of Wessex, is not even named in her husband's biography, and like many of her predecessors, is unnamed in the sources and fails to appear in the charter evidence. This long tradition of excluding royal women from a position at the court of Wessex prompted Charles the Bald (823–877) to consecrate his daughter, Judith (d. 870), before she departed West Francia for Wessex to marry Alfred's father and become stepmother to Alfred. But even her time there as wife firstly to Æthelwulf (856–858) and then to his son, Æthelbald (858–860), albeit a short career, has left little evidence of her activities at the West Saxon court.[21] The wife of the king of Wessex was not even referred to as queen (even though by definition, this was her position). Asser offers the cautionary and largely fictional tale of Eadburh (d. 802), daughter of Offa, King of Mercia, to explain why Wessex did not have queens.[22] Eadburh married Beorhtric of Wessex and became a dominant and tyrannical presence at his court, eventually poisoning her husband and fleeing to the court of Charlemagne.[23] Although the story served to justify the succession of Alfred's grandfather to the throne of Wessex following Beorhtric's death, it also illuminated the weakness of women and justified the prevention of the attainment of political power for Wessex royal women. Unlike these royal women of Wessex, Æthelflæd appears to have been politically active from the 890s and was no mere passive consort in Mercia. The suggestion is that husband and wife ruled Mercia jointly.[24] Accepting Alfred as their overlord, Alfred in turn acknowledged his son-in-law and daughter as Lord and Lady of Mercia.[25]

In the *Mercian Register*, Æthelflæd was styled 'Lady of the Mercians' or *Myrcna hlæfdige* in Old English. This was the female equivalent of Æthelred's male title, Lord of the Mercians, or *hlaford*.[26] The word *hlæfdige* means bread-kneader, and the male equivalent, *hlaford*, translates as bread guardian.[27] These Old English titles, denoting positions of authority, reflect the evolution of Anglo-Saxon rulership from its roots in the household structure and offer a domesticated model of governance wherein the Lord oversees the provision of food and the Lady is responsible for its preparation. Within their gendered roles, the pair work in partnership to provide nourishment and sustenance for the population. Although Æthelflæd could hardly have been expected to actually make her own bread, the title offers an insight into the significant role of the Mercian Lady as the provider for her people and one who assumes responsibility for their welfare as their leader and ruler.[28] The Wessex sources fall short of referring to the couple as king or queen, but their activities are indicative of such a status, such as the minting of coins, the issuing of diplomas and the building of fortifications, all activities usually associated with kingship. However, other sources originating from neighbouring kingdoms, such as the *Welsh Annals* and the *Irish Annals*, do use the terms king and queen to describe Æthelflæd and her husband.[29] Together, Æthelflæd and Æthelred exercised most, if not all, of the powers of a king and queen, and Æthelflæd continued to enjoy such powers after her husband's death.[30]

Æthelflæd may have been influenced by the tradition of historical record-keeping in her father's kingdom to commission her own chronicle, known as the *Mercian Register*. Within this annal, we learn of Æthelflæd's deeds and those of her family (her own deeds are often absent from other contemporary chronicles, particularly those compiled in Wessex). Æthelflæd may have imported something of a literary culture to Mercia from Wessex and, like her father, appears to have been intent on leaving a lasting imprint on the kingdom over which she ruled.[31] Æthelflæd and Æthelred not only followed Alfred's literary policies but also became his closest military allies and shared in his ambition of pushing back the Vikings.

After Alfred's death in 899, Æthelflæd's brother, Edward the Elder, succeeded their father, and the Mercian couple worked closely with Edward to further Alfred's ambitions for a united Anglo-Saxon England and to expand this realm. Despite making substantial progress, at the time of Alfred's death, the Danelaw still comprised East Anglia, the southern part of Northumbria and much of the Midlands. Pushing north, the allies used the Roman technique of following a chain of fortifications, with the Mercians on the left flank and Edward on the right. The Mercians faced off against not only Vikings but also other foes, such as the Welsh, the Irish, the Scots and the Norse (Scandinavian settlers as opposed to Vikings who served in the Viking armies).[32] Æthelflæd and her husband rebuilt or reclaimed fourteen forts between 902 and 918, thereby securing Mercia and Wessex.[33] In keeping with her father's defence plan of creating burhs or strongholds throughout the kingdom, offering protection against the Vikings, Æthelflæd and Æthelred created an English burh at Gloucester between 881 and 889 with an additional burh constructed at Worcester in 889.[34] The pair rebuilt urban centres such as Worcester, Gloucester and Chester, fundamental to the success of the Wessex-Mercian alliance.[35]

From 902 until her death, the *Mercian Register* records Æthelflæd acting alone or closely with her brother, Edward, on military endeavours as Æthelred was incapacitated by an illness that would eventually lead to his death in 911.[36] It appears that Æthelflæd was working on behalf of her husband; we might understand this arrangement as Æthelflæd serving in the capacity of regent whilst Æthelred was incapable of ruling. An interesting interaction between the Norse people and Æthelflæd can be found in the *Annals of Ireland*. In 902, the Norse leader, Ingimund, had sought the permission of Æthelflæd to settle his people on lands close to Chester.[37] It is significant that the source describes Ingimund engaging in diplomacy not with Æthelred, Edward, or a male representative of Æthelflæd, but with Æthelflæd herself, identified in the annals as 'Queen of the Saxons'.[38] Æthelflæd agreed to Ingimund's request, and his people settled in the Wirral, likely forming a useful defence for Æthelflæd against their Viking cousins.[39] But fearing that peace between herself and the Norse would be short-lived, she began to restore Chester, embarking on an extensive building programme and brought her army to settle in the city. Through diplomacy, she also sought peace from the Scottish, Welsh and Irish. But as the city of Chester grew and became more and more prosperous, it became a tantalising lure for the Norse who made attempts on the city. The *Annals of Ireland* contains a colourful description of a skirmish at the city walls as the inhabitants of Chester threw 'down all the beehives in the town upon the besiegers, which prevented them from moving their hands or legs from the number of bees which stung them'.[40] The Norse siege of Chester, which began around 907, was ultimately repelled through Æthelflæd's strategic foresight and effective planning, enabling her to confront the Norse threat successfully and secure their expulsion from the region.[41] This victory was a watershed moment for the Lady of the Mercians. It seems her reputation as a courageous leader and brilliant strategist, the protector and defender of her people, acting alone without her husband, was created here.[42]

Chester was secure, and now with Æthelred remaining inactive, Æthelflæd joined her brother, Edward, and in 909 the pair launched an aggressive attack into Northumbria in Danelaw territory. Working together, they recovered the body of St Oswald (d. 642) from Lindsey and brought the relic to the abbey dedicated to the saint in Gloucester, built by Æthelflæd and Æthelred.[43] This incursion into Viking territory prompted a retaliatory response from the Danes as armies from Northumbria ravaged parts of Mercia.[44] In August 910, a Wessex-Mercian army faced the Vikings and claimed victory at the Battle of Tettenhall. The *Anglo-Saxon Chronicle* indicates that Edward was not present on this occasion; rather, he sent forces from Mercia and Wessex.[45] It is possible then that Æthelflæd led the Anglo-Saxon forces on this occasion, perhaps with the assistance of the Mercian ealdormen, albeit she is not named as doing so by the *Mercian Register* or the *Anglo-Saxon Chronicle*.[46] The victory was significant, and the *Anglo-Saxon Chronicle* noted the deaths of several Viking kings and noblemen.[47]

Æthelred's death in 911 transformed his wife's position from that of a regent into an independent ruler, as a regnant. Unlike her mother, who withdrew from public life following her husband's death, it is probable that Æthelflæd continued to enjoy the status of a junior in a partnership with her younger brother, Edward.[48] She apparently held all the qualities required for rulership, even if that position traditionally belonged to a man. The people of Mercia were evidently content with her rulership, and so was her brother, for Edward, as her overlord, could quite easily have replaced Æthelflæd as the ruler of Mercia with a man. Nevertheless, there is a suggestion that Edward needed to be convinced, or compensated for this arrangement, for the *Anglo-Saxon Chronicle* tells us that when Æthelred died, 'King Edward took over London and Oxford and all the lands which belonged thereto'.[49] These lands had been given to Æthelred by Alfred. Æthelflæd's exalted role in the Mercian kingdom was at odds with the perception of the capabilities of women in her brother's kingdom, her homeland, as discussed above. This divergence in notions of the role of women could explain Edward's receipt of Oxford and London as a form of reimbursement for the unusual situation in Mercia. It could also explain the events which were to unfold following Æthelflæd's death, as discussed below.

Æthelflæd, now ruling Mercia alone, with the approval of her brother, her overlord, continued to be styled as 'Lady of the Mercians'. The first known example in English history of a woman ruling a kingdom as regnant. With the dawn of Æthelflæd's sole rulership, brother and sister continued to co-operate, furthering their father's policy of driving back the Vikings. As Edward continued to push north along the eastern flank, Æthelflæd mirrored his actions on the western flank. The pair created a pincer movement, securing Mercian and Wessex lands and establishing new territories in previously held Viking territory such as East Anglia. A coordinated construction programme commenced with the building of burhs to secure Wessex and Mercia.[50] In 912, Æthelflæd constructed a burh at Bridgnorth and several others at an unlocated place referred to as *Scergeat* to hinder Viking crossings at the River Severn.[51] The following year, she constructed a burh at Stafford and fortified Tamworth. In 914, Æthelflæd can be found building a burh at

Eddisbury and another 100 miles south at Warwick, and in the following year, she further strengthened her northern defences with a burh at Runcorn.[52]

The sources give us a glimpse into Æthelflæd's activities that extended beyond military matters and reveal an interesting interaction with her neighbours in the Welsh kingdom of Brycheiniog. Brycheiniog was perhaps operating under the overlordship of Mercia. The incident involved the unnamed King of Brycheiniog and Abbot Ecgerht, on 16 June 916, the festival of St Quiricus, the Martyr's Day. Perhaps in highlighting this feast day of a child martyr, the author sought to emphasise the abbot's innocence.[53] The *Anglo-Saxon Chronicle* claimed the abbot:

> who had done nothing to deserve it, was slain together with his companions. Three days later, Æthelflæd sent an army into Wales and stormed Brecenanmere, and there captured the wife of the king and thirty-three other persons.[54]

This account is significant for several reasons. Firstly, this illustrates Æthelflæd acting independently of Edward, or indeed of any other male; she orders the retaliatory move for the insult to her in the murder of one who likely fell under her protection or was associated with her court. Secondly, this is a rare example of female rulers taking captives, and rarer still it stands as an example of one female capturing another in the medieval period.[55] The chronicle does not inform us if the king was present when the attack occurred, but in taking his wife and presumably members of her household or entourage, the king or a high-status delegate would be forced to enter Mercia to secure their release. This would be a very public performance, and Æthelflæd's objective for this display would be to ascertain public acknowledgement of Mercia's superior status to that of Brycheiniog.[56] Within this incident, we see diplomacy in action, and although we do not know the outcome of this hostage situation, it offers us a great insight into Æthelflæd's political activities and her formidable and vengeful character as experienced by her contemporaries.

The Vikings at Derby experienced something of her legendary spirit when the city fell to her in 917. Here she experienced personal loss rarely referred to in the *Anglo-Saxon Chronicle,* which records she lost 'four of her thegns, who were dear to her'.[57] However, despite suffering such losses, the capture of Derby was a significant step towards the unification of England, for Derby was one of the five Viking boroughs in the north-east Midlands bordering the north-east Mercian territory, and as the first of these boroughs to fall, more would swiftly follow.[58]

Building upon her success at Derby, Æthelflæd besieged the second of the 'Five Boroughs', Leicester, in 918, and the city reportedly fell to her 'by peaceful means; and the majority of the Danish forces that owed allegiance to it became subject to her'.[59] The *Anglo-Saxon Chronicle* is mute on why precisely the Vikings of Leicester submitted to Æthelflæd without a fight, perhaps we should assume that her reputation was sufficient.[60]

In the same year (918): 'The people of York had promised her to accept her rule, some of them engaged themselves to do so by pledge, others ratifying it with oaths'.[61] As was the case in Derby and Leicester, the Vikings in York submitted not to Edward, but to Æthelflæd. It was she who secured the surrender of these territories, but sadly, she would not live to see the fruits of her labours. Before Æthelflæd could see the surrender of York and the completion of her and her brother's project, the Lady of the Mercians died on 12 June 918 at Tamworth. Unfortunately, the sources are silent regarding the nature of her death. We are told that following her death, her body was transported some 100 miles from Tamworth to be buried alongside Æthelred in the minster at Gloucester that the couple had founded together.[62]

What followed was unprecedented. For the first time in English history, a woman succeeded another woman as Ælfwynn succeeded her mother as ruler of Mercia. The inhabitants of Mercia appear to have been content with this arrangement, and there is no record of any opposition to Ælfwynn's succession within her own kingdom. However, Ælfwynn's uncle, Edward, was seemingly unhappy. In 919, the *Mercian Register* notes that under Edward's orders, she was 'deprived of all authority in Mercia: she was taken to Wessex three weeks before Christmas'.[63] The tone of the *Mercian Register* suggests a degree of bitterness, likely reflecting the resentment of the Mercians at the perceived humiliation of their ruler, removed from power and supplanted by her overlord, Edward. Mercia had enjoyed a degree of autonomy, albeit answerable to an overlord, but crucially, the fact that the ruler of their kingdom was a woman had been inconsequential for almost two decades. Ælfwynn disappears from the historical record; she likely entered the religious life, as no mention of her marriage is recorded.[64]

We can speculate as to why Edward decided to remove Ælfwynn from power. By this point, Edward had adult sons, including his eldest son, Æthelstan (*c*.893–939), who needed to be provided for in terms of inheritance; this may have informed his decision. Once Edward took Mercia, it became enveloped into Wessex under Edward's rulership, thus paving the way for the unification of England. These factors undoubtedly played a part, but perhaps the most convincing theory for Edward's decision stemmed not in Wessex, but in Mercia. Æthelflæd was evidently a most capable woman who held the reins of power, initially as a regent for her husband and then as a ruler in her own right. Ælfwynn's name, alongside Æthelflæd's, appears among the witness list of charters in Princes Risborough (903/4), Worcester (904) and Weardburh (915).[65] Her presence tells us that Ælfwynn travelled with her mother on occasion and indicates that Æthelflæd was perhaps training her daughter for her eventual role as Mercian ruler.

But Ælfwynn may not have possessed those qualities required for rulership that her mother was imbued with. Edward seemingly had confidence in his sister;

however, Ælfwynn may have fallen short of Edward's expectations of a ruler and thus he made the decision to remove her from power. Edward was a seasoned ruler with a wealth of military experience, and Mercia had seen an explosion in territorial gains under Æthelflæd. Nevertheless, the Vikings were a continuing and ever-threatening presence within the British Isles. These factors may have contributed to the Mercian acceptance of the removal of their inexperienced ruler in favour of a more seasoned warrior, alongside whom they were accustomed to fighting.[66]

One of the ongoing scholarly debates concerning Æthelflæd centres on the extent of her involvement in warfare. Neither the *Anglo-Saxon Chronicle* nor the *Mercian Register* depict her donning armour or leading troops from the front. This suggests that her military involvement was limited to a leadership role exercised through strategy and command rather than through direct participation in hand-to-hand combat. An example of her reputation as an effective military commander appears in the *Irish Annals*. According to this later source, at the Second Battle of Corbridge in 918, Æthelflæd pursued a group of Vikings into a wooded area. When the enemy attempted to conceal themselves among the trees, the account records:

> The Queen ordered them [the soldiers under her command] to cut all the wood down with their swords and axes. And they did so accordingly. They first cut down the wood, and [afterwards] killed all the Pagans who were in the wood. In this manner did the Queen kill all the Pagans, so that her fame spread abroad in every direction.[67]

Although not contemporaneous, this account reflects the enduring posthumous reputation of Æthelflæd as an authoritative military leader. Twelfth-century sources, such as Henry of Huntingdon, upon whom much of our later understanding of Æthelflæd depends, praised her as a conqueror and implied that Æthelflæd was directing military operations. These portrayals indicate that she exercised authority as a strategist, possibly in collaboration with experienced military advisers such as the Mercian ealdormen, particularly after her husband's incapacitation and eventual death. While the role of women as military leaders in the medieval period was exceptional, it was not without precedent. Matilda of Tuscany and Sikelgaita similarly directed military operations.

There are several examples of women directing military activities in the early medieval period. For example, the *Anglo-Saxon Chronicle* contains a brief but tantalising note for the year 722: 'This year Queen Ethelburga destroyed Taunton, which Ina had formerly built'.[68] William of Malmesbury tells us that she was the wife of Ina, but little else is known of her and her activities, or indeed why she destroyed Taunton. Notably, the chronicles appear unconcerned with her sex, suggesting that female involvement in directing military affairs, while unusual, was not viewed as extraordinary.[69] Nevertheless, there is little evidence of such women taking up arms and fighting shoulder to shoulder with the seasoned warriors they commanded. Women probably only took up arms when circumstances required.

In 2018, a statue was unveiled in Tamworth as part of the celebrations in the town to mark 1100 years since Æthelflæd's death. The impressive 6-metre-high figure of Æthelflæd dons battlefield attire, shield on her back, she holds a sword in one hand and a spear in the other, pointing towards the town. This exciting way of representing Æthelflæd draws upon the image of the warrior queen so many of us are familiar with. And I should think Æthelflæd would be extremely pleased with how she has been depicted; she was a military leader and commander, a fearsome ruler with an impressive reputation, commanding respect in a male-dominated world.

A century earlier, Æthelflæd had been remembered in a slightly different way by the people of Tamworth. In a statue erected in 1913 in the grounds of Tamworth Castle, Æthelflæd appears holding a sword. But another figure appears beside her, upon whom she lovingly looks down. That figure is Æthelstan, her nephew, the eldest son of her brother, Edward. She tenderly embraces the boy and thus offers another dimension to Æthelflæd, as a maternal figure. Sword in hand, she was remembered as a warrior but also as a nurturing foster mother.

Æthelflæd is accorded many titles, one of which is 'Mother of England', indicative of her role as foster mother to Æthelstan. Following Edward's death in 924, Æthelstan was elected ruler of Mercia and his half-brother, Ælfweard, Edward's eldest son from his second marriage, was acknowledged as King of Wessex.[70] Ælfweard, swiftly followed his father to the grave in the same year and Æthelstan then assumed the rulership of Wessex, but not immediately. Æthelstan initially acted solely as a ruler and king of Mercia whilst he waited for the approval of the leading men of Wessex.[71] William of Malmesbury is the only source who tells us that Æthelstan was raised at the Mercian court; nevertheless, this is entirely plausible. If we consider the possibility that Æthelflæd herself spent a substantial amount of her childhood in the Mercian court, we might be witnessing a tradition of royal Wessex children receiving their education in this neighbouring kingdom. Æthelflæd was destined to rule Mercia, and perhaps when arrangements were made for Æthelstan's education in Mercia, his father may have envisaged a similar destiny for the boy. According to William of Malmesbury, Æthelstan joined his uncle, Æthelred, on campaign as soon as he was able to bear arms and later assisted Æthelflæd in her military endeavours.[72] Æthelstan may have spent much of his childhood at Æthelflæd's court to familiarise himself with the Mercian people and learn their traditions and customs. Æthelstan may have represented his father's interests at the Mercian court following Edward's seizure of power following the death of Æthelflæd.[73] He was presumably rather well acquainted with them, for they were the first to accept his kingship in 924. Possibly considered an outsider to the kingdom, he was not crowned king of Wessex until September 925.[74]

Æthelflæd's fostering of her nephew renders her an important part of his narrative. Æthelstan ruled over Mercia, Wessex and East Anglia, thanks to the efforts of his father and aunt, and throughout the course of his reign, through military means as well as diplomacy, he added Northumbria to his domains, making him the first king of England. No doubt some of his qualities as a successful ruler were acquired from his aunt's example. Æthelflæd's military endeavours in conjunction with her brother paved the way for Æthelstan's eventual unification of England. Æthelflæd, 'Mother of the English', could have left no greater legacy than this.

Æthelflæd stood out among her contemporaries as a successful ruler, imbued with leadership qualities, who presented a fearless stance against the Vikings, despite the limitations placed upon her because of her sex. She was partially responsible for the eventual unification of England, and it was through her actions as the ruler of Mercia that her nephew was eventually credited as the first king of the English. Æthelflæd embodied all the qualities required of rulership, including those of a great military tactician. We may have no evidence of her personally fighting in the thick of battle, but that does not in any way diminish her military achievements. Her title 'Lady' was later used by Empress Matilda from 1141, perhaps as a compromising way of assuring her authority without going as far as to call herself queen. Unlike Æthelflæd, Matilda failed to acquire the kingdom bequeathed to her, and such a feat would not again be accomplished until the coronation of Queen Mary I in 1553. Æthelflæd is remembered as a woman ahead of her time, a woman who challenged the conventional norms of her day and provides a fascinating glimpse into the tumultuous Anglo-Saxon past.

Chapter 2

Emma of Normandy (*c*.990–1052)

Early English queen consorts are often invisible. They infrequently appear in contemporary sources, and when they do, some are nameless. That is not true of Emma of Normandy, the only woman to have been queen of England on two separate occasions. She first married King Æthelred II (966–1016), known to history as the 'Unready'. This epithet is a misinterpretation of the Old English *unræd*, which more precisely means 'poor counsel', a deliberate pun on Æthelred's given name, meaning 'noble counsel', thus highlighting the perceived contradiction between his name and the quality of his rule.[1] Æthelred is remembered as a poor king who failed to halt the Viking attacks and, under his watch, the Danes completed their conquest of England (1016). However, the context of his difficulties is often overlooked.[2] Emma then married Æthelred's replacement, the Danish invader, Cnut (994–1035). Emma is largely visible to us as she commissioned the *Encomium Emmae Reginae* 'In Praise of Queen Emma' (hereafter referred to as the *Encomium*).[3] An unknown ecclesiast authored the text, but Emma herself was the chief source of information. Although dismissed by some historians as a piece of propaganda, the *Encomium* remains a valuable source, offering insight into how Emma wished to shape her legacy and represent her political agency.

Emma was the daughter of Richard I of Normandy (932–996), making her the granddaughter of William Longsword (d. 942) and the great-granddaughter of the renowned Viking Rollo (d. 930), the first ruler of Normandy. Emma's mother was Gunnor, Richard's second wife, and together they had a total of eight children.[4] Gunnor was of Danish origin and a seemingly formidable woman in her own right. Richard died in 996, and Gunnor survived him by around thirty years. As a widow, she witnessed charters and likely had a hand in the prosperous marriages of her three daughters. Significantly, Gunnor was a joint commissioner of Dudo's panegyric work *History of the Normans,* which painted her husband and his forebears in a glowing light.[5] Although we do not know how much time Emma spent with her mother throughout her childhood, Gunnor was a politically powerful woman in her widowhood and undoubtedly offered lessons that Emma would use in her later life.[6]

Richard I was succeeded in 996 by his son, Richard II, thus making Emma the sister of the Duke of Normandy as she approached her teens and a desirable bride for any ruler. Through marriage, Richard II used his siblings to create a network of powerful allies. Æthelred had several sons with his first wife, and so the need to reproduce sons was not a driving factor behind this marriage. Rather, Æthelred sought an alliance with Normandy to halt the ceaseless Viking attacks on English shores. Æthelred is traditionally remembered as the king who adopted a policy of paying tribute to the Vikings, a strategy that ultimately failed and even encouraged continued raids. His marriage to Emma signals a policy change. This union was forged to create a strong alliance with Normandy, whose Viking heritage and sympathies often led them to shelter their Scandinavian cousins, thereby creating a base from which to attack English shores. A treaty, ratified by the Pope, had been made with England by Emma's father in 991, but this pact did not cease Viking attacks. Richard II broke this treaty in 1000 by allowing a Viking fleet into Normandy. It was clear that a new, much stronger treaty was required if Æthelred was to halt the Viking attacks and in 1002, he married Emma.[7]

We cannot be certain of Emma's age at the time of her wedding. But if we assume that Emma was no younger than 12 years of age upon her marriage to Æthelred in 1002, the canonical minimum age for a girl, we can date her birth to before the year 990.[8] Anglo-Saxon kings tended to marry the daughters of the nobility from within their kingdom, and Emma's arrival marked the first significant French influence on the Anglo-Saxon court to have a profound effect on the destiny of the English monarchy.[9] Before Emma arrived in England in 1002, the last foreign bride to marry an English king was Judith, daughter of Charles the Bald, the Carolingian king. Judith could count amongst her stepchildren the future King Alfred the Great. She wed Æthelwulf of Wessex in 856 when she was 12 years old and although she was crowned queen, she found no political position for herself at the court of Wessex.[10]

Often, royal brides were much younger than their husbands, especially if this was the bride's first marriage. Serial monogamy was common in the early medieval period, and it was not uncommon for kings to dismiss previous wives in favour of a new alliance and a new marriage. Like her mother and Judith, Emma was a second wife. Æthelred's first wife had either passed away or had been dismissed shortly before 1002. Æthelred was around 36 years old at the time of his marriage to Emma, making him potentially at least twenty years her senior. Upon her arrival in her new kingdom, Emma took the Old English name Ælfgifu, although Emma continued to use her Norman name for the most part throughout her life. Ælfgifu was the name of Æthelred's grandmother. The act of taking on an Old English name was undoubtedly intended to warm the English subjects to Emma, whose status as a foreigner was likely a disadvantage to her personally. It offered Emma a connection to a prior English consort, a connection she could not claim through blood. Although Normandy was an increasingly powerful kingdom in the early eleventh century, their dukes had not attained the status of kings. Emma was in effect 'marrying up' and her name change was indicative of her social and political climb. Emma's marriage to Æthelred would increase the status of her family, and thus Emma's brother, Richard, would have been keen to ensure she was crowned.[11] This was especially important as Æthelred had sons from his first marriage. A coronation would ensure that Emma's children, as the offspring of two anointed parents, had a strong claim to the English throne.

Emma gave birth to Edward (who would later be known as the Confessor) before 1005. A daughter, Godgifu, was born around 1007, and another son, Alfred, arrived sometime before 1013. At a time of increasing pressure from the Danes, Emma's son's names are significant – both Edward the Elder and Alfred the Great were successful rulers and renowned for their achievements in pushing back the Vikings.[12]

Alas, Emma's marriage to Æthelred did not cure the Viking problem. Not long after the marriage, Emma's brother Richard agreed to a peace treaty with Swein Forkbeard (963–1014) and offered him safe harbour in Normandy.[13] In the ninth and tenth centuries, increasing numbers of Scandinavians had come to settle in the British Isles. But during Æthelred's reign, several Scandinavian mercenaries had arrived in his kingdom and had given the king cause for concern. Men such as Pallig, a brother-in-law to Swein Forkbeard. Pallig was hired by Æthelred as a mercenary, but betrayed Æthelred, joined a Scandinavian force and attacked Devon. Perhaps justifiably, Æthelred had become concerned about an alleged plot to overthrow him.[14] In response to this perceived threat, Æthelred ordered the execution of all Danish men in England on 13 November 1002. This became known as 'The St Brice's Day Massacre'. Æthelred may have felt emboldened by his marriage to Emma and thus in a position to finally rid himself of these unwanted elements within his kingdom.[15] According to tradition, Swein's sister was killed in the massacre, and Swein used this loss to justify his attack on England the following year and subsequent attacks in the years that followed.[16] By late 1013, Swein had completed his conquest of England.

After Swein's successful capture of the English throne, Emma and her children were sent to Normandy. Æthelred followed, but his older sons from his first marriage remained in England.[17] Swein's reign was short-lived; he died in February 1014, and Æthelred, Emma and their children were able to return to England. Swein's son, Cnut, was his father's successor and was declared king by his Danish army. Cnut, however, withdrew his army to Denmark and would not return to claim his perceived inheritance until the following year. Æthelred resumed his kingship with Emma at his side.

But Æthelred's second reign would be short-lived. In the summer of 1015, Cnut arrived in England with a fleet and attacked the kingdom of Wessex, the power base of Æthelred's forebearers. Æthelred died in London on 23 April 1016, having lost much of his kingdom to Cnut. At the time of Æthelred's death, London was the only part of England under his control.[18] By 1014, Æthelred had lost Ecgberht, Edgard, Eadred and Æthelstan, his sons from his first marriage. The eldest survivor of Emma's stepsons was Edmund Ironside (*c.*990–1016), a nickname given to him, according to the *Anglo-Saxon Chronicle*, for his valour.[19] Edmund took up the defence of England in his father's stead. After suffering a crushing defeat at the hands of Cnut at Ashingdon, Essex, Edmund was forced to accept Cnut's terms – the division of England. Edmund was to rule Wessex and the regions in the south of England, and Cnut, Mercia and the north. This arrangement was short-lived, for Edmund died in November 1016, allowing Cnut to take the entirety of England for himself. It is not clear whether Emma left England at this time, although the sources do suggest she left for Normandy with her two sons, Edward and Alfred, who are recorded as fleeing to their mother's ancestral lands.[20] It was at this crucial moment in English history that we see Emma take charge of her destiny.

As the wife of Æthelred, Emma seemingly exercised limited political control; she appears infrequently and sporadically in the charters of her first husband's reign.[21] However, as Æthelred's widow, Emma became a key political player. The *Anglo-Saxon Chronicle* tells us that in 1017, Cnut became king and 'commanded the widow of the late king Æthelred, Richard's daughter, to be brought to him so that she might become his queen'.[22] This simple statement suggests that Emma had little choice or agency in the matter. The *Encomium* offers a different interpretation of these events. In Emma's own words, once he had taken England, Cnut sought a worthy bride. Eventually, Cnut set his sights on Emma.

> Wooers were sent to the lady, royal gifts were sent, furthermore precatory messages were sent. But she refused ever to become the bride of Cnut, unless he would affirm to her by oath, that he would never set up the son of any other wife other than herself to rule after him.[23]

For Emma knew that Cnut had sons by another woman, Ælfgifu of Northampton (1006–1036). Ælfgifu belonged to a powerful Mercian family. Cnut's marriage to Ælfgifu was an attempt by Swein Forkbeard to consolidate his political power in the north following his invasion in 1013.[24] Cnut and Ælfgifu had two sons, Harold Harefoot (1015–1040) and Svein (1016–1035). The precise nature of this marriage has been debated by historians. The *Encomium* suggests this was not a proper marriage at all, and that Ælfgifu was Cnut's concubine.[25] This is one possibility. Another is that Ælfgifu was Cnut's wife in a very formal and proper sense, and she was set aside by Cnut once a more politically advantageous marriage came along. Serial monogamy was not unusual among tenth and eleventh-century aristocrats and royalty. The union could have been an arrangement unique to Scandinavians, which ensured the legitimacy of any children and the woman's status, but had a certain amount of flexibility, enabling the man to cast her aside once a better opportunity came along.[26] Nevertheless, Emma was rightly concerned about the threat that Harold and Svein posed to her children as heirs to the English throne. Cnut did not set Ælfgifu aside once he married Emma. He entrusted her to rule Norway with their son, Svein, in 1030 as his regents. All this suggests that Ælfgifu was more than a concubine. Through the *Encomium*, Emma then presents herself as a powerful woman with political agency as Æthelred's widow who drove a hard bargain. She understood her value and, in her words, 'wisely providing for her offspring, knew in her wisdom how to make arrangements in advance, which were to be their advantage'.[27] This is a very different woman from the one presented by the *Anglo-Saxon Chronicle,* who was 'brought' or 'fetched' to be Cnut's wife. It should be noted that the *Encomium* was written in 1041–2, after the death of Cnut, and it was easy to present Emma as a demanding negotiator, given the eventual course of events.

Cnut and Emma were married in 1017. Emma's value as a consort lay foremost in her status as the anointed queen of England, a position that imbued her with symbolic legitimacy. Through this marriage, Cnut was able to establish a sense of dynastic continuity, aligning his newly established Danish regime with the royal lineage of Æthelred and his predecessors. Although Cnut acquired the kingdom through military conquest, his union with Emma served to further legitimise his rule by associating it with the existing Anglo-Saxon monarchy. Furthermore, Emma brought political utility; her experience within the English court and familiarity with its administrative structures made her an invaluable asset to the governance of the kingdom.[28] Emma, like Cnut, was originally a foreigner to England. Her earlier experience navigating the cultural and political complexities of the English court would have been highly beneficial to Cnut as he worked to establish and legitimise his rule in a newly conquered kingdom.

In 1017, Cnut faced many potential threats to his throne, not least of all from Emma's sons with Æthelred: Edward and Alfred. Marrying Emma served to neutralise the threat from her sons, now living in exile in Normandy. The marriage also brought about a treaty with Normandy, and Cnut was assured that Richard would not assist Edward and Alfred in any attempts to take the throne of England. But Emma's sons were not the only potential claimants to the throne. Edmund Ironside left two infant sons, Edward Ætheling and Edmund. Details of their movements immediately after their father's death are unclear, but the *Anglo-Saxon Chronicle* claims Edward (presumably along with Edmund) was eventually banished to Hungary, where he was raised.[29] Although only small children in 1017, Cnut was acutely aware of the possibility that these boys could be used to rally support among the English nobility in resistance to his rule.

Emma's Danish maternal heritage presumably meant she was fluent in the language. This shared linguistic and cultural familiarity likely facilitated smoother communication and strengthened her suitability as queen consort. The couple appear to have been at least amicable, if not on friendly terms, throughout their marriage. However, there is no evidence that Cnut left Emma to act as regent in England during his absence.[30] Interestingly, as noted above, Cnut did send his first wife, Ælfgifu, to rule Norway as his regent with their son, Svein.[31] Furthermore, Cnut did not invite her sons, Edward and Alfred, back to court, which could suggest Cnut never completely trusted Emma.[32]

Nevertheless, it appears that Emma was much more politically powerful and visible as the wife of Cnut than she ever had been as Æthelred's consort. The charters give some evidence of her changing status under Cnut. In Æthelred's reign, Emma is normally referred to as *conlaterna regis*, meaning 'king's wife'. This title firmly identifies her as the bride of Æthelred, whose power and authority rest on her position as his wife. Seldom is she accorded the title *regina*, meaning queen, in Æthelred's reign. Yet as the wife of Cnut, she is almost always referred to by this title.[33] Moreover, the sources often referred to Cnut and Emma as a pair, suggesting there was an acknowledgement among contemporaries that Cnut needed Emma as much as Emma needed Cnut.[34] This implies Emma's political status changed; under Cnut, she was an independent political player, a powerful woman in her own right. This sense of their balanced relationship was depicted in an illustration contained within the *New Minster Liber Vitae*, created in 1031. In this image, Cnut and Emma are depicted as the centrepiece of the illustration, both have their hands on a crucifix placed on an altar. The illustration signifies the duality of their relationship as understood by their contemporaries, and more significantly, their subjects.[35]

Yet, despite this acknowledgement as a powerful woman, like all women of her time, Emma's power rested upon her status as a wife and a mother. Emma's status undoubtedly increased when she fulfilled her queenly duty of providing Cnut with a son, Harthacnut, who was born in 1018. She also bore Cnut a daughter, Gunhilda (*c.*1020–1038), who during her short life was the wife of the Holy Roman Emperor, Henry III. In 1023, Emma and Harthacnut oversaw the relocation of Archbishop Ælfheah's body to Canterbury in recognition of his sanctity. This was very much a symbolic act, and the occasion does seem to indicate publicly that Harthacnut was Cnut's formal heir.[36] The pomp and ceremony of this event under the watchful eyes of her subjects undoubtedly brought Emma great joy and a sense of immense pride.

Cnut died in 1035, and Emma was widowed once more, but this time, she found herself in a much stronger position than she had in 1016. Emma immediately set to work to secure the succession of her youngest son, Harthacnut, but this was not an easy path. Harthacnut had been sent by his father to rule Denmark and was not present in England at the time of the death of his father. Harold Harefoot, Cnut's eldest son by Ælfgifu, who was on English soil, claimed the kingdom as Cnut's son and heir. He was, unsurprisingly, supported by his mother, Ælfgifu and the influential Earl Leofric of Mercia. Naturally, Emma supported Harthacnut and attracted the support of the powerful Earl Godwin (1001–1053), the father of King Harold II of England who would die at the Battle of Hastings. According to the *Anglo-Saxon Chronicle*, Emma was residing in Winchester at the time of Cnut's death and had the foresight to seize Cnut's treasures.[37] Without the protection of Harthacnut, Emma was alone, awaiting his arrival. As she waited, Harold had all of Cnut's valuables taken from her.[38] In Harthacnut's absence, a witan was held in Oxford, and the kingdom was divided between the two half-brothers. Harold was to rule Mercia and Northumbria and Harthacnut was given Wessex.[39] Harold had the distinct advantage of his presence in England in these years immediately preceding his father's death, and in Harthacnut's absence, he enveloped the entirety of the kingdom and was accepted as sole king in 1037.

Emma was likely responsible for the propaganda that circulated, intending to damage Harold's status. The *Anglo-Saxon Chronicle* describes Harold as a man who 'claimed to be Cnut's son … although it was not true'.[40] The *Encomium* goes even further, claiming Harold was not the son of either Cnut or Ælfgifu, but the child of a servant who was slipped into Ælfgifu's bed in secret.[41] Ælfgifu's position rested solely upon her status as Harold's mother, and Emma used motherhood, or a lack thereof, to delegitimise her rival.

Emma's reasons for her hatred towards Harold ran deeper than political dispute; it was personal. In 1036, Emma's sons from her marriage to Æthelred, Edward and Alfred, sailed from Normandy to England. The motive behind their decision to leave the safety of Normandy remains unclear. In the *Encomium*, Emma tells us that Harold sent a letter to her sons in Normandy under false pretences, forging her name to make it appear as though she had invited them to return to England. Unsurprisingly, she sought to distance herself from any involvement in their arrival, given subsequent events.[42] More likely, either Emma sent for them or they decided, independent of Emma, to take the opportunity afforded them by the political turmoil in England to attempt to claim the throne for themselves.[43] The brothers travelled separately, and as Edward went to his mother at Winchester, Alfred landed at Dover. On his way to meet Emma at Winchester, Alfred and his company were entertained by Godwin, a supposed ally of Emma. Godwin then betrayed Alfred and gave him to Harold. Alfred's men were mutilated, sold or killed. Alfred was blinded, a significant act as a punishment given to rebels.[44] But it was also used to bar potential candidates to the throne from inheriting, essentially rendering them unworthy of kingship. Alfred was then handed over to the care of the monks of Ely, where he died and was buried. This version of events, as told by the *Anglo-Saxon Chronicle*, identifies Godwin as largely to blame for Alfred's death.[45] Emma's version of events in the *Encomium* is slightly different. She places the blame for the whole incident squarely on the shoulders of Harold, the author of the forged letter luring her son into a fatal trap. In her version of events, Godwin entertains Alfred and his men and does his utmost to protect Emma's son. Harold then seizes Alfred from Godwin's protection and had him killed.[46]

This differing version of events is significant. Emma's fortunes following the death of Cnut were often bound to Godwin's. The two were allies at the time of the composition of the *Encomium,* and it seems that Emma was attempting to remove any blame for this incident from Godwin, her ally, and in turn herself. Indeed, this incident may explain Edward's treatment of his mother in later years. Edward had spent most of his life in exile in Normandy with Alfred, and one can imagine a close bond between the brothers. It seems Edward and other contemporaries blamed Emma for her son's death, and the *Encomium* was used by Emma to distance herself from any involvement in the episode. With the death of his younger brother, Edward returned to Normandy and would not revisit his native shores until 1041.

As part of his takeover of the entire kingdom in 1037, Harold drove Emma from England and into exile. Taking pity on the isolated, downcast Emma, the *Anglo-Saxon Chronicle* tells us she was eventually 'driven from the country without any mercy to face the raging winter'.[47] Interestingly, she sought refuge not with her eldest son, Edward, in Normandy, but instead with relatives in Bruges.[48] Perhaps Emma could not face Edward in light of the recent death of his brother, Alfred. In Bruges, Emma awaited Harthacnut who had begun to amass military forces to present a challenge to Harold. But before he could make his move, luck was on the side of Emma and Harthacnut. Harold died in March 1040, allowing Harthacnut to make his return to England as king in June of that year.

It was as the king's mother that Emma reached the peak of her power ruling alongside Harthacnut. Emma was fortunate that Harthacnut was still unmarried and could therefore easily position herself as queen alongside her son. Indeed, it was Emma's queenship that had secured Cnut's position as king decades earlier, and she was still an anointed queen. In witness lists, her authority is recognised, and she is referred to as *mater regis,* king's mother. Her power was different from that of her son's, but by no means lesser.[49] From a duke's daughter in the relatively new kingdom of Normandy, Emma had risen to the position of king's wife, twice. She had endured exile on numerous occasions and now had reached the pinnacle of her political career, enjoying the powerful position as mother of a king and co-ruler.

However, all was not as she had longed for and her rule, alongside Harthacnut's, was largely unpopular and marked by factionalism.[50] The new king arrived in England with sixty-two warships and to pay for their crews, Harthacnut levied a tax. Two of his housecarls who were given the task of collecting this tax were killed in Worcester. Harthacnut retaliated by harrying Worcester and the surrounding area. He was considered an oath breaker for betraying Earl Eadwulf after promising him safety.[51] In a move that many found incredibly distasteful, perhaps in response to the death of Alfred, or in retaliation of his taking the kingdom in 1037 and the treatment of his mother, or a combination of all these factors, Harthacnut had Harold's body exhumed and cast into a swamp.[52] The *Anglo-Saxon Chronicle* summed up the rule of Harthacnut: 'He never did anything worthy of a king while he reigned'.[53]

In a move that was probably intended to bolster Emma and Harthacnut's popularity, Edward was invited back to England in 1041 to rule jointly with Emma and Harthacnut in a triumvirate. Edward also brought additional legitimacy as the only surviving son of the last English king. Emma was an incredibly useful element within this triumvirate; unlike her sons, who had spent much of their childhood abroad (Edward in Normandy and Harthacnut in Denmark), Emma had spent most of her life in England. Although she originally came to England as a foreigner, she undoubtedly considered England to be her home. Emma understood the complex workings of the Anglo-Danish court and knew how to gain the support of the nobility. Significantly, she was England's queen. Seemingly, Harthacnut was warm towards Edward, as he had been towards Alfred when he was alive. As a threat to his kingship, Harthacnut could have conspired to have his half-brothers killed; indeed, the deaths of Anglo-Saxon princes were rather commonplace. Perhaps it was Emma who was responsible for cultivating this brotherly love between Harthacnut and Edward, which resulted in Edward as Harthacnut's designated heir.

It was at this time, in 1041 or 1042, that the *Encomium* was written. Remaining completely silent on Emma's first marriage to Æthelred, instead, the *Encomium* focuses on Emma's marriage to Cnut and the fruits of this union, namely Harthacnut. Emma's eldest son, Edward, is named and features within the text without reference to his father. The *Encomium* is traditionally thought to have been compiled in Flanders, but more recently it has been proposed that, given the author's awareness of the fast-developing political situation in the Anglo-Danish court, it is possible that the author was writing in England.[54] And although historians have disputed the occupation of the author, traditionally referred to as The Encomiast, the manuscript's frontispiece depicts a tonsured figure presenting the work to his patron, Emma, suggesting he was a monk, probably from St-Omer in Flanders.[55]

The *Encomium*, written in Latin, presents the Danish invasion of England as a positive step and offers a praiseworthy account of those responsible for the invasion – Cnut and his father, Swein Forkbeard. Emma emerges in the text in the aftermath of the Danish conquest as a figure who restores peace following a period of warfare and instability in England, thereby fulfilling one of the primary expectations of queenship: the role of peacemaker and intercessor. In her marriage negotiations with Cnut, Emma presents herself as a figure of considerable political authority, actively participating in and shaping the terms of the union.[56] Although the author addresses the work to Emma, the work functions primarily as a defence of both Emma and Harthacnut, crafted with the intent of serving as a rhetorical tool in defence of her conduct.[57] The *Encomium* presents Harthacnut regaining a kingdom wrongfully taken from him after the death of the 'tyrant' Harold and concludes with England ruled by a triumvirate comprised of Emma, Harthacnut and Edward. The text emphasises co-operation and unity: 'having no disagreement between them, enjoy the ready amenities of the kingdom. Here there *is* loyalty among sharers of the rule, here the bond of motherly and brotherly love is of strength indestructible'.[58]

This triumvirate was demonstrated beautifully in an illustration in the frontispiece of the *Encomium*. Emma assumes a powerful, masculine pose sitting open-legged in the fashion of contemporary kings. Her two surviving sons, Edward and Harthacnut, now ruling jointly with her, watch on in the background as Emma is presented with the text. The *Encomium* was as much addressed to them as it was a defence of her actions. In many ways, this illustration depicts Emma's hopes for the future, one in which she sees her two sons guided by her, offering her wisdom and political acumen in a political climate fraught with difficulties. Soon after the *Encomium* was completed and this image was created, Emma's fortunes would be very much reversed from the wise, powerful queen to a shadow of her former self, cast into the shadows of politics.

In June 1042, Harthacnut collapsed at a celebratory feast and died. He was only 24 years of age. Emma entered the final and most difficult phase of her life, as mother to King Edward the Confessor. Edward was now Emma's only surviving son, and it was solely upon him that she now relied for power. Whereas Harthacnut was a young man in his early twenties in 1040 when he gained the kingdom, Edward was a fully grown man in his late thirties when he ascended in 1042.[59] Until 1036, when he came to England, Edward had not seen his mother since her marriage to Cnut in 1017. He had been raised by his mother's kin in a foreign land. Edward lived in exile while his mother continued to hold one of the most powerful positions in his kingdom and enjoyed a new life with her new family. It is difficult to envisage a particularly close relationship between Emma and her eldest son, and Edward may have held Emma at least partially responsible for the death of his brother, Alfred.

The *Anglo-Saxon Chronicle* tells us that in 1043, following his coronation, Edward, known to history as 'The Confessor' confiscated all his mother's lands and possessions for himself. The reason given by the source: 'because she had been too strict with the king, her son, in that she had done less for him than he wished, both before his accession and afterwards'.[60] Emma's actions before 1043 suggested she favoured her new Danish family. By endorsing Harthacnut's claim to the throne over that of Edward's equally forceful claim as Æthelred's son, Emma appears to have demonstrated a preference for Harthacnut. One could argue that Emma sought to eradicate Edward's father from history altogether, indicated by his total absence from her narrative. The fact that Edward and Alfred remained alive, albeit in exile, suggests strong intercession on their behalf. Emma may have sent her eldest boys into exile for their protection, thereby removing them from the clutches of Cnut should he perceive any threat to his position. Nevertheless, Edward felt utterly sidelined by his mother and was arguably only requested to return to his homeland once Emma needed him to strengthen her position.

In depriving Emma of her possessions and her property in 1043, Edward forced Emma, a dowager queen, into retirement. There was nothing unusual about this. However, the sources suggest this was more than just forcibly retiring Emma.[61] One rumour likely circulating in Emma's lifetime accuses her of plotting with Magnus of Norway to overthrow Edward. This accusation seems unfounded and may attest more to ideas linking Emma to Denmark as the wife and mother of Danish kings than anything else.[62] Significantly, the *Anglo-Saxon Chronicle* mentions Bishop Stigand's fall immediately following Emma's. Edward deprived him of his see and his possessions 'because he [Stigand] was his mother's closest confidant, and she, as was supposed, followed his advice'.[63] Emma appears to have been working with Stigand, the Bishop of East Anglia, perhaps to make a power play herself, or at least, it is suggested that this was what Edward thought. Whether Edward's suspicions had any justification or not, Edward recognised his mother as a powerful woman who had attracted the support of influential men such as Stigand.[64] Forcibly removing his mother from power seemed to him the only option to neutralise this maternal threat. Edward sought to remove the shackles of an experienced yet overbearing mother of whom he harboured much resentment.

For the remainder of her life, Emma resided in Winchester on lands given to her by Æthelred. She did regain a position at court, but no longer as the powerful queen she had once been. In 1045, Edward took Godwin's daughter, Edith, as his wife, and thus a new queen was at court, leaving no place for Emma. A twelfth-century source accuses Emma of having a sexual affair with Ælfwine, Bishop of Winchester in her later years. To prove her innocence, Emma underwent the ordeal of hot ploughshares, walking over nine red-hot ploughshares barefoot. Emma allegedly emerged unscathed due to the intercession of St Swithun.[65] This episode cannot be found in contemporary sources and is perhaps a later fabrication intended to explain the fall of the formidable Emma.

Emma died on 6 March 1052 and was laid to rest in The Old Minster at Winchester, alongside her husband Cnut and their son Harthacnut. Emma lived in a period of profound transformation, marked by two major invasions of eleventh-century England, in both of which she played a significant role. During the 1016 invasion, she relied on political acumen to ensure her survival and united an invaded kingdom under its conqueror. In the year of Emma's death, her great-nephew, Duke William of Normandy (1028–1087), visited England. He had spent a substantial part of his childhood with Edward during the latter's exile in Normandy, Emma's homeland. It is entirely plausible that, as William claimed, Edward the Confessor designated William as his heir, which prompted England's second invasion in

1066. Normandy had sheltered Edward and his brother Alfred since childhood, a consequence of Emma's decision to send them into exile for their protection. Though not culpable, Emma played a significant role in shaping the conditions that made the Norman Conquest of 1066 possible. As the key figure connecting the English and Norman courts, she fostered the familial ties that would later prove politically decisive.

Emma, twice queen of England, was a kingmaker; the mother of two kings and the great aunt of the conqueror who would change the trajectory of English history forever. Emma was very much at the centre of eleventh-century English politics, and without her political acumen, her two sons would not have attained the throne. Two images of Emma have survived, and she is the earliest English queen of whom we have a pictorial representation. Her foresight in commissioning her version of events and her ability to survive one of the most turbulent times in English history make her one of the most fascinating and formidable women of the medieval period.

Chapter 3

Empress Matilda (1102–1167)

Here lies Henry's daughter,
wife and mother,
great by birth, greater by marriage,
But greatest by motherhood.[1]

This was the epitaph inscribed upon the tomb of Empress Matilda by the order of her son, King Henry II (1133–1189). This inscription places Matilda firmly within the gender norms of her period, described only in her relationship to men first as a daughter, then as a wife and then as a mother. Yet there is an acknowledgement in these words that Matilda herself was an essential lynchpin in the Norman-Angevin Dynasty. Matilda possessed qualities classified as inherently male; she was an accomplished military tactician and a ruler, albeit ruling on behalf of her male relatives.[2] Although Matilda never did acquire the crown, she nevertheless was the first woman to make a serious claim to the throne in her own right.

Matilda was the eldest child born in 1102 to parents King Henry I of England (*c.*1068–1135) and his first wife, Edith-Matilda of Scotland (1080–1118), daughter of the King of Scotland, Malcolm III. This made Matilda the granddaughter of William the Conqueror on her father's side and the great-granddaughter of Edmund Ironside on her mother's side. Matilda could claim as her ancestors the legendary Rollo, the founder of the Norman dynasty, and the Anglo-Saxon king, Alfred the Great. Her father was the third king to rule the Conqueror's newly-founded Norman dynasty in England. Matilda was very much the personification of the combination of this new world, which merged Normans and Anglo-Saxons as the memory of the Conquest of 1066 was beginning to fade.

We know little about Matilda's early life. Likely, she would have been taught letters and morals at an early age within her mother's court, presumably alongside her brother, William, who was born a year or so after her.[3] Edith-Matilda was a very capable consort; on numerous occasions, she acted as regent during her husband's absences.[4] She offered her daughter a wonderful role model of a woman exercising real political power in a male-dominated world.

Matilda's illustrious parentage means that she was marked for a prestigious marriage, the primary path to greatness for twelfth-century women. A worthy groom was found for Matilda, who would enhance her father's status and offer an important alliance. Matilda was betrothed to Henry V, king of Germany (and from 1111 also the Holy Roman Emperor) by proxy at Easter 1109. The following year, the 8-year-old Matilda left England for her new home and her new life in Germany, accompanied by a splendid retinue of ecclesiastics and knights.[5]

Matilda must have felt daunted by the splendour of the occasion as she met her future husband in the bustling city of Liège, in modern-day Belgium, in February 1110. Henry, fifteen years older than his future bride, made every effort to welcome and settle her into her new role. Matilda performed her first act as the future queen at Liege by interceding on behalf of the disgraced Godfrey of Lotharingia.[6] Interceding at court was a time-honoured duty of any queen, and in doing so, the 8-year-old exhibited the powers of her newly acquired position. Matilda was crowned later that same year as queen of Germany.[7]

Henry was intent on shaping Matilda into an active consort, capable of supporting him in the complex governance of his extensive realms, a role traditionally embraced by German queens. Her early presence at court allowed Henry to mould her according to his needs. Over the following four years, Matilda received rigorous training under the guidance of Archbishop Bruno of Trier, a trusted adviser of Henry. She was instructed in the German language, court customs, and the responsibilities expected of an Empress.[8] Germany quickly became home to the young Matilda, consequently, contemporary chronicler, Orderic Vitalis, claimed Matilda was much loved by her subjects and earned the affectionate epithet of 'the good Matilda'.[9]

Matilda reached the canonical age for marriage in 1114 when she was 12 years of age, and she wed Henry V at Worms that January. Since Matilda was of canonical age and Henry V did not have a son and heir, it is reasonable to assume their marriage was consummated promptly. However, in their eleven years of marriage, the couple had no surviving children.[10] It is a testament to Matilda that Henry did not repudiate his wife as rulers were accustomed to doing when no offspring arose from their marriage. Indeed, Orderic Vitalis noted that Henry 'loved his noble wife deeply'.[11] Matilda was someone Henry could undoubtedly trust as is evidenced by his faith in her as regent during his absence on campaign.[12] And in turn, Matilda was a devoted wife, supporting Henry throughout his dispute with the Papacy known as the Investiture Controversy, a quarrel he had inherited from his father, Henry IV.[13]

In March 1117, the royal couple made their way to Rome. Henry had been crowned Emperor in 1111, but Matilda had yet to celebrate her imperial coronation, and it was tradition for the Emperor to undergo a crown-wearing ceremony if he was in the holy city on a feast day. As the couple approached the city, Pope Paschal promptly left, and Matilda was instead crowned by the Archbishop of Braga, the highest-ranking ecclesiastic on hand.[14] Theoretically, an imperial coronation could only be performed by the Pope in Rome, and so Matilda's status as an empress was rather dubious. For this reason, she continued to be referred to as Queen of the Romans (another title used for the queen of Germany).[15] Nevertheless, her coronation was performed in Rome and by an archbishop, which was sufficient for Matilda, her husband and her Anglo-Norman family. From this time on, Matilda styled herself 'Empress Matilda' and evidently this coronation increased her sense of her own political standing and status. Henry left for Germany that same year, but Matilda, still only 16 years old, remained in Italy until 1119 to represent Henry's interests. Matilda was precisely the consort Henry had envisaged; she witnessed charters, interceded, and in Italy acted as judge and ruled with vice-regal powers.[16]

After eleven years of marriage, Henry died on 23 May 1125 with his wife beside him. He entrusted the imperial insignia to Matilda until a new king could be crowned.[17] Widowed without providing an heir to the throne, there was little reason for Matilda to remain in Germany, and so her father recalled the 23-year-old widow to his court. In her long absence, the situation in England had changed dramatically.

In 1118, Matilda's mother, Edith-Matilda, passed away, and two years later, William, Matilda's younger brother, drowned aboard a vessel sailing from Normandy to England in what became known as The White Ship Disaster. All 300 passengers on board, save for one, perished, and the captain allowed himself to be drowned rather than face the wrath of the king. A child was sent to deliver the news to Henry I, so it might soften the blow. The distraught king took himself into his private chambers and gave over to grief at the loss of his only legitimate son and heir.[18] In response to the disaster, in January 1121 Henry quickly remarried in the hopes of producing another male heir. His new wife was Adeliza (*c*.1103–1151), daughter of Count Godfrey of Lotharingia (the same Godfrey whom Matilda had petitioned on behalf of, upon her arrival at Liege many years before). Despite Adeliza's youth (she was close to her stepdaughter, Matilda, in age), no children were born of the marriage. When Matilda returned to England in 1126, her father, now in his fifties, sensed that time was not on his side and he needed to establish an heir, and soon.

Henry's thoughts turned towards Matilda as his successor to England and Normandy. Although the chroniclers and Henry recognised that Matilda's sex would bring some additional problems to the succession, Matilda's sex did not necessarily bar her from the throne.[19] While not common, the twelfth century saw some women succeed their fathers. Urraca of León-Castile (1081–1126) ruled in her own right from 1109 until her death in 1126 as the designated heir of her father. Despite her marriage to two different rulers, it was Urraca who held the reins of power. Melisende of Jerusalem (1105–1161), another contemporary of Matilda, found herself one-third of a ruling triumvirate along with her husband,

Fulk of Anjou (who would later become Matilda's father-in-law) and her eldest son, Baldwin III. Fulk died in 1143, and Melisende continued to rule with Baldwin. Melisende believed throughout her life, even once her eldest son came of age, that she was the heir to her father's kingdom. She was more than just a mere transmitter of blood from one king (her father) to the next (her son).[20] Although a female succeeding to the English throne was unprecedented, aristocratic women could and did wield power through inheritance.

Spending time with his daughter, now a stranger in her homeland after her long absence, Henry could see Matilda possessed all the necessary skills required for rulership, even though that role was traditionally assigned to men. It was because of Matilda's abilities and experience that Henry felt confident in publicly declaring his daughter as his heir. In January 1127, Henry asked his leading nobles and ecclesiastics to swear oaths of loyalty to Matilda as they had sworn to recognise her brother as their father's heir before his premature death. They pledged that, should Henry and Adeliza produce no sons, Matilda would succeed him.[21]

None would dare to refuse to swear the oath as Henry, renowned for his ferocious temper, stood before them.[22] And why would they refuse; although not a man, Matilda possessed all the requirements of rulership – bloodline, training, and experience. Furthermore, she was the embodiment of the Norman, Scottish, and Anglo-Saxon royal bloodlines, and her status as Empress only enhanced the prestige of her kingdom.[23] After a century of dynastic upheaval, the nobles were eager to establish a secure and stable monarchy.[24] Amongst them was Stephen, Count of Blois (1096–1154), Henry's favourite nephew. After the oaths were taken, Henry entrusted his illegitimate son, Robert of Gloucester (1090–1147), with the tall task of ensuring Matilda would succeed their father upon his death without a glitch.[25]

Like her contemporaries, Urraca and Melisende, Matilda's position as her father's heir would be much more secure if she were married and produced sons. Geoffrey (1113–1151), the son of Count Fulk V of Anjou, was selected as Matilda's groom. An alliance with Anjou was strategically desirable, as the marriage would strengthen ties between England and Anjou against Henry's nephew, William Clito, Count of Flanders, a persistent threat to Henry's kingship and a claimant to the succession.[26] Geoffrey was approximately eleven years younger than Matilda. As the recent widow of the Holy Roman Emperor, she may have viewed marriage to the son of a mere count as a social demotion. While her first marriage had elevated her status, this union represented a step down the social hierarchy. Nevertheless, Matilda was compelled to set aside any personal resentment in favour of the broader political advantages the alliance offered.

As Matilda arrived in Anjou for the occasion of her wedding, Fulk abdicated to marry Melisende of Jerusalem, thus rendering Geoffrey the new Count of Anjou. While Geoffrey's advancement may have caught Matilda's attention, it was unlikely to impress her; her former imperial status rendered his rank as count comparatively insignificant. Yet despite any reservations Matilda may have had, the couple were married in Le Mans in June 1128. Matilda was a strong-willed 26-year-old widow with remarkable life experience as an empress. Geoffrey, a mere untested youth of 15, was quite the contrast to her first husband.[27]

Geoffrey's intended role following Henry's death is uncertain. Unlike Matilda, he received no oaths of allegiance, nor is there evidence that Henry envisioned Geoffrey inheriting England or Normandy or ruling jointly with Matilda.[28] The succession plan appeared unchanged after their marriage – Matilda was to succeed her father, with Geoffrey's role limited to supporting her claim and producing heirs, particularly sons, who would eventually inherit. This dynastic strategy underpinned Henry's hopes as well as those of the nobility. Although childless from her first marriage, and the possibility of barrenness could not be dismissed, Matilda was only 26, meaning the desired outcome could still be achieved.[29]

Following her second marriage, Matilda continued to style herself in charters as 'Empress', often followed by the words 'daughter of King Henry', rejecting the lesser title of countess. Her self-identification marked her out as an independent female lord.[30] Matilda's superior status was acknowledged by her husband, which was often useful to Geoffrey, who referred to himself on one occasion as 'the husband of Matilda, daughter of the King of the English and former wife of Henry, Roman emperor'.[31] The mature and proud Matilda, Norman heiress, was a stark contrast to the inexperienced Geoffrey, scolded in a letter from his father-in-law for his wish to journey on pilgrimage rather than governing his kingdom.[32] The pair were evidently mismatched and consequently, Matilda left Anjou and Geoffrey for Normandy in 1129 while Geoffrey remained in Anjou, fathering a son with his mistress.[33]

In 1131, Matilda travelled to England, where oaths reaffirming her status as Henry's heir were renewed, notably without mention of Geoffrey. The council subsequently resolved that she return to her husband, to which she acquiesced.[34] The couple's differences seem to have been sufficiently set aside for a son was born to them in Le Mans in March 1133. He was named Henry after his maternal grandfather. Another son, Geoffrey, soon followed (1134–1158). Matilda fell gravely ill following Geoffrey's birth and almost lost her life. She made a recovery and bore another son, William FitzEmpress (1136–1164) two years later.

Matilda and Geoffrey learned to live and work in partnership, and Matilda even took her husband's side in 1135 against her father in a dispute regarding Matilda's dowry.[35] Henry visited his hunting lodge in Lyons-la-Forêt during this dispute, and according to Henry of Huntingdon:

> he partook of some lampreys, of which he was fond, though they always disagreed with him; and though his physician recommended him to abstain, the king would not submit to his salutary advice.[36]

Henry fell ill and went to the grave on 1 December 1135 after a short illness. Notwithstanding their earlier quarrel, Henry spent his final hours doing all he could to secure his daughter's succession.[37] Despite Henry's attempts in the final decade of his life to ensure the continuation of his dynasty, his death flung England into a bitter civil war. Henry's failure to accede control of his daughter's dowry of lands and castles in England and Normandy was a fatal mistake. In doing so, he had failed to allow Matilda to secure for herself a power base from which she could stake her claim as the heir of her father.[38]

Matilda was in Anjou when she received the news of her father's death. Unfortunately for Matilda, an unbeknownst rival claimant was geographically closer to England, her cousin, Stephen of Blois. Stephen was in Boulogne when he heard the news of his uncle's death and made for England. Considering the time it took for news to travel, Stephen could have learned of his uncle's death within three days and reached England within a week.[39] As Stephen's grandfather, William the Conqueror, had learnt, proximity was key to success. William had initially lost the throne to Harold Godwinson, who was in England upon the death of Edward the Confessor (January 1066). He was able to garner support to arrange a speedy coronation, the day after Edward's death. A king was much more difficult to remove once he had been crowned and coronated. Likewise, brothers William Rufus and Henry I himself had seized the English throne, on both occasions excluding their older brother, Robert Curthose.

Arriving in England, Stephen convinced the nobility that Henry had a change of heart regarding the succession on his deathbed and had named Stephen his successor (the same argument Harold Godwinson had used against William the Conqueror).[40] Stephen was duly crowned on 22 December 1135 by the Archbishop of Canterbury at Westminster Abbey, and he further consolidated his position with a papal blessing from Pope Innocent II in July 1136.[41] Stephen was widely popular; he had a blood claim as the grandson of William the Conqueror and was considered preferable to a woman. Moreover, he had acquired exceptional qualities which made him an excellent candidate for the throne; he was affable, generous to his nobles and had been tested in battle.

Over on the Continent, around three months pregnant with her third child, Matilda probably only heard the news of her father's sudden passing when Stephen was already in England.[42] Having nearly died during the birth of her second son, Matilda likely exercised caution, delaying any swift action or sea voyage to England for the sake of her health.[43] Through the latter days of 1135 and into 1136, Matilda and Geoffrey worked together to secure Normandy, obtaining a foothold in the duchy which would be used as a springboard from which to launch expeditions into England over the coming five years.[44] Matilda's sex worked against her in 1135; the nobility easily abandoned her as her father's heir because she was a woman, and her pregnancy prevented her from travelling and disputing her cousin's usurpation of her throne.[45] Yet Matilda would not be silenced.

Matilda's claim rested on the oaths her father had extracted from the magnates, including Stephen, who had sworn to uphold her succession. Yet even before Henry's death, some questioned the validity of these oaths, arguing that Matilda's 1128 marriage to Geoffrey, arranged without their counsel, nullified their earlier promises.[46] In early 1139, Matilda made an appeal to Pope Innocent II at the Second Lateran Council, declaring that Stephen and his supporters were oath breakers. Stephen's defence argued that Matilda could not be her father's legitimate heir because her mother had taken religious vows as a nun, a point denied by Matilda's representatives. Notably, Stephen's defence was based on hereditary principles rather than Matilda's sex, which was not a legal barrier.[47] The Pope showed little concern for these petty squabbles and declared that his earlier acknowledgement of Stephen's coronation still stood.[48] Some nobles now considered their earlier oaths null and void; however, Stephen did not enjoy the support of all the nobility.

Matilda's father holds the record for fathering the most known illegitimate children of any English monarch.[49] The eldest of these identifiable twenty-five illegitimate children was Robert, the first earl of Gloucester, a staunch supporter of his half-sister, Matilda and her greatest ally. In the immediate aftermath of Henry's death, Robert paid homage to Stephen, likely in a bid to protect his own lands and wealth. However, the relationship between Stephen and Robert turned sour in 1137. The pair were together in Normandy that year when a confrontation between the two men broke out. Allegedly, Robert had accused Stephen of trying to dispose of him. In May 1138, Robert informed the king that his allegiance now lay with his sister, Matilda, and not with him.[50] Robert publicly called Stephen an oath breaker and usurper. It was likely loyalty to his father that drove Robert to defect to the cause of his half-sister.[51] This was a terrible blow for Stephen and his cause. Robert was one of the richest and most powerful of the Anglo-Norman nobles, and his abandonment of Stephen marked the beginnings of the first English Civil War, which was later coined 'The Anarchy'.

With Robert on side, Matilda now decided to make a move in a bid for the English throne. Matilda and her half-brother sailed from Normandy to England in September 1139, leaving Matilda's husband and three young sons in Anjou. A woman ousting a crowned monarch from power was unheard of, even if he was a usurper. Matilda had now decided to transform herself from her father's heir, wrongfully cast aside, into a female king, a ruler in her own right and an attractive alternative to the usurper of her throne.[52]

In response to Robert's change of allegiance, Kent and the southwest of England rebelled against Stephen, while King David of Scotland, Matilda's maternal uncle, launched an invasion from the north. Matilda and Robert landed on the Sussex coast in September 1139. Arriving in secret, they made their way to Arundel Castle in Sussex, held by Matilda's stepmother, Adeliza, now recently wed to William d'Aubigny. Publicly, William and Adeliza supported Stephen, but privately,

Adeliza was a vehement supporter of her stepdaughter. Matilda was welcomed into Arundel Castle as Robert quietly ventured on to one of his fortresses in Bristol to meet his supporters.[53]

In response, Stephen marched to Arundel and surrounded the castle. Stephen's brother, Henry, Bishop of Winchester (*c*.1096–1171), warned him of the optics and political implications of besieging two women in the castle. For once, Matilda's sex worked to her advantage.[54] The decision was taken to permit Matilda to meet Robert in Bristol, no doubt informed by Stephen's sense of chivalry. Matilda was escorted to her brother by her cousin, Henry Bishop of Winchester, with Stephen hot on her heels.[55]

Matilda made Gloucester Castle her base of operations and as she rallied support, her presence within the kingdom was a powerful call to arms. Chief among her supporters was Brian Fitz Count and Miles of Gloucester, who, along with Robert of Gloucester, were among the most militarily capable and loyal in England.[56] Through them, Matilda held much of the southwest of England and Robert convinced Welshmen to intervene in this English dispute and throw their support behind Matilda.[57] Stephen controlled much of the southeast, while much of the remaining territory was held by nobles who remained neutral.

In January 1141, Ranulf, Earl of Chester, seized Lincoln Castle from Stephen's control and Stephen responded by laying siege to the castle. Ranulf escaped and requested reinforcements from his father-in-law, Robert of Gloucester, who promptly responded. Robert and Ranulf brought their forces to meet Stephen at Lincoln. The Battle of Lincoln was fought on 2 February 1141, and Matilda was victorious. Stephen himself was captured by Ranulf and handed over to Matilda's custody and imprisoned in Bristol Castle.[58] Geoffrey continued to strengthen Matilda's stronghold in Normandy, made all the easier by Stephen's removal from power. With Stephen imprisoned and Matilda taking control of England, many of the nobles surrendered to the Angevin regime.

Matilda struck a deal with Henry's brother and her own cousin, Henry, Bishop of Winchester, now papal legate. Matilda agreed to consult Henry on all important issues concerning governance and, in exchange, Henry offered his support and gave up the royal treasury.[59] In a Church Council held in March 1141, presided over by Henry, it was decided that Matilda would be referred to as 'Lady of the English', and it was here she was formally offered the crown and her coronation was planned for June 1141. Matilda continued to use the titles 'Empress' and 'Daughter of King Henry', which denoted her former lofty status as the wife of the Holy Roman Emperor and as her father's designated and therefore rightful heir.[60] The title 'Lady of the English' was problematic for her contemporaries; it recognised Matilda as a female ruler independent of any male relative. It was considered permissible for women to wield power and authority, but only if they were doing so on behalf of a male, usually as a regent for their husband or son.[61] However, at this moment,

Matilda was acting alone, in her own interests, and this subversion of the social order may explain why Matilda would never be crowned.

To secure her coronation, Matilda had to gain access to London before making her way to Westminster. The Londoners had requested that their financial obligations to the Crown be reduced. Matilda responded by demanding more from them. Matilda's financial demands followed by her refusal to grant Stephen's son, Eustace, lands owed to him shocked the Londoners and they considered this unwomanly behaviour.[62] The author of the pro-Stephen contemporary chronicle, the *Gesta Stephani*, used gender to criticise the Empress during her confrontation with the Londoners:

> She, with a grim look, her forehead wrinkled into a frown, every
> trace of a woman's gentleness removed from her face.[63]

Although she had undertaken a role traditionally assigned to men and Matilda did possess characteristics traditionally associated with men, it was considered she had become too masculine and had completely abandoned all sense of femininity:

> She at once put on an extremely arrogant demeanour instead of the
> modest gait and bearing proper to the gentle sex, began to walk and
> speak and do all things more stiffly and more haughtily than she had
> been wont.[64]

For the author of the *Gesta Stephani* the absence of femininity in Matilda's character not only rendered her unnatural, but more importantly, indicated that she was a bad ruler. Interestingly, Stephen's queen, Matilda of Boulogne (1105–1152), who took control of Stephen's army and engaged in negotiation and diplomacy to bring about his release, was praised by the same author for exhibiting manly qualities. He commented upon her 'manly courage' and of possessing 'a manly heart in a woman's body'.[65] But Queen Matilda was acting on behalf of her husband and thereby in a way that was considered acceptable and not in a subverted way, unlike the Empress, who acted on her own authority in her quest for power.

The Londoners, feeling alienated by the Empress, decided to throw in their lot with Queen Matilda and her retaliatory force. As the Londoners revolted, Empress Matilda retreated to Oxford. Henry, Bishop of Winchester, unsurprisingly changed sides once again and joined his sister-in-law in her efforts to remove the Empress. Matilda's failure to reach an agreement with the Londoners was to be her downfall. At the height of her power, when her coronation was within her grasp, Matilda had shown herself to be lacking in political judgement and wisdom.[66]

Matilda and Robert besieged the bishop in his castle at Winchester in July 1141. Their supporters were surrounded by Queen Matilda's forces and the Londoners.

Matilda escaped, but Robert was captured in September 1141 and later exchanged for Stephen, restoring the stalemate that had persisted since her arrival in England.[67] In 1142, Robert sailed to Normandy to seek the aid of Geoffrey, who had continued to fight his wife's cause in the duchy. The risk appeared minimal; Stephen had been taken ill since the spring, and an attack seemed unlikely. Whilst there, Robert assisted Geoffrey in his conquest of the region. Robert returned to England with 300 men and his nephew, Matilda's eldest son, Henry.[68]

During Robert's absence, Matilda was besieged by Stephen's forces at Oxford, while Stephen also seized Wareham Castle, cutting her off from Normandy. Upon his return, Robert recaptured Wareham and assembled a relief force to rescue Matilda. With supplies dwindling and her position desperate, Matilda escaped Oxford in December 1142, crossing the frozen Thames by night, dressed in white to evade detection with only three knights.[69] She walked for around eight miles to Abingdon before riding onto Devizes Castle, which became her base of operations for the next six years.

In 1142, with her eldest son now in England, Matilda's attitude changed, and she bequeathed her claims to England and Normandy to Henry.[70] Matilda had perhaps recognised that her claim to the throne as a woman would only be acceptable if she was seen to be working on behalf of a male, and this change of course may have been agreed upon by Robert and Geoffrey during their time together in Normandy.[71] Matilda had come tantalisingly close to the throne but had failed to secure her coronation. Henry's presence in England was symbolic of her quest; she was now a lynchpin in a dynastic struggle, passing the throne from her father, Henry I, to her son, Henry II. Her son's succession became the reason for the war.[72] Seeing a way beyond female rulership, Matilda gained traction in England for her cause or the cause of her son. Henry would remain in England, learning from his mother's example, until he returned to his father in Normandy in 1144.

The years 1143–1146 saw a stalemate in England. Matilda held the southwest of England, and Stephen ruled the rest of the kingdom.[73] In December 1143, Matilda lost Miles of Gloucester, who was mortally wounded in a hunting accident. In 1147, her half-brother, Robert, died of a fever in Bristol.[74] The loss of two of her most ardent supporters was a huge blow for Matilda, and she retired to Normandy in March 1148.

In September 1151, Geoffrey took their son Henry to Paris to have him formally recognised as the Duke of Normandy. On their return to Normandy, Geoffrey became ill and died suddenly, leaving Henry the new Count of Anjou. Henry continued to assert his claim to the English throne until November 1153, when he was recognised as Stephen's heir. Stephen's eldest son, Eustace, had died in August of the previous year and his wife, Matilda, three months before that. Stephen was grief-stricken and exhausted. Henry agreed to permit Stephen's son William to inherit the lands his father had held during the reign of Henry I, and Stephen was to remain king until his death. Henry did not have to wait for long, as Stephen died on 25 October 1154 and Henry became King Henry II of England.[75]

Matilda remained in Normandy and often acted as regent for her son there in his absence. The newly crowned Henry II relied upon his mother for advice; she was, after all, a shrewd politician with decades of experience in matters of state.[76] Her authority in Normandy was acknowledged, and she was often credited with the role of peacemaker.[77] Matilda was a mediator between her son and Thomas Beckett when the former friends spectacularly fell out in 1164.[78] Matilda remained active in politics until her death in September 1167, and although not queen herself, she remained an influential figure and no doubt an intimidating presence at her son's court.

A near contemporary source, Ralph of Diss, described Matilda as having 'masculine courage in a female body'.[79] The manly skills Matilda had acquired that made her a viable candidate as the heir of her father had been acquired through conventional means, her first marriage. Matilda's attempts at the seizure of the English throne were thwarted because she tried to claim the throne for herself, initially acting without the authority of a male or on behalf of one. Although not explicitly mentioned by the chroniclers, the suggestion is that contemporaries were not ready for a female ruling in her own right. The *Gesta Stephani* made every effort to portray Matilda as un-throne-worthy, beyond her sex, suggesting her personality was an obstacle; however, this pro-Stephen account cannot be taken as a true reflection of Matilda's character. Nevertheless, contemporary accounts of Matilda's refusal to retreat and allow her cousin Stephen to retain the throne offer us a glimpse into medieval ideas about gender and how women, like Matilda, who wielded authority, were considered, regardless of their obvious partiality. Despite being designated heir by her father, it was widely recognised that her status as mother to a potential king and then mother to a consecrated king (Henry II) allowed Matilda to exercise the greatest power, because this was the accepted means by which royal women could do so.[80] This is borne out by her epitaph, which explicitly places Matilda within the context of acceptable channels of female power; as daughter, wife and mother.

Chapter 4

Eleanor of Aquitaine (*c.*1124–1204)

Eleanor of Aquitaine was the only woman crowned queen of both France and England, as the wife of Louis VII of France (1120–1180) and Henry II of England (1133–1189). As a result of these alliances, she was also mother to three English kings: Henry the Young King, Richard I and John. Eleanor was not just a significant historical figure because of her relationship to these men; unusually, she was an heiress in her own right. A formidable woman, she went on crusade with her first husband, travelling to the far reaches of Christendom. When her second marriage proved unsuccessful, she had her sons rebel against their father, resulting in her imprisonment for fifteen years. She assisted her sons in their respective reigns and proved to be a wonderful adviser and great political ally. A victim of her own power and success, contemporary commentators could only consider a powerful woman a threat to the social order and therefore offered scandalous reports of her alleged adulterous behaviour. Her life was remarkable and inimitable.

Eleanor was the second child and eldest daughter of William X, Duke of Aquitaine and Count of Poitou (*c.*1099–1137), and his wife Eleanor (d.1130), a descendant of the Viscounts of Châtellerault. The young Eleanor came from a long line of formidable duchesses of Aquitaine, unafraid to confront and leave their adulterous husbands, ruling on behalf of ineffectual spouses, performing the role of regent for their minor sons and even laying claim to lordships as was their hereditary right.[1] Born into the vibrant court at Poitiers in around 1124, Eleanor's forebearers, the dukes of Aquitaine, were credited for their patronage of literature and the development of courtly love and poetry. Literature in this region was unusually secular rather than ecclesiastical in nature and topic, and Eleanor's grandfather, Duke William IX, was reported to be the first troubadour.[2] Eleanor inherited this love of literature, and books became all the more readily available throughout her life, a period known as the twelfth-century Renaissance.[3] Eleanor participated in this European-wide phenomenon as a great patron of writers and poets.[4]

Eleanor's older brother, William, died as a child sometime in the 1120s and with no other brothers, Eleanor took his place as their father's heir. Widowed in 1130, Duke William embarked on a pilgrimage to Santiago de Compostela in 1137, but he died before he could reach his destination. This left his eldest daughter, Eleanor, a wealthy heiress to lands which covered approximately one-third of modern-day France, the largest territory in the country. They spanned from central modern-day France to the Pyrenees and included the economically prosperous County of Poitou and the ports of La Rochelle, Bordeaux and Bayonne.[5] An orphan now around 13 years of age, Eleanor was placed under the protection of King Louis VI of France. Louis married Eleanor to his son, the 16-year-old Louis, on 25 July 1137 in Bordeaux, and the couple became the Duke and Duchess of Aquitaine. The king died in the same year, and Louis was crowned King Louis VII of France and Eleanor, Queen of France, in December 1137.

Far from the vibrant and exciting court of her upbringing in Poitiers, Eleanor found herself in the more sombre Parisian court, and her husband proved to be far less exciting than she had undoubtedly hoped for. William of Newburgh, looking back on the marriage decades later, suggested Eleanor felt she 'had married a monk, not a king'.[6] Like Eleanor, Louis had been thrust into the position of heir to his father following the death of an older brother. Louis was originally destined for a career in the Church.[7] This may explain his apparent piety and Louis' perhaps misogynistic attitude in preventing his wife from exercising any political influence as his queen and even relegating her to a secondary role in her birthright as a duchess of Aquitaine.[8] However, the young and inexperienced Louis could be easily influenced, and there is every reason to believe his young wife learnt how to persuade her husband early on in their marriage.[9]

Initially, the marriage appears to have been a relatively happy one. The couple welcomed their first child, a girl, Marie (1145–1198), following the intercessory prayers of (later Saint) Bernard of Clairvaux (1090–1153). But Eleanor and Louis' relationship with Bernard had not always been so friendly. The royal couple had experienced the wrath of Bernard in 1142 following an incident in Vitry. Eleanor's younger sister, Petronilla, had joined Eleanor at the French court and had caught the eye of the king's cousin, Raoul of Vermandois, a married man some two decades her senior. Raoul repudiated his wife, Eleanor of Champagne, in favour of Petronilla and married his young lover, prompting the Pope to excommunicate the newlyweds. Eleanor leapt to the defence of her sister, insisting that the charge be lifted. The incident caused great offence to Eleanor of Champagne's family, the most prominent member of which was Count Theobald IV of Champagne, prompting a war between Raoul and his ex-in-laws.[10] Louis, perhaps at the behest of Eleanor, took the side of Raoul, and Louis laid waste to the town of Vitry-en-Perthois in the county of Champagne in 1142. Unknown to Louis, the inhabitants of the town had taken refuge in a church which he set alight, killing hundreds of innocents. Bernard chided Louis, asking him:

> From whom but the devil could this advice come under which you
> are acting, advice which causes burnings upon burnings, slaughter
> upon slaughter.[11]

Bernard understood that Eleanor had influenced Louis throughout this incident, and the couple would not reconcile with the leading cleric until 1144. It was said that Louis was so grief-stricken by the burning of the church in Vitry-en-Perthois that he wept and vowed to go on a pilgrimage to Jerusalem to atone for this great sin.[12]

Louis did not need to wait long for his call to the Holy Land, for in 1145, news reached the West of the fall of Edessa, one of the four Christian-held states that comprised the Holy Land; consequently, the Second Crusade was called. Bernard of Clairvaux gave a sermon in March 1146 at Vézelay promoting the expedition, and here, in a very public ceremony, Louis took the cross. Eleanor accompanied her husband on the expedition, a decision that raises questions about her motivations. A woman of considerable will, she may have viewed the journey as an opportunity for adventure. According to some chroniclers, the appeal of travelling in the company of numerous men may also have played a role.[13] The decision may not have been Eleanor's; Louis was said to be infatuated with his wife, and his 'over-urgent longing for his young wife' meant he could not leave her behind.[14] He may have been influenced by political considerations, perhaps fearing his headstrong wife might challenge Louis' appointed regent, Abbot Suger, for the role.[15] If the decision to go was hers, Eleanor may have been moved by deep devotion and perhaps had hoped that by enduring a perilous and most uncomfortable journey, she might be rewarded with the safe arrival of a son and heir for Louis.[16] Eleanor brought much-needed wealth to Louis' crusade, and her participation in the expedition attracted the involvement of Aquitanian nobles. However, the chroniclers complained that Eleanor's participation encouraged other women to join their husbands on the crusade. The inclusion of so many women stirred the imaginations of commentators who concluded that the expedition had been transformed into a cesspit of sin and sexual impropriety.[17]

Setting out on 11 June 1147, the now 25-year-old Eleanor was on the brink of the adventure of a lifetime. Louis' French contingent was as many as between 25,000 and 50,000 crusaders and pilgrims recruited from Louis and Eleanor's lands.[18] The royal couple reached Constantinople on 4 October 1147 after five months of travelling and were entertained there by the Emperor Manuel and his Empress, Irene. The Byzantine author, Niketas Choniates, writing his account half a decade after their visit, claimed:

> Females were numbered among them, riding horseback in the manner
> of men, not on coverlets sidesaddle but unashamedly astride, and

bearing lances and weapons as men do; dressed in masculine garb, they conveyed a wholly martial appearance, more mannish than the Amazons. One stood out from the rest as another Penthesilea and from the embroidered gold which ran around the hem and fringes of her garment was called Goldfoot'.[19]

Here lies the root of the legend of Eleanor riding at the head of an Amazonian cohort. Niketas does not explicitly mention Eleanor in this context. However, many historians have posited that the author was alluding to Eleanor indirectly as the one who stood out as another Penthesilea, queen of the Amazons. Criticising these women in gendered terms, they are masculine and thereby unnatural in their appearance and their actions.[20] Eleanor's participation in the crusade itself was considered unnatural and unbecoming of a woman, and thereby the comparison drawn between her and the Amazon women fits with wider criticism of her.

After the fiasco on Mount Cadmus, in January 1148, in which Eleanor's vassal, Geoffrey of Rancon, was blamed for his failure to safely lead the army across the mountain pass, Louis and Eleanor boarded a ship from Attalia to Antioch.[21] The couple were greeted warmly by Raymond of Poitiers (*c.*1105–1149), Eleanor's uncle and the ruler of the principality of Antioch. Raymond, merely nine years older than Eleanor, was said to be tall and 'handsome far beyond all the kings and princes of the world'.[22] His court would have been exotic and filled with familiar faces from Poitou, and Raymond spoke Eleanor's native tongue, Occitan.

The original objective of the Second Crusade was to rescue Edessa, but by the time Louis and Eleanor had reached the Holy Land, Edessa was a lost cause. In May 1148, Raymond suggested the key to success in the region was to assault Aleppo. Louis rejected this notion, hell-bent on reaching Jerusalem and fulfilling his crusading vow. Eleanor supported Raymond's proposition, probably because it made tactical sense.[23] Comfortable in her uncle's court, she initially refused to acquiesce to Louis' demand that she accompany him to Jerusalem; consequently, rumours began to circulate of a love affair between Eleanor and her uncle. William of Tyre, writing some thirty years after the event, accused Raymond of trying to steal Eleanor from her husband, whom he described as 'a foolish woman … she disregarded her marriage vows and was unfaithful to her husband'.[24] But Eleanor's refusal to join Louis is consistent with her character; Eleanor was independently minded, and there is every reason to believe she saw herself as a policy maker independent from Louis and perhaps had offered to support Raymond.[25] However, somewhat inevitably, these political or strategic considerations were not discussed by contemporary chroniclers. Instead, they depicted Eleanor's dealings with her uncle as evidence of a sexual relationship, drawing on established stereotypes about women's moral shortcomings.

Twelfth-century chronicler John of Salisbury claimed that when pushed to leave for Jerusalem with Louis, Eleanor threatened him with divorce:

> she mentioned their kinship, saying it was not lawful for them to
> remain together as man and wife since they were related in the fourth
> and fifth degrees.[26]

Eleanor had no agency in the arrangement of her marriage to Louis, but she was determined to steer its course and bring it to an end if it suited her needs. Louis was furious with his wife and was prepared to divorce her; however, his advisors persuaded him to desist from this course of action. Likely, Louis needed Eleanor's finances to continue the expedition. Eventually, Louis forced Eleanor to join him as he travelled on to Jerusalem.[27]

Once the couple reached Jerusalem, it was decided that, as Edessa was now a lost cause, the crusade should concentrate its efforts on Damascus. The expedition had been a disaster from the outset, and at Damascus in July 1148, the crusaders found their luck had not improved. Running low on supplies and gaining no ground, Louis and his forces retreated. Some suggested that Raymond was determined to ensure Louis' crusade was unsuccessful and that he was responsible for the defeat by proposing the crusaders attack from a disadvantageous position.[28] Louis remained with Eleanor in Jerusalem for a year after this defeat, visiting the holy sites within the kingdom.

In April 1149, the couple left Jerusalem and travelled west on different ships within a Sicilian fleet, suggesting that their relationship was strained at this point. When Eleanor's ship was taken captive by the Byzantines, in conflict with Roger II of Sicily, she was rescued, not by her husband, but by the Sicilians. Eleanor suffered further misfortunes when her ship was caught in a storm and pushed onto the western shores of Sicily while Louis landed on the Italian mainland. This whole ordeal was likely responsible for Eleanor's sudden illness, and her troubles worsened when she learned of the death of her uncle Raymond, killed by Nur ad-Din during the campaign Louis had refused to support. She was cared for by Roger of Sicily in his palace in Palermo and eventually made her way to join her husband on the Italian mainland in September 1149.[29] The couple then travelled to Rome, where Pope Eugenius III tried to repair the fractured marriage and offered something akin to marriage counselling, hearing the complaints of each party and even remarrying the couple. He then forbade the couple to divorce and encouraged them to get their marriage back on track.[30] Eugenius' intervention appears to have worked, for the couple conceived their second child, another daughter, Alice (1150–1198), during this visit. The couple returned to Paris in November 1149 after a long two-year absence.

Louis' costly crusade had been a complete failure. Chroniclers suggested the blame for the failure lay in the sexual sins of its participants, particularly

Eleanor. Chroniclers portrayed her alleged sexual deviance as the reason for God's withdrawal of favour from the crusade, thereby absolving Louis of blame and justifying his repudiation of her upon their return as one who 'behaved not like a queen but more like a harlot'.[31] More likely, the divorce stemmed from the couple's failure to produce a male heir. In March 1152, a council of bishops annulled the marriage on the grounds of consanguinity, an issue Eleanor had previously raised while in Antioch. The legitimacy of her two daughters was affirmed by the council and it was decreed they would remain in the custody of their father; Eleanor probably never saw them again.[32] Ironically, the lack of a son enabled Eleanor to escape an unhappy marriage. If she had given birth to a son, Louis probably would not have sought a divorce from her, as the legitimacy of the boy could easily be called into question.[33]

Now a divorced woman, Eleanor departed for her lands in Poitou, taking with her one of the wealthiest and most powerful kingdoms in all of France. Whilst travelling to Poitou, she narrowly evaded capture, firstly by Thibault of Champagne and then by Geoffrey of Plantagenet, both wishing to marry her.[34] Eleanor was in a precarious position and, considering her options, she sent word to Henry, son of Empress Matilda and Geoffrey of Anjou, heir to the English throne and the Duchy of Normandy, offering him her hand in marriage. Henry joined Eleanor at Poitiers and the pair were married at the cathedral there on 18 May 1152, some eight weeks after Eleanor's divorce from Louis.[35]

It has been suggested that this marriage had been planned when the couple first met in the summer of 1151, when Henry came with his father to Louis' court to pay homage.[36] Eleanor, then almost 30 years old, stuck in an unhappy marriage, may have fallen for Henry, now in his late teens, described by contemporaries as 'striking rather than handsome in appearance with reddish coloured hair. He was strong in appearance thanks to his stalwart chest and limbs'.[37] Eleanor may have been physically attracted to Henry, but her more immediate concern was to find a suitable husband to rule her lands alongside her. As Henry's senior by a decade or so, she may have had ambitions to establish herself as the dominant partner, a role she had undertaken in the early years of her first marriage.[38] Henry's status improved in September 1151 when his father, Geoffrey of Anjou, died in his prime, aged just 39. Henry was now the ruler of the Angevin Empire, and this kingdom would expand to include England with the death of King Stephen in 1154. Eleanor and Henry remained vassals of Louis. Louis, feeling threatened by the lands accumulated by the newlyweds, responded by forming a coalition with Henry's enemies.[39]

In what must have been a horrific blow to her former husband, Eleanor conceived a child within seven months of her marriage to Henry and gave birth to a boy, named William, in August 1153. His name evoked the Dukes of Aquitaine, and Henry's great-grandfather, William, Duke of Normandy.[40] William was made

Count of Poitiers but died in infancy. Following the death of King Stephen in October 1154, Henry and Eleanor were crowned together in December of that year at Westminster Abbey. Eleanor was heavily pregnant at the time and the following February, gave birth to another son, Henry the Young King (1155–1183). Over the following eleven years, Eleanor gave Henry an additional six children: Matilda (1156–1189), married to Henry, Duke of Saxony and Bavaria; Richard (1157–1199), who would become King Richard I, the Lionheart; Geoffrey (1158–1186), Duke of Brittany; her namesake, Eleanor (1162–1214), later queen of Castile; Joan (1165–1199), later queen of Sicily; and the youngest of her children, John (1166–1216), another future king of England. Through her children, Eleanor boasted descendants in all major kingdoms in Western Europe, including France, Castile and the Holy Roman Empire. Together, Henry and Eleanor established the House of Plantagenet that would outlive all expectations, ruling England until 1485 when Richard III died at the Battle of Bosworth.

The birth of eight children within thirteen years would suggest that Eleanor and Henry enjoyed an amicable if not friendly relationship in the early years of their marriage. Henry was known to have had a succession of mistresses, and, as this was an accepted part of kingship, this cannot be used to suggest their marriage was an unhappy one. Henry undoubtedly trusted in Eleanor's abilities, for during Eleanor's childbearing years, she was also politically active, often serving as Henry's official regent in England during his absences abroad.[41] Likely the result of the more experienced and older Eleanor over her younger husband, she encouraged Henry to put down revolts in Aquitaine and pressured him to assert his rights to Toulouse on her behalf in 1159.[42] Eleanor frequently travelled with some of her children from her second marriage, suggesting she was largely involved in their upbringing.[43]

A large brood of sons ensured the dynasty would continue, but it also complicated the issue of succession. Primogeniture was not yet a firmly established system, and Henry and Eleanor had created a huge empire that encompassed England, Normandy, Anjou, Aquitaine, Toulouse and Brittany. Henry decided to bequeath parts of the Angevin Empire to his eldest sons in preference to leaving all of it to one of them. This move would also ease relations with Louis, who feared the growing influence of the Angevin Empire. In 1169, Henry's decision regarding the future of his Empire was ratified in a treaty signed by both Eleanor's current husband and her first husband in Montmirail, France. The eldest surviving son, Henry (known as the Young King), was crowned king in June 1170, during his father's lifetime and would rule jointly with his father. Upon his father's death, the Young King was to succeed his father's throne in England and the duchies of Normandy and Anjou. To foster good relations with Eleanor's first husband, Henry the Young King married Margaret of France, Louis' daughter from his second marriage.[44]

Eleanor and Henry's second surviving son, Richard, was destined to inherit Eleanor's Duchy of Aquitaine as a kingdom independent from England, Normandy and Anjou. Richard was now 11 years of age and betrothed to Louis' youngest daughter from his second marriage, Alice. The couple's third eldest son, Geoffrey, would become the Duke of Brittany through his marriage to Constance, daughter of Conan IV of Brittany. At this time, no provision was made for the youngest son of the family, John, accordingly nicknamed Lackland for his lack of prospects.

In 1168, Henry installed Eleanor as ruler of her ancestral lands of Aquitaine, which had become increasingly volatile, where she remained until 1174. From this time on, Eleanor was primarily concerned with furthering the interests of her children rather than those of Henry.[45] Her son, Richard, accompanied her where he was to be trained as ruler there under Eleanor's tutelage. At this time, Eleanor issued charters in her own name, sometimes in association with Henry or Richard, but very much acting on her own authority.[46] Richard was Eleanor's favourite child, and his time spent under his mother's instruction no doubt strengthened an existing loving bond. In June 1172, at the age of 14, Richard was acknowledged as the Duke of Aquitaine at a ceremony held in Poitiers and then followed by another in Limoges.[47]

Seemingly, a woman acting on her own authority was a cause for suspicion, and it was during Eleanor's time governing Aquitaine that rumours once again began to circulate regarding her conduct. A Book known as *The Art of Courtly Love* is said to be the basis for the notion that Eleanor and her eldest daughter from her first marriage, Marie of Champagne, presided over judicial courts of love held in Aquitaine, where lovers brought their quarrels.[48] Although most historians since the mid-nineteenth century have dismissed notions of these courts as pure fantasy, the enduring myth of these courts persisted in academia even as late as the 1950s and continue to appear in popular literature.[49] What they represent is contemporary and near-contemporary concerns regarding courtly love and the threat of women as seductresses who disobey their husbands. In many ways, Eleanor's unusual circumstances as an heiress in her own right, coupled with her strong personality and independent will, personified this kind of woman among her contemporaries.

As Eleanor successfully governed Aquitaine, her husband was about to meet his greatest challenge from his sons, which would shake the Angevin Empire to its core. In February 1173, Henry II met Count Humbert of Maurienne in Montferrat to celebrate the engagement of Henry's 5-year-old son, John, to Count Humbert's infant daughter. Humbert enquired what John would be bringing to this prestigious union. Henry announced his intention to hand over three castles in strategic locations in Chinon, Loudun, and Mirebeau to John upon the marriage. As these were part of the Young King's expected inheritance, the decision provoked his fury; already denied control over his patrimony, the further loss of these castles was perceived as a profound insult.[50] The Young King, financially dependent upon his father and unable to support or control his own household, was a perpetual youth caught in the purse strings of his father. He was king in name, but denied the full powers of a king; he felt he was treated as a child and prevented from attaining manhood.[51] The Young King made his fury publicly known and demanded part of his inheritance, either England, Normandy or Anjou. His father, not yet 40 years of age himself, refused.[52] The Young King secretly fled to the court of his father-in-law, Louis VII, who gladly took in the troublesome son of his former wife. Henry II prepared for war.

Richard and Geoffrey, aged around 14 and 12 respectively, living under the protection of their mother, also fled to the Parisian court, and contemporaries suggested this was done at the advice of Eleanor.[53] Henry came to the natural conclusion that Eleanor had been conspiring with her sons. But she had every reason to rebel, for Eleanor suspected her husband had intended to envelop Aquitaine into the English kingdom rather than forming part of the inheritance of Aquitaine she would pass on to Richard. This was an insult to Eleanor and her Aquitaine nobles.[54] Eleanor called her own supporters to take up arms.

It was suggested by commentators that Eleanor was at least partly responsible for this rebellion. She was said to have had an inappropriate relationship with another of her uncles, Ralph, Lord of Faye-la-Vineuse, an influential man at Henry's court who had a reputation as a despoiler of churches, and was accused of creating a rift between Eleanor and Henry.[55] According to Matthew Paris, both Eleanor and Ralph encouraged the Young King to rebel, saying: 'It is not fitting that a king, whoever he may be, should be seen [as] unable to exercise in his kingdom the power he has a right to'.[56] Including Ralph in this scheme takes something away from Eleanor's influence over her sons and undermines her position. Peter of Blois reminded Eleanor of her duty as a wife to submit to the king: 'For we know that unless you return to your husband you will be the cause of a general ruin'.[57] Eleanor is framed as a disobedient wife rather than a mother looking after the interests of her children. Depicted as the worst kind of woman, unwifelike and unfeminine, her disobedience threatened the stability of society, and her association with yet another uncle served only to highlight the depravity of the queen rather than consider her as a policy maker.

A settlement was eventually reached on 8 September 1174 between Henry II, his sons and Louis VII and a peace treaty was signed at Montlouis. Henry II was generous in his concessions. Although the Young King did not obtain what he desired – control of England, Normandy and Anjou – he was accorded an increase in lands and revenues. Henry was similarly generous to all his sons.[58] Notably, Eleanor was absent from the peace treaty, neither physically present nor mentioned in its terms. Henry had completely removed Eleanor from the equation, reducing her to a non-player in a game in which she had been so dominant for decades. Her fate during the rebellion of 1173–1174, therefore, becomes a critical point of inquiry.

At the outbreak of the rebellion, Eleanor chose not to remain in Poitiers to retain Aquitaine as a power base for herself and her sons. Instead, she set out for Paris but was intercepted by Henry's forces and placed in his custody. According to the contemporary chronicler Gervase of Canterbury, Eleanor had taken the disguise of a man.[59] The truth behind this element of the story is less relevant than its symbolism; Eleanor was once again acting unnaturally, subverting social norms by disguising herself as a man. Henry decided to imprison his now 50-year-old queen in summer 1173 after contemplating a divorce. Imprisoned at the royal residence of Salisbury Castle (also known as Old Sarum), Eleanor was permitted some freedoms.[60] She was afforded an allowance which was the equivalent of the salary of a minor baron, and the pipe rolls of 1178 note her expenses, which included a fine robe for herself and her maid.[61]

In June 1183, the Young King died of dysentery, but not before he dictated a letter to his father requesting lenient treatment of his mother.[62] Her eldest son's final plea to his father may explain Henry's more reliant attitude towards Eleanor in the years that followed. Still under Henry's custody, in 1184, she travelled to Winchester to visit her daughter Matilda and her husband, the Duke of Saxony, and she attended the Christmas royal court at Westminster along with her children. Henry recognised Eleanor's power as a political weapon, and her presence on this occasion served to ease growing tensions between their sons.[63] Henry again used Eleanor and her influence the following year to settle a dispute between Richard, now heir to his father's throne and the Duchies of Normandy and Anjou and John. In a rearrangement of inheritance following the death of the Young King, Richard refused to relinquish control of Aquitaine, where he had spent the past decade consolidating his authority, to John. Furthermore, giving up the Duchy of Aquitaine would render him in the same position his elder brother had been in, reliant on his father and awaiting his death before he could assert any real authority and control.[64] Richard returned to Aquitaine, where he enjoyed the support of the nobility with whom he had fostered good relations. John, with the support of their brother Geoffrey, pursued military action to secure Aquitaine, reigniting armed conflict within the Angevin Empire. Henry called Eleanor to Normandy and ordered Richard to meet his parents there, which he dutifully did in April 1185. Henry ordered Richard to surrender Aquitaine to his mother, the only person who could not threaten Richard's position as duke, for she was the Duchess of Aquitaine.[65] This was an astute move from Henry; it ensured a settlement without humiliating Richard. Although Eleanor was still technically the prisoner of her husband, this event did once again thrust Eleanor into political life and was a demonstration of her continued significance in the politics of the Angevin Empire.

Tensions between father and sons were unresolved when Henry II died at Chinon in July 1189. On his deathbed, he acknowledged Richard as his heir. Eleanor's favourite son was now the king of England and the duke of Normandy, Anjou and Aquitaine, ruling over the vast Angevin Empire. Richard immediately sent word that his mother, now at least in her mid-sixties, was to be released from imprisonment after fifteen years, and she was afforded unlimited freedoms, with 'the power of doing whatever she wished in the kingdom'.[66] With decades of political experience, Eleanor was a force to be reckoned with, and no one was better placed to dominate royal officials and to hold the reins of government in England until Richard could make the journey to his newly acquired kingdom.[67] Her long-standing close relationship with Richard increased her power and influence. Free now from the physical restraints placed on her by her husband and the societal bonds of marriage, Eleanor, the widow, was ready once again to embark on a political career and take the limelight.

Throughout Richard's reign, Eleanor assumed the role of regent across the Angevin Empire, and although she was not accorded an official title, her position as anointed queen held sufficient authority. To reinforce her status, Richard ordered that 'the queen's word should be law in all matters'.[68] Eleanor immediately set about repairing the damage of abuses committed by her husband in England and securing England for her son. Between the death of her husband and her death in 1204, Eleanor maintained significant political influence. Her activities from her late sixties until her death in her early eighties were notable for her time and unmatched by any contemporary ruler.[69]

In July 1190, Richard left for the Holy Land to embark on the Third Crusade. During Richard's absence, Eleanor busied herself with securing Richard's dynasty and the pressing concern of his lack of a wife. Richard had been betrothed to Alice of France, sister of the new king of France, Philip II, but her alleged sexual relationship with Henry II rendered this match untenable.[70] A wife was found for Richard in the kingdom of Navarre with Berengaria, the daughter of King Sancho VI. Eleanor can be located in Bordeaux in autumn 1190, and from there, the sexagenarian set off on a 200-mile journey south across the Pyrenees to Pamplona, Navarre, to collect her new daughter-in-law. The two women then crossed the Pyrenees and the Alps before arriving to meet Richard in Sicily.[71]

Eleanor spent some time there at the place where she had landed four decades ago on the return journey from her own crusade. As Eleanor set sail for Normandy by way of Rome, Richard and Berengaria were married on the island of Cyprus, and there a new queen of England was crowned. Yet, unusually, Eleanor's powerful position within the Angevin Empire remained unchanged. After arriving in Normandy, Eleanor crossed to England in February 1192 to personally confront John, who, in Richard's absence, was attempting to claim the throne and align himself with King Philip. Threatening to remove John's lands and castles should he continue on this treacherous path, Eleanor brought John into line, according to Richard of Devizes: 'through her own tears and the prayers of the nobles'.[72] Interestingly, the author here portrays Eleanor's combination of feminine persuasion – her tears, with her political influence – the support of the nobles.

Fearing for the security of his throne, Richard concluded his crusade in October 1192 and set sail for home. While travelling through Germany in December 1192, Richard was captured and imprisoned by Duke Leopold of Austria, whom he had offended during the siege of Acre by replacing Leopold's flag with his own. Leopold handed Richard over to the custody of the German Emperor, Henry VI, another of Richard's rivals.[73] Learning of her son's imprisonment, Eleanor wrote to Pope Celestine III demanding Papal protection for Richard as a crusader. In a striking assertion of authority, she styled herself as 'Eleanor, by the wrath of God, queen of England, duchess of Normandy, countess of Anjou and unhappy mother'.[74] Eleanor swiftly made contact with her son and collected Richard's huge ransom of 100,000 marks by levying a tax. While estimates vary, this sum would equate to nearly £1 billion today, double Richard's annual income from England.[75] In January 1194, in a powerful move indicative of her authority and strength of character, Eleanor personally travelled to Speyer to hand over the ransom money in exchange for her son.

Richard ruled with his mother's support for five more years until he sustained a fatal wound during the siege of Châlus-Chabrol. Feeling death approaching, he sent word not to his wife, but to his mother, who duly joined her son.[76] After naming John as his heir and successor, Richard died on 6 April 1199. Richard was buried by his father's side at Eleanor's residence of Fontevraud, and it was left to Eleanor, now in her mid-seventies, to ensure the smooth succession of her youngest and problematic only surviving son, John.

John's succession was disputed by the 12-year-old Arthur of Brittany, Eleanor's grandson, the son of Geoffrey, who had died in 1186. Whilst John secured Normandy, supporters of Arthur had invaded Anjou and Maine. Despite her advanced age, Eleanor remained committed to defending the Angevin Empire, leading an expedition to devastate territories that had supported Arthur's claim.[77] Whilst John headed to Westminster to celebrate his coronation on 25 May 1199, Eleanor secured the Duchy of Aquitaine and embarked on a tour of her lands in Aquitaine, travelling some 1000 miles. And in September 1199, Eleanor formally recognised John as her heir to the Duchy of Aquitaine.[78]

A treaty between John and the French king was agreed in May 1200, which neutralised Arthur of Brittany. To ratify the treaty, Philip requested a granddaughter of Eleanor's by her daughter, Eleanor of Castile, as a bride for his son, Louis. Eleanor was then sent on this highly significant diplomatic mission to choose one of her granddaughters as the future queen of France. The ageing Eleanor travelled to Castile and then returned north with her granddaughter, Blanche of Castile.

But the journey must have been too much for the formidable Eleanor, who paused at Bordeaux whilst Blanche continued to Normandy to meet her future husband.[79] In one of her final political acts, concluding a career spanning seven decades, Eleanor visited Mirebeau, close to the border of Anjou and Poitiers, in July 1202, where she was besieged by her grandson, Arthur. Eleanor, now almost 80 years of age and as defiant as ever, refused to surrender the fortress to Arthur and awaited John's rescue.[80]

Eleanor spent the remaining two years of her life watching the Angevin Empire disintegrate under John's rule. By the end of 1202, John had lost Anjou, Maine, Touraine and Poitou and by the end of 1203, Normandy had been lost too. In the final weeks of her life, Eleanor took the veil and retired from public life. She died on 31 March 1204 at the age of 80. She had led one of the most remarkable lives of anyone of her age. As a woman, she enjoyed unprecedented power and ruled over a duchy that was the envy of the kings of France. As a mother to three English kings, she wielded a power most ruling men of her age could only dare to dream of. One of the richest women of the medieval period, Eleanor secured a dynasty that would endure in England until the Battle of Bosworth in 1485. Hers was an example followed by her daughters and granddaughters, yet her life, governed by unimaginable riches and power, was inimitable.

Chapter 5

Isabella of France (*c.*1295–1358)

> She-wolf of France, with unrelenting fangs,
> That tear'st the bowels of thy mangled.[1]

This unfair assessment of Isabella of France, queen consort of King Edward II (1284–1327) of England, penned by Thomas Gray in his poem 'The Bard' in 1757, has endured throughout the centuries. Isabella shares the epithet 'She-wolf' with another later queen featured within this book, Margaret of Anjou. Both women were of French origin and were wed to ineffectual, weak kings, and consequently, both women fought to secure the succession of their sons in a volatile political climate. One might argue that weak kings make for strong consorts. Nevertheless, contemporaries presented both women as overreaching; their actions were considered to be driven by a desire for personal power, ignoring the wider considerations of their maternal role in safeguarding the succession of their sons.

Isabella of France was born around 1295 to King Philip IV of France and Queen Joan I of Navarre, a title and kingdom Joan held in her own right as well as Countess of Brie, Bigorre and Champagne.[2] One of seven children, Isabella was the only daughter of the couple to survive into adulthood. Unsurprisingly, we know little of her upbringing and early life. We do know she was well-educated as befitting her station, and her acquisition of books in her later life would attest to her love for literature. Contemporary chronicler Froissart gave her a flattering portrait describing her as 'one of the fairest ladies of the world'.[3]

The 23-year-old King Edward II of England married the 12 or 13-year-old Isabella in Boulogne-sur-Mer in northern France on 25 January 1308 in a magnificent ceremony attended by monarchs and dignitaries from throughout Western Europe. The marriage ratified a treaty between England and France, arranged by their parents at the behest of Pope Boniface VIII in 1298.[4] In the month following their marriage, the newlywed couple sailed to England for their joint coronation, and Philip's daughter was the personification of the splendour and wealth of the Parisian court. She arrived with seven crowns, several head coverings and luxurious gowns amongst a collection of other ornate luxury items.[5] But despite the magnificence of the celebrations and the warm welcome Isabella received in her new kingdom, tensions were already brewing. Isabella complained to her father that her new husband failed to properly provide for her financially in the first year of their marriage. This was, however, soon remedied. Edward eventually awarded his wife the county of Ponthieu in France, and when Edward I's widow, Queen Margaret, Edward's stepmother, died in 1318, Isabella was given the usual dower lands in England.[6]

After an initial uneasy start, Isabella and Edward appear to have got along rather well in the early years of their marriage. They sent gifts to each other, wrote to each other when apart and spent a reasonable amount of time together at various times in their marriage.[7] When visiting the court of her father in 1313, one Parisian chronicler recalled how Edward arrived late for a meeting with his father-in-law, for he had overslept after making love to his wife throughout the night.[8] During that same visit to France, the couple were sleeping in a pavilion during a visit to Pontoise, which caught fire. A naked Edward scooped his wife into his arms and carried her from the flames, later claiming 'love made him do it'.[9]

In the first decade of their marriage, Isabella performed the queenly roles of both intercessor and peacemaker to perfection. Undertaking the role of mediator between her husband and her family in France, Isabella made the trip across the channel on multiple occasions to further Edward's interests in her father's court. She played an active political role in administering the kingdom and acted as a substitute for the king and his chancellor in 1319 during his war with the Scots, and then again in 1321 during Edward's war with the Marcher Lords.[10] Edward's close relationship with Isabella and his confidence in her political abilities are evidenced by his entrustment of the Great Seal (a symbol of the king's approval of state documents) to his wife on several occasions.[11] Together, the couple had five children, four of whom survived infancy: Edward (1312–1377); John (1316–1336); Eleanor (1318–1355); and Joan (1321–1362).

Yet despite outward appearances, it was evident to contemporaries that Isabella and Edward were a mismatch. Isabella was a strong, dominant personality who acted in accordance with her royal dignity, whereas Edward's unusual behaviours and personality were not synonymous with the office of kingship and provided a stark contrast to the behaviour of his wife. During a trial in 1315, Robert, a messenger of the king's household, was charged with contempt of the Crown for suggesting Edward could not be expected to be victorious in battle because he did not hear Mass but instead spent his time 'idling and applying himself to making ditches and digging and other improper occupations'.[12] One contemporary chronicler claimed Edward enjoyed the company of singers and jesters, craftsmen and harlots. Moreover, he was swayed by the counsel of others rather than his own.[13] The appearance of a pretender to the throne, John of Powderham, in 1318 raised further suspicions about Edward. Powderham claimed to be the real King Edward, hidden as a baby after he had been mauled by a pig and suffered facial disfigurement. He claimed the present king was a low-born child who had been raised in his place.[14] Although dismissed as incredulous, Edward's alleged low birth seemed to explain his degenerate behaviour, his preference for commoners and ill company and reflected wider doubts regarding his suitability for kingship.[15] Such rumours and suspicions did little to bolster Edward's authority at a time when tensions were growing between himself and the nobility.

Piers Gaveston (*c*.1284–1312), a Gaston knight, had attracted the hatred of the English baronage as a foreigner and favourite of the new king. Exiled in February 1307 by King Edward I, who disapproved of their relationship, one of the first acts of the new King Edward II, following his father's death in July of that year was to recall Gaveston and grant him the earldom of Cornwall. Determined to welcome Gaveston into the royal family, Edward awarded his favourite with a prestigious marriage to Edward's niece, Margaret de Clare, in November 1307.[16] These acts elevated Gaveston's place at Edward's court and increased his social status and were done without the consent of the English nobility to their further annoyance.[17]

Gaveston caused great offence to both the baronage and the new queen at the coronation of the royal couple on 25 February 1308, where Gaveston wore purple silks (a colour symbolic of rulership) and was seated next to Edward at the coronation feast.[18] An offended Isabella complained in correspondence to her father that Gaveston had taken her place.[19] Isabella was joined in her indignation by her uncles who had attended her coronation and complained 'that the king frequented Piers's couch more than the queen's'.[20] The barons arrived at Westminster in April 1308 with a large armed force and demanded that Edward once again exile his favourite, which Edward did reluctantly.[21] But this arrangement would be short-lived as Edward recalled Piers from exile in 1309.

The author of the *Anonimalle Chronicle* spoke disparagingly of Edward: 'This king loved with all his heart certain people whose company his father had frequently forbidden him, among them a certain sir Piers Gaveston'.[22] Another contemporary, the *Westminster Chronicler*, wrote of Edward and Gaveston's love as an 'illicit and sinful union which led to the rejection of the sweet embraces of his wife'.[23] Others referred to Edward as a sodomite who sinned excessively.[24] As a result of these and similar accounts, Edward is often identified as gay, with many concluding that Edward II and Gaveston enjoyed a sexual relationship. Such assumptions are problematic and anachronistic given that our attitude towards sexuality is so different from our medieval forebears. What contemporaries were primarily concerned with was ensuring the continuation of the dynasty and the stability of the kingdom. Whatever his sexual preferences, Edward had conceived an illegitimate child, probably before his marriage to Isabella, named Adam, and he was rumoured to have had an affair with Elanor de Clare. No contemporary suggested Edward was unable to perform sexually with women, and he had several legitimate children with Isabella, thereby securing his dynasty.[25] However, his behaviour, sexual and otherwise, was considered unnatural, degenerate and un-kingly, and this posed a threat to the established order and the kingdom at large. Failing to live up to the impressive military reputation of his father, Edward would stumble from one military defeat to another throughout his reign, and his inability to secure victory and secure his borders rendered him a weak and ineffectual king. Edward's defeat by the Scots at the Battle of Bannockburn (1314) is often remembered as one of England's most humiliating defeats, and contemporaries perceived defeat in battle as an indication of the absence of manliness and God's favour. Edward's perceived lack of divine approval was seen as a sign of God's punishment of England, and particularly its king, an interpretation potentially fuelled by rumours of his sexual transgressions. It is impossible to say whether the relationship between Edward and Gaveston was homosexual in nature, but Edward's favourable treatment of Gaveston at the expense of others was a disruption of power and patronage which lay at the centre of medieval government.[26] This fundamental source of noble opposition encouraged critics to scrutinise Edward further, including suspicions of a sexual relationship with his favourite as evidence of his unsuitability to rule.[27] His perceived sexual transgressions thus became part of a broader critique of his kingship.

Edward's kingship was directly challenged in 1311 when a group of twenty-one barons known as the Ordainers presented the king with forty-one grievances aimed at reforming his government. Number twenty on the list related specifically to Gaveston, who, it was claimed, had 'led the lord king astray, advised the lord king badly, and persuaded him deceitfully and in many ways to do wrong'.[28] Gaveston was exiled and became symbolic of the corruption of Edward's government.[29]

Gaveston was soon recalled, and by spring 1312, he joined the royal couple in York as they celebrated Isabella's first pregnancy. Isabella was seemingly coexisting with Gaveston.[30] But the barons, led by Thomas of Lancaster, one of the most powerful and wealthiest men in the realm, and Isabella's uncle, planned to permanently remove Gaveston and restore proper order, resuming their place as counsellors to the king. Isabella was so loyal to her husband, who refused to acquiesce to the baronial demands to abandon Gaveston, that Lancaster considered her to be his enemy.[31] She fled with Edward and Gaveston, first to Scarborough, then, leaving Gaveston at Scarborough Castle, Edward placed her in the safe confines of Tynemouth Priory. The barons besieged Scarborough, and Gaveston eventually surrendered. He was taken to Warwick Castle, put on trial and condemned to death as a traitor in June 1312. Although Edward was reconciled with the barons:

> he was greatly angered and annoyed and he secretly contemplated in
> his heart all the time how to revenge himself when he should see the
> opportunity on those who had assented to his death.[32]

In November of that year, Isabella gave birth to a son and heir, Prince Edward. With the interference of Gaveston removed from the king and now mother to the heir to the throne, she enjoyed the unrivalled attention of her husband.

Following Gaveston's death, Isabella took a more active role on the political stage, performing the role of regent during her husband's absence. Isabella's strength lay in diplomacy and in this regard was an invaluable asset to Edward's government. In 1313 and 1320, the royal couple travelled to France to the court of Isabella's father and later brother. Edward sought French support in his continuing struggles with the barons, which dominated domestic affairs. Isabella's presence was paramount to Edward's success as the mediator between her natal and marital families and kingdoms. Isabella was also a great peacemaker at home and performed the queenly function of mediator between Edward and Thomas of Lancaster on several occasions. In 1318, an easing of tensions between the two was 'achieved at the request of the lady queen', resulting in the Treaty of Leake.[33] But the rise of a new favourite would restore hostilities between Edward and his barons and bring additional pressures to the English monarch.

Hugh Despenser the Younger (1286–1326) was appointed chamberlain to Edward in October 1318, a powerful court position that ultimately controlled access to the king. Despenser was ruthless, not above imprisoning his rivals or confiscating their lands and used his proximity to the king to further his own interests and those of his family. Despenser's influence over the king, reminiscent of Gaveston's control over Edward, caused the barons to leave the royal court in protest.[34] Initially, Isabella continued to work in partnership with Edward and participated in a ruse to enable her husband to gain entry to Leeds Castle in Kent, held by Bartholomew Badlesmere, an ally of Lancaster and one who had abandoned the royal court. Isabella arrived at Leeds Castle in October 1321, allegedly en route to Canterbury, and was denied entry. A skirmish ensued, and Edward enacted retribution for this insult to his wife by successfully besieging the castle, thereby renewing his conflict with the barons.[35] The civil war that followed became known as the 'Despenser War'. Playing the role of peacemaker once again, Isabella publicly threw herself at Edward's feet and begged for peace for the people within the kingdom. This highly stylised feminine spectacle of queenly behaviour did much to bolster her reputation amongst her English subjects.[36] But on this occasion, Isabella took the side of the barons and begged Edward to exile the Despenser family and restore peace with the barons. The king reluctantly assented to her request and pardoned the barons, but Despenser's exile would be short-lived, returning before the year ended.[37]

Upon his return to court, Despenser would not permit Isabella's influence to continue and from 1321, he limited Isabella's contact with the king. The sources show Gaveston's time in the spotlight had little impact on Isabella; she still had regular access to the king and performed intercession regularly, whereas during

Despenser's ascendancy, Isabella is largely absent from the Patent Rolls and incidents of her intercession fall to zero in some years between 1321 and 1325.[38]

In October 1322, Isabella was placed in jeopardy, when Robert Bruce launched a surprise attack on Edward during his visit to Rievaulx Abbey in North Yorkshire. Sent to Tynemouth Priory for her safety, she soon found herself besieged by Scottish forces. Initially, Despenser was to be sent by Edward to defend the queen, but the king's plans changed, and Henry de Sully was sent in his place.[39] Either Isabella hated Despenser to such an extent by this point that she could not bear to have his men protect her, or de Sully, who had recently arrived from the French court, was considered a more favourable option.[40] This incident proved utterly humiliating for Isabella, Edward and the English, with Isabella, along with her ladies, narrowly escaping the clutches of the Scots.[41] Up until 1322, the royal couple worked in partnership, but from 1323, their relationship deteriorated, and the evidence suggests a separation occurred.[42] On occasion, Edward treated Despenser as though he were his consort, and contemporary sources hint at a sexual relationship between the king and his favourite.[43]

Despenser persuaded Edward to remove Isabella's lands from her control in September 1324. He removed her French servants and, in an even greater insult, removed her children from her custody.[44] Despenser's wife, Eleanor de Clare, was appointed Isabella's housekeeper, enabling Despenser to have eyes and ears on the queen.[45] Pope John XXII wrote in admonishing terms to Despenser, condemning the cruel treatment of the queen.[46] Isabella's indignity grew, driving her to seek retribution.

An excuse to leave the confines of England was granted in 1325. Isabella's brother, Charles IV, now king of France, invaded Aquitaine, leading to a brief conflict with Edward known as the War of Saint-Sardos. Isabella had endured such ill-treatment but had disguised her indignation to such an extent that Edward and Despenser were convinced she could be trusted to represent her husband's interests at the French court.[47] Securing a treaty between her brother and her husband, Isabella then sent for her son, Prince Edward, who joined his mother at the French court to pay homage to the French king for Gascony and Ponthieu.[48] It is unclear whether Isabella had hatched plans to lead a rebellion against her husband before her departure for France or whether these schemes were hatched once she found like-minded individuals discontent with the reign of Edward. Nevertheless, she became a rallying call for disaffected nobles in exile, whether that was her intention or not. One such man was Roger Mortimer (1287–1330), who had led the Marcher Lords in revolt in the Despenser War.

Mortimer strongly opposed the Despensers and their hold over the king and was arrested in Shrewsbury in 1322 for his leading role in the Despenser War. Mortimer was spared the gallows and instead sentenced to life in prison in the Tower of London. The following year, in a remarkable feat, Mortimer escaped, fleeing to

France – he remains one of the few to have escaped the confines of the infamous prison. His escape became symbolic of the struggle against the Despensers, and he became a figurehead and leading member of the cause.[49]

The precise nature of Isabella's relationship with Mortimer is ambiguous. Although Edward's relationships with his favourites are often the subject of intense debate, it is often assumed by historians, with little in the way of scrutiny of the evidence, that Isabella was unfaithful to her husband.[50] Certainly, the pair became allies drawn together by their shared hatred of Despenser and his family. Some contemporary chroniclers, such as *The Chronicle of Geoffrey Le Baker of Swinbrook,* hostile to the pair, presented their sexual relationship as common knowledge: 'she had found comfort in the unlawful embraces of Roger Mortimer, and was just as unwilling to return to England as was Mortimer'.[51] However, as more modern historians have noted, the evidence is not so clear-cut.[52] Nor should we take at face value the notion that Mortimer was calling the shots. Again, sources critical of the pair claimed Isabella was 'ruled in all things by the counsel of Roger Mortimer'.[53] It is noteworthy that, here, contemporaries concluded that the time Isabella and Mortimer spent together was evidence not just of plotting against Edward, but of a love affair. This approach rests on stereotypes about women's essentially fleshly and sexual rather than intellectual and rational natures; by these standards, an affair was the obvious explanation. The narrative of Isabella forsaking her husband under Mortimer's influence suited these views, yet evidence suggests she may have acted strategically to pursue her own ambitions. Indeed, she succeeded in convincing Edward and Despenser of her submissiveness to the point of ensuring the king sent their son to join her in France.[54]

Once news reached Edward of Isabella's alleged antics in France, he demanded she return to England. Isabella refused and in 1325 responded:

> …someone has come between my husband and myself and is trying to break this bond; I declare that I will not return until this intruder is removed, but, discarding my marriage garment, I shall put on the robes of widowhood and mourning until I am avenged of this Pharisee.[55]

Isabella was careful to construct an image of herself as the dutiful wife and the injured party, wearing black clothing publicly, and claiming to have lost her husband to Despenser.[56] This naturally infuriated Edward, who rescinded all financial support to his wife. Notably, Isabella did not blame the king for the marital discord – criticising the king directly would have done little for her image, but she cites Despenser's evil counsel as the reason for the separation.[57] Isabella's supporter, Bishop Orleton, publicly claimed in a sermon that she had been unable to return to Edward for fear of her life at the hands of her husband

and Despenser. Orleton went so far as to claim that Edward carried with him a knife concealed in his shoe to kill Isabella, and declared that if he had no weapon, he would strangle her.[58] This very public image of the wronged queen, the grieving widow, further cast Edward into the characterisation of the degenerate and inept king.[59] Significantly, Isabella called for the restoration of the traditional medieval government, with the king at the head and his queen, his wife, by his side. She presented Despenser as the subverter of traditional and normal societal values by his influence over the king. This subversion not only had negative ramifications for Edward's marriage in that Isabella was driven away, but also, more importantly, for the kingdom overall.

Edward, in turn sought to discredit the reputation of his wife by accusing her of adultery. In a letter to the Sheriff of Nottingham of February 1326 (one of many he distributed throughout his lands), he wrote: '...the queen is adopting the counsel of Mortimer, the king's notorious enemy and rebel, and of other rebels ... to aggrieve and destroy the king's men and his people'.[60] Edward complained of his wife's sojourn in France to his brother-in-law, Charles IV of France. Edward insisted Isabella had no reason to leave him, her relationship with Despenser was friendly, and he asked the king to listen to his pleas for the return of his wife, 'without having regard to the wilful pleasure of [the] woman'.[61] In this narrative, Isabella's affair with Mortimer was cast as the primary cause of the marital breakdown, positioning Edward as the innocent victim. Rumours of Isabella's affair had wider implications and highlighted Edward's failings as a king; unsuited to rule a kingdom if he was unable to rule his own wife. Edwards' inability to enjoy exclusive sexual access to his wife rendered him not only unmanly by contemporary standards, but also, by extension, unkinglike.[62]

Charles refused to send his sister back to England, and although he was willing to offer shelter to Isabella and her allies, his brotherly affection fell short of supporting her plans in 1326 to launch an invasion of England. Unlike Empress Matilda two centuries before her, Isabella was only a consort to the king and could claim no hereditary power in England for herself. Similarly to Matilda's change of tack, Isabella carefully projected an image of a devoted mother who acted only in the interests of her son. She defied her husband, not necessarily for her own sake, but for that of Prince Edward.

Without Charles' financial backing for her planned invasion, Isabella travelled to the court of her cousin Joan's husband, Count William of Hainault, Holland and Zeeland in summer 1326. There, they arranged the marriage of Isabella's son, Prince Edward, to the Count's daughter, Philippa of Hainault. Count William furnished Isabella with a substantial dowry, and using these funds, along with a loan from Charles, she hired mercenaries to fill the invasion fleet provided by Count William.[63] Isabella, Mortimer and Prince Edward accompanied the invading force and landed on the English shores of Kent on 24 September 1326.

Isabella arrived at the head of the fleet as a wife and queen whose purpose was to overthrow her husband with the help of her alleged lover and son. Under any other king, Isabella would have been sent back to France or imprisoned in disgrace as a usurper and disrupter of the natural order. But Edward's deep unpopularity shielded her. Ultimately, Isabella won the hearts of her subjects by convincingly presenting herself as the lady in distress, on a moral campaign to remove Despenser and his evil influence over the king.[64] The little resistance she met was overcome by her supporters.[65] The invading party made their way to London, taking towns and cities as they progressed. On 2 October, Edward, along with Despenser, fled the capital and headed west. When Isabella reached London, Edward's authority had crumbled, and the city was handed to her.[66] Bristol fell to Isabella on 26 October 1326 as Edward and Despenser fled to Wales to seek refuge. Nonetheless, Isabella and her forces were in hot pursuit, and the two now dishevelled figures were captured near Llantrisant on 16 November 1326.[67] Despenser met a gruesome end at Hereford on 25 November. Without trial, he was hanged, drawn and quartered before Isabella. Perhaps indicative of Despenser's alleged sexual relationship with the king, he was castrated, and his genitals were thrown into a fire.[68] Edward was imprisoned in Kenilworth Castle, and parliament was summoned in January 1327, where Edward II either abdicated or was forcibly deposed, and it was decreed that his minor son would replace him as King Edward III.[69] The deposition of an anointed post-conquest king of England was unprecedented, and consequently, Edward's fate was much debated.[70]

Edward II was spared execution; indeed, the execution of an anointed king of England was unthinkable. Instead, he was to face a life of imprisonment, and three plots to rescue the former king were almost successful in April, July and September 1327.[71] As long as Edward remained alive, he was a threat to the new regime, and it was unsurprising news when, on 21 September 1327, Edward II was found dead at Berkeley Castle. Much ink has been spilt over the nature of Edward's death, and many historians have come to the natural conclusion that Isabella and Mortimer had a hand in his death. Soon after his death, rumours began to circulate that Edward died via a hot poker inserted into his anus. Edward's death by anal rape has been interpreted by many as a reference to his sexual identity. Because this rumour was committed to paper so soon after Edward's death (from 1333) it gives the tale some merit, but it did not become the prevailing narrative until a generation later.[72] Other explanations, such as illness or an accident, were put forward to explain the king's death. Some even claimed that Edward had escaped his imprisonment, and a look-alike was murdered in his place until the former king could be found. This theory is supported by contemporary evidence, which claimed Edward's close friends and family were kept away from the king's corpse whilst it was on display.[73] The circumstances surrounding Edward's death remain one of the greatest mysteries of the Middle Ages.

The 14-year-old Edward III celebrated his coronation in February 1327. Isabella was to take a pivotal role in his new government, undertaking the role of regent along with Mortimer, either as her ally or lover. Isabella seized the Despensers' lands, much of which she kept for herself, and others she assigned to Mortimer. She transferred many of the royal lands to herself, leaving Edward only one-third of the share.[74] Her insatiable greed contributed to the unpopularity of her regime with Mortimer. Other factors, such as her peace treaty with France (1327) and her secret recognition of Robert Bruce as king of Scotland (1328) and thereby her abandonment of England's claims to Scotland, disgruntled many of the barons from whom she had found support in 1326.[75] To add insult to injury, Isabella kept for herself most of the reparation money the Crown received from Scotland.[76] Mortimer accused Edward II's brother, Edmund of Kent, of plotting against the government and executed him in 1330.[77] This appears to have been the final straw for Edward, who could no longer tolerate the unpopular regime of his mother and Mortimer. Now, a man aged 17 and no longer a minor, Edward sought not only freedom but retribution.

Edward ordered Mortimer to be seized from Isabella's chambers at Nottingham Castle on 18 October 1330, and Isabella reportedly begged her son to 'have pity on gentle Mortimer'.[78] Mortimer was accused of sowing discord between Edward and Isabella and was held responsible for the murder of Edward II. He was executed for treason on 29 November 1330.[79] Isabella was distanced from blame and was only mentioned indirectly in the list of charges. Edward initially forced Isabella to hand over her dower lands, and for the following two years she remained secluded either because Edward perceived her as a threat to his new regime or because, as has been suggested, she suffered a mental breakdown following Mortimer's death.[80] But she was not impoverished or imprisoned as some earlier historians had maintained; her financial independence was restored, and by 1337 her annual revenue had reached the level of those she had enjoyed as consort.[81] Isabella was no longer a significant political figure, however, following Mortimer's fall, she enjoyed the life of a conventional dowager queen along with the financial benefits and freedoms that came with that role for the remaining twenty-eight years of her life.[82] Although her experimental triumvirate with Edward and Mortimer failed, Isabella was ultimately forgiven by her son for the overthrow and murder of his father and he made frequent visits to her in her later years.[83]

Isabella succumbed to illness in 1358 and met her end at Hertford Castle on 23 August of that year. Her daughter, Joan, Queen of Scotland, with whom she enjoyed a close relationship, was at her side at the end. She was buried with all due pomp and ceremony at the Franciscan Church at Newgate, and her husband's heart was placed within her casket.

Isabella is known to history as the 'She-wolf'; ruthless, vindictive and politically driven. She-wolves are fiercely protective of their cubs, and although Isabella was politically astute and undoubtedly harboured political ambitions of her own, she understood the patriarchal world within which she operated and at least presented a convincing façade of the wronged wife and a devoted mother acting in the interests of her son and her kingdom.

The sources offer us glimpses of Isabella's character, which indicate she was not the power-driven usurper her critics portrayed her as. Isabella was a great supporter of the Franciscans in England to the extent that she was remembered as the mother and protector of the Order. Her generous donations to the Order appear to have been beyond mere queenly conventions of patronage and show a real gratitude and devotion towards its members.[84] Isabella enjoyed travelling and made various pilgrimages, including a visit to Canterbury in 1321 and two visits to the cathedral in the final year of her life. The story of Isabella's discovery of a Scottish orphan during her travels who she cared for, dressed and then sent to be educated in London is often cited by historians who challenge the notion of Isabella the cold-hearted she-wolf.[85]

Yet Isabella demonstrated political ruthlessness. Her decision to order and reportedly witness the gruesome execution of Hugh Despenser the Younger, who was castrated, disembowelled, and beheaded, may appear unqueenly by traditional standards. However, her presence likely served as a calculated display of authority, signalling her capacity for leadership and her resolve to exact retribution on those who opposed her.

Isabella was only able to achieve the overthrow of her husband precisely because of Edward's failings. It would have been inconceivable to consider the possibility of a consort removing any other medieval king in this manner, regardless of the strength of character of that consort. Edward II's failure to make gains on his father's acquisitions in Scotland and his poor military record, coupled with his un-kingly conduct and his unwavering devotion to certain favourites, rendered him unfit for office by contemporary standards and thereby served to justify Isabella's actions.

To some contemporaries, she was the liberator of the kingdom from a sinful, tyrannical king. However, to others, Isabella was a power-hungry woman who acted against the natural order in usurping her husband, her king. Much has been made over the centuries regarding her relationship with Mortimer, and contemporaries ultimately concluded Isabella, a member of the weaker sex, was naturally swayed by Mortimer. Yet these assumptions overlook Isabella's political abilities and experience and fail to uncritically acknowledge her pivotal role in securing the succession of her son.

Women Who Fought

Chapter 6

Sikelgaita (*c*.1040–1090)

The phrase 'Halt! Be men!', reportedly exclaimed by Sikelgaita, is particularly striking and has contributed significantly to the enduring scholarly interest in her. As the wife of Robert Guiscard (1015–1085), Sikelgaita has drawn the attention of historians examining the political and military roles of women in the eleventh century. For some women who feature in this book, such as Eleanor of Aquitaine and Empress Matilda, we have a wealth of evidence regarding their lives and deeds. In the case of others, such as Sikelgaita (sometimes spelt Sichelgaita, or referred to as Gaita), we have little to go on. She lacks a dedicated biography, and aside from a few, albeit significant, scholarly articles, she has attracted limited attention from historians. Yet her life is so fascinating, and her deeds are so extraordinary that her story simply must be told.

Sikelgaita was born around 1040 into a region recently tossed into turmoil thanks to the arrival of several disparate groups of Normans. With limited lands and resources in their homeland, Normandy, coupled with the Byzantine Empire's struggle with the relatively recent Muslim invaders in the region, had drawn the Normans, ever the opportunists, to southern Italy. These newcomers, all living up to the fearsome reputation of their Viking forebears, jeopardised the security of the Lombard kingdom of Salerno, a vibrant city in south-west Italy and the largest kingdom in southern Italy. This was the realm of Prince Guaimar IV of Salerno (*c*.1013–1052), who fathered Sikelgaita by his wife Gemma of Capua. Guaimar died in 1052, and his son and successor, Gisulf II (*c*.1030–1090), sought to secure his position in the region through the marriage of his female relatives to Norman leaders. Robert Guiscard rose to prominence as the preeminent Norman leader in southern Italy, a trajectory famously recounted by Anna Comnena as a rags-to-riches narrative. She accurately describes Guiscard as the landless son of a minor Norman noble, who departed his homeland accompanied by merely five knights and thirty foot soldiers, embarking on a quest to secure fortune and status in a foreign land.[1] Guiscard would eventually succeed his brother, Humphrey, as Count of Apulia and Calabria in 1057. And, in return for his loyalty to the Papacy, Pope Nicholas II conferred upon Guiscard the more prestigious title Duke of Apulia and Calabria.[2] Guiscard had risen from the shadows as the sixth of twelve sons of a petty nobleman, a meteoric rise few could claim in a single generation.[3]

Guiscard proposed marriage to Sikelgaita, Gisulf's sister in the latter 1050s, but according to Guiscard's biographer, William of Apulia, Gisulf was initially hesitant to marry his sister to Guiscard: 'because the Gauls [Normans] seemed to him a race fierce and barbarous, cruel and inhuman in mind, and the repudiation of his first wife imposed a pause before one gave a second!'[4] Guiscard's first wife was a Norman woman named Alverada, by whom he had a son, Bohemond of Taranto (*c*.1052–1111) and a daughter, Emma. A marriage to Sikelgaita was more politically advantageous, and so an annulment of this first marriage was arranged on the basis of consanguinity. A convenient excuse for Guiscard, who could not have been too concerned about the closeness of their relationship, as Sikelgaita was the sister of his brother, Drogo's wife.[5]

Gisulf cast his reservations aside, and the marriage was celebrated in 1058 with the hope of fostering a good relationship with the unpredictable Normans.[6] Gisulf hoped the marriage would ward off William of the Principate, another powerful Norman newcomer and Guiscard's half-brother, who had designs on Salerno.[7] Not only did the marriage offer security for Sikelgaita's family and ensure future political advantages for Sikelgaita herself, but it also helped to secure Guiscard's authority in the region. Far from operating as a united force in southern Italy, rivalries existed amongst Norman lords who looked only to further their own ambitions in the region.[8] His marriage to Sikelgaita provided Guiscard with a sense of authority and legitimacy in the eyes of the Lombards and the Normans.[9] The match effectively made him an heir to the Principality of Salerno and provided him with a stable political foothold among the Lombards.[10] As the chronicler, William Apulia, neatly summarised:

> A marriage of such grandeur much augmented Robert's noble reputation, and people who had previously had to be constrained to serve him now rendered to him the obedience due to his ancestors. For the Lombard people knew that Italy had been subject to his wife's grandfathers and great-grandfathers.[11]

Sikelgaita was around 18 years old at the time of this marriage. We know little of her life before marriage, but there is no evidence to suggest she received any sort of official military training.[12] She probably received an education and training suited to her intended purpose in life, which was to marry and bear children. Together, the couple had a total of ten children: three sons and seven daughters. Their eldest son, Roger Borsa (1060–1111), would go on to fulfil his father's ambitions and become the ruler of southern Italy. Sikelgaita is largely absent from the historical record in the early years of her marriage; this is hardly surprising, as she was preoccupied with providing Guiscard with ample heirs. However, from the mid-1060s, we begin to see her presence in historical documents. For instance, in 1065, she witnessed a charter alongside Guiscard at St Maria at Matina in Calabria. She is noted as the 'daughter of Guaimar of Salerno' rather than being identified as Robert's wife.[13] This implies that her status was essential to Guiscard's legitimacy and a vital component of her husband's power.

Sikelgaita's children enhanced her power and prestige; however, her offspring faced fierce competition from Bohemond, Guiscard's heir presumptive. Sikelgaita used her power and influence to further the prospects of her own children at the expense of her stepson throughout her life. When Guiscard almost died in 1073, his wife made Guiscard's vassals swear allegiance to her eldest son, Roger Borsa, thereby excluding Bohemond and ensuring her son would become the heir to all his father's conquests in southern Italy.[14]

As a Lombard princess, Sikelgaita held substantial regional influence, but she also possessed excellent political skills, which Guiscard relied on frequently, and in one notable example, in an attempt to secure peace with her brother, Gisulf. Despite the alliance forged through marriage, Gisulf soon fell afoul of the Normans, like many before him, and came to regard Guiscard as more of an adversary than an ally. Guiscard's incursions into Amalfi, where he held strategic interests, led to a territorial dispute with Gisulf, prompting Sikelgaita to intervene as mediator. Gisulf's hostile response to arbitration came with a threat to make his sister a widow. A furious Guiscard laid siege to his brother-in-law's stronghold of Salerno in 1076, and the city fell to him eight months later in March 1077.[15] After the complete surrender of the city, Guiscard and his wife made Salerno their Capital, but Guiscard's actions were deemed unjust by the Papacy, and for this conquest, he was excommunicated by successive Popes.[16]

Capturing Salerno by force, Guiscard then looked to consolidate his hold over the region, and Sikelgaita, the Lombard princess who commanded the respect of her fellow natives, used her ancestral roots to lend authority and legitimacy to her husband's rule. In numerous charters, which were issued in her native Salerno, Sikelgaita is referred to either as 'duchess' or, more intriguingly, as 'duke'.[17] Although duke was a title typically used by men, the title could, on occasion, be used by women. Sikelgaita's use of this title suggests Guiscard was using his wife's status to legitimise his position as ruler of the city. Furthermore, it was an acknowledgement that her status was perhaps equal to his own.[18] He had obtained the city rightfully not only by conquest but also by marriage. This made his marriage to Sikelgaita equally as essential to his position in Salerno as was his military conquest of the region.

It has been established that Sikelgaita was an invaluable political ally to her husband, but she is also noted for her involvement in the military activities of Guiscard. The first reference to Sikelgaita's direct involvement in military activities can be found in the pro-Norman account of William of Apulia in events he described as occurring in 1080. Significantly, Sikelgaita's child-bearing years were now over when she appears to have entered the military arena. In this year, Peter II of Trani, Guiscard's arch-enemy, seized the city of Trani, which Guiscard had taken from him in 1073.[19] William tells us that Guiscard: 'left his wife at this siege. He went to Taranto, not without many troops, and besieged it by land and by sea'.[20] William does not explicitly state that Sikelgaita took part in any fighting, but Guiscard certainly placed her in command of the siege. The siege was later hailed a success with the surrender of Peter II, and the city was delivered to Sikelgaita.[21] From this, we can infer that Sikelgaita had some expertise and perhaps some experience as a commander. As a native Lombard princess whose family once ruled Trani, perhaps Sikelgaita was the right person for this job; it was hoped she could win over the people and negotiate a surrender with the least amount of bloodshed and bring a swift victory for her husband. Undoubtedly, her authority was instrumental to Guiscard's success.

Women taking charge of sieges and acting on the authority of their husbands in this role was uncommon, but not unique. As this book aims to show, women could and occasionally did assume roles traditionally reserved for men, but only when acting on behalf of a male relative, as Sikelgaita did for Guiscard. Guiscard was one of the most famous and formidable Normans in southern Italy with grand military ambitions. Yet despite frequent campaigning, he managed to produce a large family with Sikelgaita. This would then suggest that she did indeed accompany her husband on military campaigns. This was not particularly unusual; Anna Comnena herself accompanied her father, along with her mother, Irene on military expeditions. Anna reassures the reader that Irene's presence on military expeditions conformed to gender stereotypes of ideal femininity, adhering to the standards and expectations of the office of empress.[22] Furthermore, Anna and Irene maintained a safe distance from the battlefield. The distinction between the sexes was enforced – the men fought, and the women worried from the sidelines. Anna reinforces the point that her mother was a 'peaceable woman' exhibiting appropriate queenly and feminine behaviour, as a woman, she was not built for warfare.[23]

We also find examples of Sikelgaita suing for peace in Anna's account. Guiscard had designs upon the Byzantine lands in southern Italy and ultimately wanted the imperial crown either for himself or for his descendants. His daughter, Olympias (later known as Helena), had been betrothed to Constantine Doukas, crowned co-ruler of the Byzantine Empire in 1071, ruling alongside his father, Michael VII. Michael was deposed in 1078 by Nikephoros III, and the engagement was cancelled. Desiring to have his daughter returned to him, Guiscard discovered she had been placed into a convent. The breaking of the arrangement gave Guiscard a pretext for war, a war he could wage on her behalf.[24] Anna tells us that Sikelgaita, along with others in his confidence, had advised him not to go to war 'on the grounds that he would be starting an unjust war and one directed against Christians'.[25] For some time, Guiscard heeded this advice, thus casting Sikelgaita as a peacemaker, an accepted feminine role. Perhaps this is no mere trope of a woman petitioning her husband to broker peace; rather, Sikelgaita was as much of a policymaker as her husband, apparently wielding power and influence in her own right by virtue of her status. Nonetheless, Sikelgaita could not contain the ambitions of one of the most formidable and ambitious warriors of the eleventh century, and in time, Guiscard prepared for war and made plans to invade Dyrrachium in 1081.

According to William of Apulia, Guiscard paused at Otranto while he awaited 'the arrival of his wife and of many counts whom he knew were going to be his companions on the march'.[26] It would appear as though Sikelgaita had been raising troops from the regions where she herself commanded authority and was an integral part of Guiscard's planned invasion.[27] Without her assistance, Guiscard would not have been able to gather an army numbering some 30,000, according to Anna.[28] He needed his wife's support for this expedition and her military assistance.

When Sikelgaita arrived at Otranto, Anna adds that she 'went on campaign with her husband and when she donned armour was indeed a formidable sight'.[29] Unlike Anna and her mother, merely bystanders to the military endeavours of her father, remaining at a safe distance from imminent danger, Sikelgaita's donning of armour suggests she appeared on the battlefield.[30] Or else, why waste armour on a non-combatant?

Guiscard arrived at the Byzantine city of Dyrrachium in October 1081 with his army and laid siege. The newly crowned Byzantine Emperor, Alexius Comnenus, Anna's father, came to meet the Normans in battle. Guiscard's eldest son, Bohemond, commanded the left wing, Guiscard the centre, and it would appear Sikelgaita was positioned on the right wing with a contingent comprising Lombards. Sikelgaita may have summoned these men, her own forces, whom Guiscard had been awaiting at Otranto.[31] Alexius' men initially gained the upper hand, causing the Norman-Lombardy forces to panic. Some of them rushed into the sea but were met by Alexius' naval allies, the Venetians. According to Anna, Sikelgaita then made her mark on the battlefield:

> There is a story that Robert's wife Gaita, who used to accompany him on campaign like another Pallas, if not a second Athena, seeing the runaways and glaring fiercely at them, shouted in a very loud voice: 'How far will ye run? Halt! Be men!' – not quite in those Homeric words, but something very like them in her own dialect. As they continued to run, she grasped a long spear and charged at full gallop against them. It brought them to their senses and they went back to fight.[32]

Guiscard's forces were victorious and inflicted a crushing defeat upon Alexius. Sikelgaita is almost credited with turning the tide of the battle in her husband's favour by Anna. But this passage has greater significance than Sikelgaita's contribution to the outcome of the battle.

Although this story at first glance may appear to be a fabrication, if we consider Sikelgaita's political position and assume that these troops were hers, rallied by her from her native Salerno, then the story becomes much more plausible. It is then plausible that the retreating troops were under her direct authority. In this light, her actions align more closely with those of a military commander seeking to rally fleeing forces. Regardless of whether the retreating soldiers were Lombards or Normans, her actions offer a rare example of a woman rallying troops amid combat. The phrase 'Halt! Be men!' is intriguing. Although Anna does admit these were not the exact words Sikelgaita used, Anna attempts to convey an intention and Sikelgaita's words in this moment, according to Anna's sources, served a specific function. Sikelgaita vocally challenges the manliness of these troops, and her actions demonstrate a complete reversal of roles; she becomes the warrior, while they exhibit traits characteristic of the weaker sex.

According to Anna, Sikelgaita shouts in the heat of battle, likely her voice would be drowned out by the shouts of the battle, and so she grabs a spear. This gave a visual aid to her command and was perhaps a spear with a banner attached to give her further visibility.[33] Anna describes her as 'Pallas, if not a second Athena', a reference to the Greek goddess who slew Pallas the giant, and perhaps offering a description of Sikelgaita's physical vigour and a metaphor for her strength and martial spirit.[34]

Anna was fascinated with the Normans and Sikelgaita; nevertheless, they were a thorn in her father's side and secured a humiliating victory against Alexius on this occasion. An alternative reading of the story is that of a critique of the Normans, depicting them as effeminate. The inference is that the Normans are deficient in strength and valour to such an extent that a woman is compelled to prompt them to fulfil their gendered and military roles.[35] Although perhaps guilty of literary embellishments, Anna did not invent the story of Sikelgaita's participation at Dyrrrachium, as her presence on this occasion was noted by other sources, such as William of Apulia:

> In this battle, Robert's wife was wounded by a stray arrow. Frightened by the wound and not expecting help, she was nearly overcome by the enemy: Fearing the dangers of death approaching close she wanted to entrust herself to her ship. God delivered her, not wanting mockery to be made of such a lady, so noble and worthy of veneration.[36]

Sikelgaita, wounded in battle, was only saved by divine intervention, a testament to the validity of Guiscard's cause according to the pro-Norman author. But a wound received in battle did not deter Sikelgaita from further military exploits. In 1085, we find her involved in a naval engagement fought between Guiscard's forces and the Venetians, allies of the Byzantine Emperor. Upon the Venetians' victory, Sikelgaita was almost captured along with her son, Guy.[37]

The leadership of troops and participation in siege warfare by women was not especially uncommon in the eleventh century. What is more exceptional, however, is the explicit documentation of women engaging directly in military affairs and present on the battlefield. References to women sustaining injuries in combat are particularly rare. In this context, Sikelgaita's active involvement in her husband's military campaigns emerges as both distinctive and noteworthy.

Nevertheless, the sources do not exclusively emphasise Sikelgaita's martial involvement or her political agency; they also construct her identity through the lens of conventional femininity, representing her as a wife and mother. In July 1085, upon falling ill with fever, Sikelgaita hastened to Guiscard's bedside to be present at the moment of his death, where she tore her face with her nails and pulled her hair.[38] This conventional, stylised feminine expression of grief can be found in many great classical literary works. While Sikelgaita assumed roles traditionally associated with masculinity when circumstances necessitated, she was also capable of embodying traits aligned with normative ideals of femininity and appropriate female conduct.

Sikelgaita had proven to be an incredibly useful ally to Guiscard as a member of the royal household of Salerno, thereby legitimising his rule in the region. She now transmitted that powerful bloodline to her son, Roger Borsa. Indeed, evidence from throughout Roger's reign reveals he considered his maternal ancestry as important as his Norman heritage.[39] Sikelgaita, the widow, employed her political influence and connections to ensure that Roger, and not Bohemond, would succeed their father. Orderic Vitalis, writing from Normandy some fifty years after events, accused Sikelgaita of poisoning Bohemond whilst Guiscard was on his deathbed. However, as Orderic tells it, Guiscard discovered his wife's crime and ordered her to send Bohemond the antidote, which she duly did, only to then poison her husband.[40] Whatever the origin of this story, either fabricated by Orderic or perhaps drawing upon similar stories in circulation in the twelfth century, it serves to illustrate Sikelgaita's anxiety around the succession, which fuelled imaginations. It highlights Sikelgaita's fundamental role in the promotion of Roger Borsa, by now around 25 years old, albeit with his own military and political experience, as a viable alternative to Bohemond, the elder son and a proven warrior with a military reputation of his own almost rivalling that of his father.[41]

Remaining politically active into her widowhood, Sikelgaita witnessed a charter in Bari in 1086 which handed control over the Jewish community in Bari to the archbishop of the city. Sikelgaita appears in the charter alongside Roger and was titled 'Duke' as in previous charters. The nature of the charter itself was a symbol of her authority; in a similar vein, her father had designated control over the Jews in Capua in 1041. Her direct involvement in this affair suggests she was reluctant to hand over power to her son and acted as regent for Roger in the immediate years following Guiscard's death.[42] Sikelgaita only relinquished power to Roger once an agreement with Bohemond had been reached in her son's favour, and Roger succeeded his father as Duke of Apulia and Calabria.[43] Retiring from politics, Sikelgaita died in April 1090 and was buried in the abbey of Montecassino.

Sikelgaita's status as the daughter of the Prince of Salerno and the bearer of a prestigious dynastic bloodline afforded her a prominent role within her husband's court. As this book has demonstrated, while females exercising authority in the Middle Ages was not the norm, it was by no means anomalous. What distinguishes Sikelgaita, however, is the extent of her active engagement in military affairs. Multiple contemporary sources attest to her presence on the battlefield, where she reportedly donned armour – presumably out of necessity, as evidenced by her having sustained an arrow wound. Sikelgaita's strategic support for Guiscard's military campaigns was closely tied to securing the succession of her son, Roger. Her astute political judgment ultimately ensured that he inherited his father's territorial acquisitions in southern Italy, secured not only through his father's military conquest but also through his mother's status as a Lombard princess.

Chapter 7

Matilda of Tuscany (*c.*1046–1115)

As this book has shown, a woman performing the role of military commander was not unheard of in the Middle Ages, but evidence of women shedding blood on the battlefield is incredibly rare. Directing military affairs is just one way in which Matilda of Tuscany challenged medieval ideas of gender and illustrates that gender theories did not necessarily equate to practice. As a ruler in her own right, Matilda enjoyed a powerful position rarely afforded to most medieval women, and her position was coveted by many male rulers of her age. The personal commentary throughout The *Vita Mathildis* (*Life of Matilda*), commissioned by Matilda and authored by the Benedictine monk Donizo, suggests Matilda was heavily involved in the composition. Although problematic as a historical source, Matilda's commissioning of the *Vita Mathildis* illustrates her awareness of the importance of constructing her own self-image.[1] By focusing on her descent from a prestigious paternal line, the *Vita Mathildis* emphasises the childless Matilda as the final member of a noble and historically significant dynasty.[2]

Matilda was born around the year 1046 to Countess Beatrice of Lotharingia (*c.*1020–1076) and Margrave Boniface III of Tuscany (*c.*985–1052). The count of several regions across northern Italy, including Lucca, Pisa, Modena, Canossa and Margrave of Tuscany, Boniface was the most powerful prince in northern Italy during his lifetime. Beatrice also boasted an illustrious heritage as the daughter of Frederick II, Duke of Upper Lorraine. Through Beatrice, Matilda claimed kinship to Henry IV, the Holy Roman Emperor and king of Germany (1050–1106), as his second cousin (their grandmothers were sisters).

Unlike many of her contemporary counterparts, Matilda's upbringing and family life were briefly recorded by contemporaries. Matilda's mother received praise for her piety, and it was perhaps under the tutelage of her mother, who cared for the sick and gave alms to the poor, that Matilda's own piety was nurtured in her youth. We know that Matilda spoke several languages in addition to her native Italian, including German, French and Latin. Matilda also received an education in theology and the fine arts.[3] This curriculum is consistent with the educational expectations for a noble-born daughter in the eleventh century and does not appear exceptional for her social standing. However, what is unusual is Matilda's tutelage in warfare. She was taught how to fight with an axe, sword, lance, and pike.[4] We might reasonably question whether the delivery of military training to young noblewomen occurred with greater frequency than has traditionally been acknowledged. Owing to a lack of surviving evidence for other eleventh-century high-status women, Matilda is recognised as an exception; however, her experience may have been reflective of wider aristocratic practices.

Disaster befell this family in 1052 upon the assassination of Boniface, Matilda's father. Matilda was the only surviving child of her parents, an older brother, Frederick, and a sister, Beatrice, also died around this time. Boniface's vast territories passed to Matilda with Beatrice as her regent. A wealthy widow and a landowner in her own right, Beatrice and her daughter were vulnerable, and in response, she acted swiftly to secure their political and territorial interests through a strategic remarriage. In 1054, Beatrice chose as her second husband her distant kinsman, Godfrey the Bearded, Duke of Lower Lorraine (*c.*997–1069). However, the marriage had taken place without the permission of the Holy Roman Emperor, Henry III, who felt threatened by this new alliance between his vassals with Beatrice's kingdoms in northern Italy and Godfrey's Lothringian kingdom to the west of the Emperor. Godfrey was temporarily dispossessed of his territories and fled the Emperor's clutches, but Beatrice and Matilda were imprisoned by Henry in 1055 for a year. This formative experience likely had a profound impact on Matilda's development, contributing to the resilience and political fortitude that would later define her.[5] Upon their release, mother and daughter returned to Italy, where Beatrice ruled their territories alongside Godfrey. To strengthen the family connection, Matilda was betrothed to her stepbrother, Godfrey the Hunchback (d.1076), with the couple marrying in 1069.[6] The couple had one child, probably a daughter, who died shortly after birth.

In 1069, following the death of Godfrey the Bearded, Beatrice was rendered a wealthy and financially independent widow. Matilda and Godfrey the Hunchback separated in 1072, and Matilda joined her mother to rule her vast ancestral lands, which stretched across northern and central Italy. A wealthy heiress ruling alongside a politically experienced mother, Matilda was taught the art of governance. Wider political and religious considerations were about to throw Matilda into the limelight and mark her as one of the most significant and incredible women of the Middle Ages.

The eleventh century was a period of profound upheaval and transformation in the history of the Christian Church, marked by some of its most consequential and eventful developments. One of the most noteworthy events of this century was the launch of the First Crusade in 1095. This marked the beginning of a conflict in the Holy Land that would last for centuries. The First Crusade found its roots earlier in that century as popes sought to establish their supremacy in the light of half a century of challenges to their authority from secular rulers. This desire for dominance became known as the Investiture Controversy, and it was a dispute that dominated the entirety of Matilda's adulthood.

From within the Church, a reform movement began to develop in the eleventh century, which found amongst some of its chief advocates a succession of popes. The primary concern of these reformists was the increasing lack of distinction between the clergy and the laity. In response, they mandated clerical celibacy as a means of demarcating the spiritual elite from the lay population and reinforcing clerical identity. Another key issue on the reformists' agenda was the buying and selling of ecclesiastical offices, a practice known as simony. Simony was perceived to undermine the spiritual authority and integrity of the Church. By allowing spiritual offices to be acquired through wealth rather than merit, the most suitable and spiritually excellent were excluded from office in favour of those who could afford to buy their way into positions of power. Akin to this was the issue of lay investiture; secular rulers, such as kings and emperors, appointed their men as bishops and into other high ecclesiastical offices, a prerogative the Church claimed for itself.

The papacy ultimately sought freedom of the Church from the interference of secular authorities whilst asserting its supremacy over secular rulers. While kings held temporal authority within their respective realms, the Church, embodied by the Pope as the successor of St Peter, claimed ultimate jurisdiction over all ecclesiastical matters, thereby challenging the autonomy of lay rulers in spiritual affairs. The assertion of papal authority within secular kingdoms raised a provocative question – 'could a pope depose a king?' The papacy's assertion of authority provoked considerable tension with secular rulers, most notably with Matilda's kinsman, Henry IV, King of Germany, who became one of the foremost challengers of papal supremacy.

Henry succeeded his father in 1054 at the age of 6, and his mother, Agnes, ruled as his regent. His position was inherently precarious and entangled him in a brutal power struggle from an early age. He was even kidnapped in 1062 by Archbishop Anno of Cologne and a group of conspirators in an attempt to seize the 11-year-old's throne.[7] As Henry grew into a man, he struggled to secure his position. He used the appointments of bishops effectively as a way of centralising power and consolidating his position. This strategy conflicted with the ideals of Pope Gregory VII (*c.*1015–1085).

Gregory VII was a zealous proponent of ecclesiastical reform, resolutely committed to eliminating the misuse of spiritual authority for political ends. His efforts to emancipate the Church from secular interference were so influential that the reform movement came to be known as the Gregorian Reform. The Gregorian Reform Movement found its chief secular proponent in Matilda, who became one of Gregory's close confidants and loyal allies. Their relationship was reportedly so close that rumours circulated of a romantic relationship between the pair.[8] Matilda and Gregory VII appear to have shared a sincere and enduring friendship that lasted until the Pontiff's death in 1085, evidenced by twelve surviving letters written by Gregory and addressed to Matilda. In one such letter, Gregory, Matilda's spiritual advisor, refers to Matilda and her mother Beatrice as 'daughters most beloved of St. Peter'.[9]

In a continuation of the policy of his predecessor, Gregory renewed the bans on clerical marriage, lay investiture and simony once he took office in 1073. Henry did not acquiesce to this request and continued to appoint his own bishops. The Investiture Controversy began in earnest in January 1076 at the Council of Worms, where Henry and his bishops condemned Gregory for bringing scandal to the Church through his overt familiarity with Matilda; they declared Gregory's election invalid and demanded he abdicate.[10]

In response to this insult, Gregory excommunicated Henry and released his subjects from their oath of loyalty, effectively declaring his kingship invalid. This act represented a direct challenge to the legitimacy of Henry's rule and marked a dramatic assertion of papal authority over secular power. Matilda was likely deeply conflicted between her spiritual obligations and her temporal duties, bound to Henry as his vassal to whom she owed homage. Matilda's secular responsibilities increased significantly in 1076 with the deaths of both her mother and her husband, leaving Matilda as the inheritor of both their territorial possessions. The territories under Matilda's sole dominion stretched from Lake Garda in the north of Italy to Tarquinia in the south, granting her significant regional power.[11] Nevertheless, wealth and a powerful lineage offered Matilda a degree of independence unavailable to many of her female contemporaries; consequently, Matilda chose not to disguise her Gregorian convictions.[12] As one of the wealthiest landowners in Italy, well-connected and incredibly pious, Matilda became Gregory's most valued and valuable proponent.

Seeking a resolution with the papacy to strengthen his own kingship following a rebellion in Saxony, Henry requested Gregory remove the ban of excommunication. Henry grew impatient as he awaited the arrival of the Pontiff and made his way to Italy. When news reached Gregory of Henry's march to Italy, and fearful that Henry's objective was to seize and imprison him, he sought Matilda's protection at Canossa, a well-fortified castle in the heart of Matilda's stronghold. Henry arrived at Canossa, seeking absolution in January 1077.[13] Matilda, a kinswoman of Henry and a close ally of Gregory, was perfectly placed to perform the role of mediator between the two factions. Matilda's involvement in these negotiations is treated in varying ways by contemporaries. Those who were supporters of the papacy were inclined to mention Matilda's involvement and that of other women present, such as Adelaide of Turin and Agnes, the mother of Henry IV. Whereas pro-imperialist authors often diminish the roles of these women or fail to mention them at all, Gregory acknowledged Matilda's significant role at this meeting, referring to her involvement in a letter to the German princes and bishops regarding the matter.[14]

Matilda found herself at the very centre of religious and political dispute, which, as was understood at the time, would have considerable consequences and dictated Church policy towards secular rulers for centuries. Her leading role in this episode, to the exclusion of males who could have been called upon to perform such a role, demonstrates she outranked her male counterparts.[15] It is important to note that within this dispute, Matilda played the role of mediator rather than intercessor. Intercession, the pleading on behalf of another, was an acceptable feminine role and often used by queens to change the king's resolve or to forward the cause of an individual. However, as a mediator at Canossa, Matilda used her own power and influence, performing an independent role to settle the dispute.[16] Matilda's role is not confined to that of a peacemaker; rather, she emerges as a policymaker in her own right. The significant role Matilda played in this affair proved difficult for contemporaries to reconcile with traditional expectations of female conduct, reflecting broader anxieties about women's participation in high politics during the medieval period. Women did, on occasion, exert power, typically done within frameworks that subordinated them to male authority, whether as wives, regents, or consorts. Matilda, however, defied these conventions; as a widow and independent heiress, she governed autonomously, without dependence on male authority, thereby challenging traditional expectations of female political conduct.

The omission of Matilda's role in the affair by pro-imperialist sources can be attributed to the profound humiliation experienced by Henry IV. In their attempts to downplay the significance of the event, they mention as few details as possible.[17] When Henry reached Canossa, he begged Gregory to withdraw the ban of excommunication. Gregory refused to do so unless Henry undertook penance. For three consecutive days (25–27 January), Henry appeared barefoot in the snow, wearing the hair shirt of a penitent at the gates of Canossa.[18] On the third day, Henry lay prostrate in the shape of a cross on the ground at the feet of the Pope. Urged into reconciliation by Abbot Hugh of Cluny and Matilda, Gregory released Henry from excommunication and, though he stopped short of recognising Henry as king, Gregory did agree to cessation of hostilities with Henry.[19] Although Henry had reconciled himself to the Church, he had done so at the expense of his dignity, and most importantly, he had acknowledged the supremacy of the Pope.[20] The settlement reached at Canossa fundamentally conflicted with Henry's sense of royal authority, and the peace that had been brokered was, unsurprisingly, short-lived.

In 1080, Gregory declared his support for Rudolf of Rheinfelden, elected as an alternative to Henry as king of Germany, or 'anti-king'. Once again, Gregory excommunicated Henry, who responded by proclaiming Gregory's Papacy invalid and had Guibert of Ravenna elected as Pope Clement III, dubbed by Gregorian supporters as the 'anti-Pope'.[21] A strange situation arose: two Popes vied for the

Papacy and for Rome, one with the backing of Henry IV and the other enjoying the continued support of the formidable Matilda. Between 1080 and 1092, Matilda became embroiled in an intermittent war with her cousin.[22] In response to her insubordination as his vassal, Henry accused Matilda of treason, forfeited her lands in Germany and initiated armed incursions into her Italian territories. The military arm of the Papacy, Matilda raised a Papal army recruiting mercenaries into her service, set up ambushes, and her forces met Henry's in battle.[23] In October 1080 Matilda suffered a significant defeat at the Battle of Volta. Emboldened by his success, Henry rampaged through northern Italy and headed south to Rome, intending to take the Holy City and there have himself crowned Holy Roman Emperor by Clement. Gregory fled the Vatican and took refuge in the nearby Castel d'Angelo. Clement was consecrated Pope in St Peter's Basilica in March 1084 and then, in turn, conferred upon Henry and his wife Praxedis the imperial coronation.[24] It was to the Normans that Gregory turned for assistance. Allied with the Papacy since 1059, they responded under the leadership of Robert Guiscard. Henry and Clement fled but opportunists by nature, the Norman troops plundered Rome, and as a result, Gregory was forced to leave Rome with his supporters.[25] As Henry retreated to his imperial lands, Gregory died in exile in May 1085, but Matilda continued to champion the ecclesiastical Reform Movement he had so fervently supported.

Matilda found an equally zealous supporter of the Gregorian Reform Movement in Pope Urban II (*c*.1035–1099), who took office in 1088 and in many ways took Gregory's place as her spiritual mentor. Matilda would once again throw her support and finances behind the Papacy as Urban contested Clement's claim to the Papacy and his occupation of the Vatican over the coming years.[26] As a means of strengthening the Papal cause in their continuing conflict with Henry, Urban persuaded a reluctant Matilda, now in her 40s, to marry Welf V of Bavaria (1072–1120) in 1089, a mere youth, twenty-six years her junior.[27] Matilda showed little interest in remarrying, as a husband would inevitably impose constraints on her authority and independence. And the prospect of marrying an inexperienced and untested 17-year-old was even less appealing. Yet, paradoxically, his youth may have served her interests; a more seasoned and influential husband would undoubtedly have curtailed her power, relegating her to a subordinate role, whereas a younger spouse could allow her to maintain dominance within the alliance. Ever the astute politician, Matilda cast aside her personal feelings, whatever they may have been, and opted for political expediency.

However, this alliance did little to deter Henry in his desire for Rome, who, himself, following his seizure of Matilda's maternal inheritance in Lorraine, launched another campaign into Italy in 1090. Focusing his efforts on the strategically vital territories held by Matilda, Henry advanced on her capital, Mantua, and seized the city in April 1091.[28] In September 1092, Matilda convened a council at Carpineti, in northern Italy. Henry had offered peace in exchange for acknowledgement of the anti-Pope, Clement III, and by extension, Urban II's deposition. After a long debate, Matilda encouraged her allies to continue the fight – such terms were abhorrent to her.[29] The tide turned, and Matilda gained the upper hand, forcing Henry to retreat. Cities in northern Italy, including Milan and Piacenza, then formed an alliance against the Emperor.[30]

Henry suffered further blows at the news that his son and heir, Conrad, had defected to Matilda's cause in 1093. A further shock came the following year when Matilda rescued Henry's second wife, Praxedis, from Henry's imprisonment and took her into her care. Praxedis made serious allegations against her husband at the Council of Piacenza in 1095, accusing him of forcing her to participate in sexual acts with others.[31] Her accusations did little to bolster Henry's reputation, who was now a spent force and abandoned his ambitions in Italy. With the threat posed by Henry diminished, Matilda no longer needed an alliance with Welf and his kin and so abandoned her marriage.[32]

One pressing question which has so far remained unanswered is what exactly was Matilda's role in military affairs? Did she assume the role of commander? Was she present on the battlefield, and did she personally engage in combat? Contemporary sources agree that Matilda assumed the role of military commander. She raised armies and demonstrated exceptional strategic acumen, playing a decisive role in shaping military policy. Her biographer, Donizo, portrays her actively recruiting mercenaries, organising the defence of key fortifications and arranging ambushes.[33] She was sometimes referred to as 'dux' or 'leader', often accompanied by laudatory epithets such as 'most prudent leader' or 'most celebrated leader', reflecting both her authority and the high regard in which she was held by her supporters and contemporaries.[34] Dux was a title usually reserved for men, which could be occasionally employed to describe powerful women.[35]

But a commander, or leader, is distinct from a soldier, who engages directly in combat. Although, for the most part, Donizo describes Matilda's activities as commander away from the battlefield, he does refer to a clash between her stepfather, Godfrey the Bearded and the Normans in 1067.[36] Here, Donizo implies that Matilda actively participated on this occasion and, for her services, was credited thereafter with the title 'daughter of St Peter'. This epithet, associated with St Peter, was reserved for those who physically took up arms in defence of the Papacy during the Investiture Controversy.[37] References to Matilda's active military participation can be found in other sources, such as a report from her friend and spiritual advisor, Anslem II of Lucca. He describes Matilda as willing to do whatever it takes to champion the reformist cause, 'even to the shedding of her own blood'.[38] To justify her actions, Matilda was on occasion labelled a *virago* by her contemporaries, as a woman whose actions were consistent with those commonly associated with masculinity and exhibited manly characteristics such as courage and bravery. Clerics, always eager to criticise women who acted in unnatural ways for subverting the gender hierarchy, were forgiving of *viragos* when they fought or acted in defence of the Church.[39]

Justifications for Matilda's engagement in traditionally masculine military activities were grounded in biblical precedent. A frequently cited example was the Old Testament figure Judith, who used her feminine charm to infiltrate the enemy camp and famously decapitated the Assyrian general Holofernes while he slept. Judith's actions were likened to Matilda's defeat of Henry as a military act of divine justice performed by a woman.[40] Anselm II of Lucca portrayed Matilda as a soldier of Christ, fighting a Holy War, just as Judith and Deborah had done, thereby rendering Matilda's subversion of conventional gender norms irrelevant.[41]

The Investiture Controversy continued beyond Matilda's death until 1122, but her direct involvement in these affairs diminished as the threat of Henry subsided. Matilda still busied herself with matters of the Church. She was no doubt a great asset to Pope Urban II as he developed his plans for a crusade in 1095. Matilda had already shown her devotion to the recovery of formerly Christian lands from Muslim hold when in 1087 she contributed troops to a Pisan-Genoese mission to modern-day Tunisia to combat Muslim forces occupying former Christian territories.[42] Matilda's dispute regarding the inheritance of the Duchy of Lorraine with the nephew of her first husband, Godfrey of Bouillon (1060–1100), who assumed a leading role in the First Crusade, may have prevented her direct participation in the expedition.[43] Moreover, her age, she was by then in her fifties, may have been a contributing factor. Although her absence from the expedition may lend support to the argument that women were effectively prohibited from participating in the crusade in a direct, personal capacity. Yet Matilda did support the cause by offering troops whilst remaining at home.

Matilda ruled as an independent woman until her death; she acted like a ruler or, in fact, as a king. Understanding the importance of visibility, Matilda travelled throughout her territories, dispensing justice, issuing charters, personally signing and sealing 139 of them.[44] Matilda spent the majority of her later years at the Monastic house of San Benedetto in Po, Lombardy. In 1113, the rumour of Matilda's death began to circulate, prompting the citizens of Mantua to rebel. However, upon witnessing the elderly Matilda leading her troops, they begged for her pardon.[45] This would be the last time Matilda saw military activity. She died in July 1115 at the age of 69 and was laid to rest at her beloved San Benedetto, a religious institution that had benefited from Matilda's generosity throughout her life. Centuries after her death, the bells were rung on the first Monday of every month in remembrance of her.[46]

Matilda ruled her own lands as an independent childless woman and made efforts during her lifetime to resolve the matter of succession. She appears to have considered Conrad, Henry IV's son, as a potential inheritor of her lands; however, he died before Matilda.[47] Following her death in 1115, Henry's second eldest son and eventual heir, Henry V, the husband of Empress Matilda, came to Italy to claim what became known for centuries after as the *Matildine Lands*.[48] Although Matilda has never been officially canonised, miracles were attributed to her after her death, and she was venerated for centuries following her death. Pope Urban VIII had her body transferred to Rome in 1633, and she became the first woman to be buried in St Peter's Basilica.[49]

Matilda's unique combination of secular authority over a vast domain and her role as the military champion of the Papacy rendered her an unparalleled figure in medieval Europe. Her exceptional position in the European political landscape afforded her a position of power in a fundamental issue which dominated eleventh-century politics: the Investiture Controversy. Matilda, who perhaps even actively participated in combat, or at least commanded her own troops, proved to be a formidable force and a significant ally for the Papacy, thwarting the lofty ambitions of the powerful Henry IV.

Chapter 8

Joan of Arc (1412–1431)

Joan of Arc is exceptional, not only for her actions throughout her short life but also as the most thoroughly documented woman of the medieval period outside of royal or noble lineage. Born into a peasant family, Joan managed to transcend gender and social class, gaining admiration across all strata of society: from peasants and clergy to nobility and royalty, including the king of France. We know so much about Joan precisely because she was tried and executed for heresy in May 1431 at Rouen, and it is through the records of the trial that we can hear Joan's voice and listen to her story. Her innocence was pronounced a quarter of a century later in the Trial of Nullification; the investigation which preceded this conclusion gave more evidence of Joan's character and personal piety from those who knew her best. Joan's life was dominated by the events of the Hundred Years' War (1337–1453) and the Armagnac–Burgundian Civil War (1407–1435); both conflicts ravaged her homeland and left France in need of a hero, or a heroine.

French fortunes in the Hundred Years' War declined upon the accession of the 11-year-old Charles VI (1368–1422) in 1380. Like his grandson, Henry VI of England, Charles suffered from sporadic bouts of mental illness throughout his adult life, rendering him intermittently unable to rule. His frequent absences from matters of the Crown left a power vacuum which those close to him sought to fill. Factions soon took up arms in familial strife known as the Armagnac-Burgundian Civil War. This internal strife enabled the English to obtain their victory at the Battle of Agincourt in 1415, and the Treaty of Troyes (1420) saw Charles VI's son and heir, Charles the Dauphin (1403–1461), disinherited in favour of the English claim. Upon the deaths of both King Henry V and King Charles VI in 1422, the infant, Henry VI, son of Catherine of Valois, daughter of Charles VI, was acknowledged as the king of France and England with regents ruling in his stead. The Burgundians, led by Philip, Duke of Burgundy (1396–1467), unable to unite with the Armagnac faction to expel the English from France, instead allied with the English and fought against the Armagnacs, who supported the restoration of the French Valois dynasty and took up the cause of Charles, the disinherited Dauphin, who would later become Charles VII. It was amidst this strife that Joan of Arc entered the pages of history, convinced of her mission to ensure the expulsion of the English from French lands and the crowning of the Dauphin.

Jehannette, known to history as Joan of Arc, was born in 1412 in the small village of Domremy in the region of Lorraine. Joan never referred to herself as 'Joan of Arc', nor is it likely she ever heard the designation applied to her; she identified only as 'la Pucelle' (the Maid) to underscore her virginity.[1] The region into which she was born was an isolated pocket of land loyal to the Dauphin's cause, surrounded by lands under Burgundian control or those of his supporters. The youngest of five children, two of Joan's brothers, Jean and Pierre, would later fight alongside her. Their parents were Jacques d'Arc and his wife Isabelle Romée. A serf and an agricultural labourer, Jacques also served as the dean of the village and the village leader. In this prominent role, Jacques collected taxes and was responsible for the defence of Domremy.[2] Although identified as peasants, the d'Arc family owned fifty acres of land, suggesting a relatively prosperous status within the village community. During her trial, Joan revealed she had many godparents, which is a testament to the family's status within their community.[3]

In an effort to emphasise Joan's religiosity, she was often incorrectly described as a shepherdess. Joan herself denied ever tending sheep or other animals in the fields.[4] Nevertheless, the conceptualisation of Joan the shepherdess conjured Biblical images as St Paul had told his followers to 'Be Shepherds of the Church of God'. The birth of Christ had been first revealed to the humble shepherds, members of this profession thereafter garnered a reputation within the Christian Church as innocent and particularly receptive to the Word of God.[5] The designation of Joan's date of birth to 6 January, the date of the Epiphany, was another way contemporaries sought to associate Joan with Christ and the Nativity.[6]

At her trial, Joan claimed she began to hear a voice she identified as the voice of God at the age of 13. Visitations from various angels and saints, including St Michael, St Catherine and St Margaret, soon followed.[7] When questioned, Joan claimed, 'the first time she heard her voice, she took a vow to keep her virginity, so long as it pleased God'.[8] Her status as a virgin was to become central to Joan's identity. Initially, reassuring Joan that she was a good child and encouraging her to attend Church regularly, they then transformed the nature of their conversations from domestic issues into political, and commanded Joan to leave her home and 'go to France' (presumably meaning the Dauphin).[9] It is possible that hallucinations and voices were triggered by the raid upon Domremy in 1425, an event which Joan had perhaps found especially traumatic.[10] At her trial, Joan recounted that her mother had relayed her father's dream that she would depart with men-at-arms, a detail often interpreted as foreshadowing her military role.[11] However, this may instead reflect Jacques's fear of his daughter's abduction and sexual assault as evidenced by his preference for her death over such a fate, thus illuminating the stark insecurities of Domremy in the 1420s.[12]

Joan had been experiencing visions for three years before she embarked on her mission to obtain an audience with the Dauphin to secure his coronation and save France. Without the knowledge of her parents, Joan travelled to the court of Robert de Baudricourt, the commander of the Dauphin-aligned garrison at the nearby Vaucouleurs, a lonely outpost in the English-Burgundian occupied Champagne on two occasions, firstly in May 1428 and then in December of that year.[13] Baudricourt initially refused to support her quest to travel to the Dauphin and suggested she should be taken 'back to her father's home and smack her'.[14] News of Joan and her mission had begun to circulate and had caught the attention of Charles II, Duke of Lorraine (1365–1431), who had incorrectly assumed she was a healer and summoned Joan to appear before him at his court in the nearby city of Nancy.[15] Joan was accompanied on this journey by her ardent supporter, Jean de Metz, who is believed to have first provided her with male attire.[16] The reason behind Joan's assumption of male dress at this stage was likely pragmatic, aimed at concealing her sex to deter possible sexual aggression.

Joan divulged little of her intentions to the duke, whose loyalties had oscillated between the Burgundians and the Dauphin. Now drawn into the Dauphin's orbit by his son-in-law, René of Anjou (1409–1480), father of Margaret of Anjou, the Duke of Lorraine favoured the Dauphin's cause. René's mother, Yolande of Aragon (1381–1442), and mother-in-law of the Dauphin, may have promoted Joan's cause at Nancy. It was perhaps through Yolande that Joan was given crucial information regarding current military and political proceedings, which would have enabled Joan to 'predict events'.[17] The duke gave Joan his blessing for her mission to travel to the Dauphin and provided her with a horse, money and an escort back to Vaucouleurs. Even at this early stage, Joan emerges as a headstrong woman, unafraid to assert herself and issue directives to those of higher social rank. Her parting admonition to the Duke of Lorraine was to dismiss his mistress and restore his wife, warning that God disapproved of his conduct.[18]

Returning to Vaucouleurs, Baudricourt had little choice but to offer Joan his support, but only after a priest had performed an exorcism to ensure she was not under demonic influence.[19] Joan had also convinced Baudricourt of the legitimacy of her quest in reminding him of a prophecy: 'that France will be destroyed by a woman, and restored by a virgin from the marches of Lorraine'.[20] The woman to destroy France was Isabeau of Bavaria, whose agreement to the conditions at Troyes had disinherited her son, Charles the Dauphin, and Joan firmly believed she was the one to rescue her nation.

Before she embarked on her 300-mile journey to Charles' palace of Chinon, the inhabitants of Vaucouleurs provided her with her own clothing designed for men:

> Joan cast aside all women's clothing and had her hair cut round (in a bowl shape), like a young man's. Then she put on a shirt, breeches,

a doublet, and hose fastened together by twenty loops, high-laced shoes, a short, knee-length robe, a close-cut hood, tight-fitting boots, long spurs, a sword, dagger, cuirass, lance, and other elements of martial equipment typical of a man-at-arms. And with these she practiced feats of arms.[21]

Again, it made practical sense for Joan to don male clothing, as part of a logical attempt to resist drawing the attention of passing travellers and to deter her companions from sexual arousal. Her haircut, too, cut an inch or so above the ears, was fashionable among fifteenth-century men and made practical sense, facilitating the use of a helmet.[22] Beyond donning male armour for practical purposes, Joan began to train for warfare, receiving some rudimentary training in combat from her travelling companions. A teenage girl, dressed in full martial armour, wielding and making full use of a sword, is unique in the source material. Joan was embracing a new identity and assuming a male role.

At the time of Joan's arrival at Chinon in February 1429, morale was low in the Armagnac camp. The English-Burgundian alliance had gained a decisive upper hand, and their victory at Orléans, an Armagnac stronghold besieged by the English-Burgundians since October 1428, seemed imminent. French forces loyal to the Dauphin, including those led by the Bastard of Orléans, made regular raids on the English stationed outside the city walls. On 12 February 1429, a failed attempt to intercept food and supplies arriving for the English soldiers was amusingly dubbed the 'Battle of the Herrings'.[23] Joan's arrival at Chinon with her compelling sense of patriotism could not have been timed better.

At her trial, Joan claimed to have known who the Dauphin was amongst the hundreds of men in attendance at Chinon 'by the counsel of her voice, which revealed him to her'.[24] It is plausible that Charles orchestrated a test of Joan's divine claims by concealing his identity. One witness would later note:

> When the King knew that she was coming, he withdrew to one side, stepping back from the others. But Joan clearly recognised him and bowed to him; she had a long meeting with him.[25]

Such courtly deceptions were not uncommon in the fifteenth century, making it entirely plausible that Charles did indulge in this game when his new guest arrived.[26] The incident works twofold; in emphasising Charles' aura of kingship and highlighting Joan's holiness and powers of divination derived from God.[27] In all likelihood, this was a staged event because Joan had probably met Charles before this much-discussed meeting.

Arriving at Chinon, Joan likely obtained a secret audience with the Dauphin and a small number of his attendants, facilitated by his mother-in-law, Yolande of Aragon. Yolande's involvement in the whole affair, from the time of Joan's arrival at Nancy, would explain how Joan obtained an audience with the Dauphin in the first instance.[28] Still uncertain of Joan's credibility, when she was publicly welcomed to court, Charles and his courtiers 'only laughed and mocked her … and considered this Joan to be simple-minded, not taking any notice of her words'.[29] Joan told the Dauphin she had been sent by God to come to save the people under siege at Orléans, chase the English from France and see the crowning of Charles at Reims, where French kings were traditionally crowned.[30] Charles had to be sure of Joan's legitimacy and be seen to be using the proper channels of doing so before he could publicly support any of her ideas. Consequently, he sent her to be questioned at Poitiers by a committee of theologians and inquisitors, where she arrived on 1 March 1429. The purpose of the proceedings was to investigate whether Joan's visions were truly divinely inspired, as she had claimed, or demonic in nature. Following three weeks of questioning, they found nothing contrary in her Catholic beliefs and suggested the Dauphin furnish her with an army and send her to Orléans, for in doing so, he had nothing to lose.[31] The confirmation of Joan's virginity by matrons under Yolande's direction validated a central aspect of her identity.[32]

Convinced of her legitimacy, Charles agreed to fulfil Joan's desire to be sent at the head of an army to lift the siege of Orléans. Charles probably arranged for Joan to receive some additional rudimentary military training to prepare her for what was to come. Witnesses would later testify that Charles had a suit of armour made for Joan, which properly fitted her body.[33] The white suit, comprising cuirass, neck plate, gauntlets and footwear, cost a staggering one hundred livres tournois. In comparison, the Duke of Orléans' armour worn at the Battle of Agincourt (1415) cost eighty-four livres tournois. Preparing a suit for a female body may explain the inflated cost of Joan's suit. Several helmets were also provided for Joan, suggesting that she was intended to play an active military role rather than serving as a symbolic figurehead for the Dauphin's cause; there was an expectation she would appear in the thick of battle.[34]

Joan was furnished with a special sword, retrieved from a hidden location in the church of Sainte-Catherine de Fierbois, upon the instruction of her voices.[35] A standard was made for Joan by her own design, the particulars of which were dictated to her by her voices. Two angels stood beside the figure of Christ, who held either a fleur-de-lys or a globe. The words 'Jesus Maria' were written on the standard made from white canvas fringed with silk on a field of fleur-de-lys.[36] At her departure for Orléans in April 1429, Joan's appearance had completely changed. Initially donning male attire for practical purposes, she had now been transformed and took on the appearance of a military leader.

Her sex did not deter recruitment; news soon spread of Joan's prophetic gifts, and she led a force of some 10,000 to 12,000 soldiers to Orléans.[37] A month before leaving for Orléans, Joan dictated a threatening letter to be sent to the English calling them to 'surrender to the Pucelle [maid], who has been sent here by God … the keys of all the good towns that you have taken and violated in France'.[38] This was the first of several aggressively toned letters Joan sent to the English at Orléans. Their response, if they gave one, has not survived. Likely, they mocked and ridiculed the French, who had now seemingly depleted their military resources and were forced to send not men, but young women to confront them. Little did it occur to them just how powerful a figure Joan would prove to be.

Joan arrived at Orléans in late April 1429, her banner held aloft, marching behind a string of priests, and she approached the city to the accompaniment of hymns and to the great relief of the besieged. Her arrival was a visual display of a heavenly-sanctioned military force, evoking the notion of Soldiers of Christ with Joan at the head, leading this divine army.[39] Joan was determined to stamp her authority and to involve herself in strategy, and immediately began by challenging the military counsel given by one who had been instrumental in efforts to lift the siege; the Bastard of Orléans.[40] Slipping through the English blockade alongside the Bastard, Joan entered the city riding her white horse with her banner preceding her and was welcomed by crowds of grateful citizens who hoped for a glimpse or a touch of their saviour.[41]

From within the city of Orléans, Joan pushed an aggressive policy and would not falter or halt her determination to lift the siege even when receiving a wound to the shoulder. Taking herself away from the battle for but several minutes, she returned holding her standard, making the English tremble in fear.[42] By 7 May 1429, the English were defeated, and on the following day, Joan watched on as the English army lifted the siege and retreated. Joan had promised the Dauphin a sign of her holiness, and the victory at Orléans was widely interpreted as confirmation of her divine inspiration. It was an important victory both strategically and symbolically for Joan and Charles. She now set her mind to her second promise to the Dauphin, his coronation at Reims, a task complicated by the fact that the city lay within Burgundian-controlled lands.

Joan met the Dauphin at Tours, and he embraced her warmly, and witnesses noted the evident affection in his manner.[43] Some advised Charles to attack Normandy, an English stronghold in France. But Joan, recognising the symbolic potency of the king as God's anointed sovereign, advised that once he had been crowned, English power in France would ebb away.[44] Furthermore, Joan claimed this was the will of God, and so Charles decided to follow the advice of his military maid and, from Tours, made his way to Reims in Joan's company.

The Duke of Alençon was appointed commander of the Dauphin's army, but Charles instructed Alençon to act in accordance with Joan.[45] Joan played an active role in the capture of Jargeau (11–12 June 1429); joining the attack on the English, Joan stood in a ditch holding her banner when she was struck on the head by a stone. Once again, wounds inflicted in the heat of battle did not deter the maid, and she

1. Statue of King Alfred the Great, Winchester (1901). (*Photograph: Ashley Firth*)

2. Æthelflæd Monument at Tamworth Castle Grounds (1913). (*Photograph: Ashley Firth*)

Above: 3. Statue of Æthelflæd, near Tamworth Railway Station (2018). (*Photograph: Ashley Firth*)

Below: 4. The ruins of St Oswald's Priory, Gloucester. (*Photograph: Ashley Firth*)

Brittene igland is ehta hund mila lang.
7 twa hund brad. 7 her synd on þis
iglande fif geþeode. englisc. 7 brit
tisc. 7 wilsc. 7 scyttisc. 7 pyhtisc. 7
boc leden. Erest weron bugend þises
landes brittes. þa coman of armenia. 7 ge sætan
suðewearde bryttene ærost. þa gelamp hit þ pyh
tas coman suþan of scithian. mid langū scipū
na manegum. 7 þa coman ærost on norþ ybernian
up. 7 þær bædo scottas þ hi ðer moston wunian. ac
hi noldan heom lyfan. forðan hi cwedon þa scottas.
we eow magon þeah hwaðere ræd gelæron. we witan
oþer egland her be easton. þer ge magon eardian gif
ge willað. 7 gif hwa eow wið stent. we eow fultumiað. þ
ge hit magon ge gangan. Da ferdon þa pihtas. 7 ge
ferdon þis land norþan weard. 7 suþan weard hit hef
don brittas. swa we ær cwedon. And þa pyhtas heom abæ
don wif æt scottum. on þa ge ræd þ hi ge curon heora
kyne cū aa on þa wif healfa. þ hi heoldon swa lange
syððan. 7 þa gelamp hit imbe geara rina. þ scotta
sum dæl ge wat of ybernian on bryttene. 7 þæs lan
des sum dæl ge eodon. 7 wes heora heretoga reoda ge
haten. from þā heo synd ge nemnode dæl reodi. Six
tegum wintrū ær þā þe crist wære acenned. gai iuli'
romana kasere mid hund ehtatigū scipū ge sohte
bryttene. þer he wes ærost ge swenced mid grimmum
ge feohte. 7 micelne dæl his heres forlædde. 7 þa he

5. A page from the Anglo-Saxon Chronicle (c.1150). (*Public domain via Wikimedia Commons*)

Left: 6. Queen Emma and her sons being received by Duke Richard II of Normandy, Cambridge University Library, Ee.3.59: fol. 4v. (*Public domain via Wikimedia Commons*)

Below: 7. The Ordeal of Queen Emma, by William Blake (1779). (*Public domain via Wikimedia Commons*)

Above: 8. 'God Begot House', reportedly the former home of Emma of Normandy, Winchester. (*Photograph: Ashley Firth*)

Right: 9. Emma receiving the *Encomium* – illumination from *Encomium Emmae Reginae* (11th-century). (*Public domain via Wikimedia Commons*)

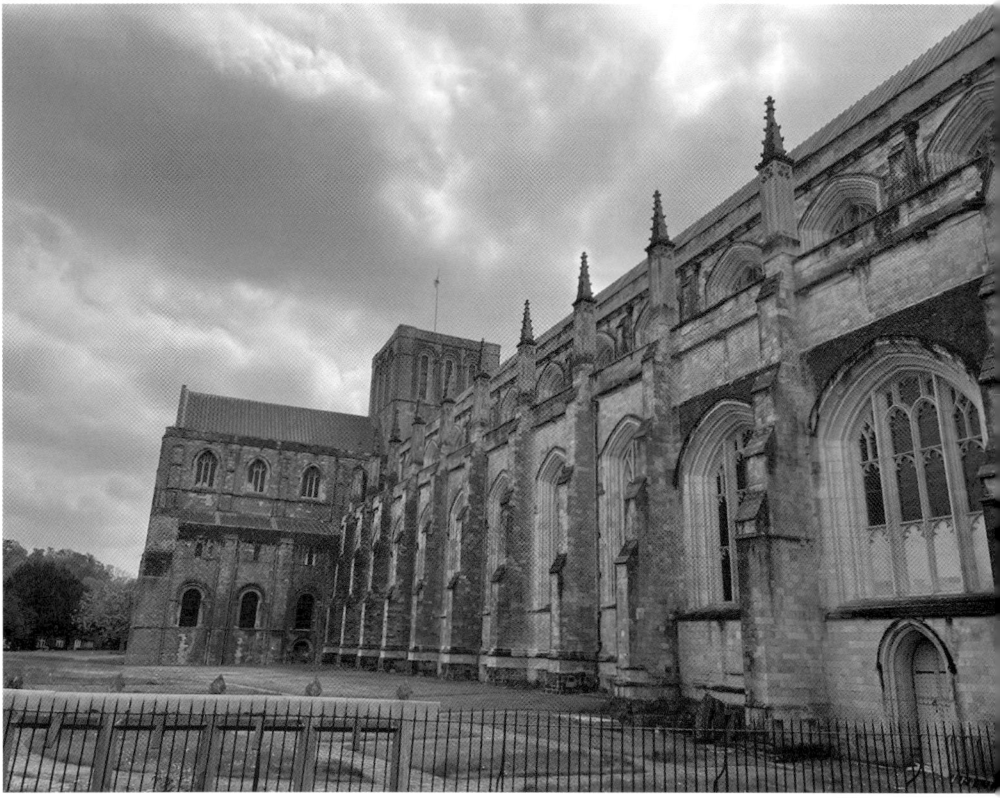

Above: 10. Winchester Cathedral, the burial place of Emma of Normandy (*Photograph: Ashley Firth*)

Left: 11. Empress Matilda at the crowning of her granddaughter, Matilda of England, as Duchess of Saxony, from the *Gospels of Henry the Lion* (circa 1188). (*Public domain via Wikimedia Commons*)

12. Wedding of Louis VII and Eleanor of Aquitaine. Chantilly, Bibliothèque du château, 0867 (0324), f. 121r. (*Public domain via Wikimedia Commons*)

13. The ruins of Old Sarum, the former prison of Eleanor of Aquitaine. (*Photograph: Ashley Firth*)

Above: 14. Isabella of France and her son, Prince Edward, paying homage to Charles IV, Illustration from an edition of Froissart's Chronicles (15th century). (*Public domain via Wikimedia Commons*)

Left: 15. Isabella of France. Detail from Jean Froissart's Chronicles (15th century). (*Public domain via Wikimedia Commons*)

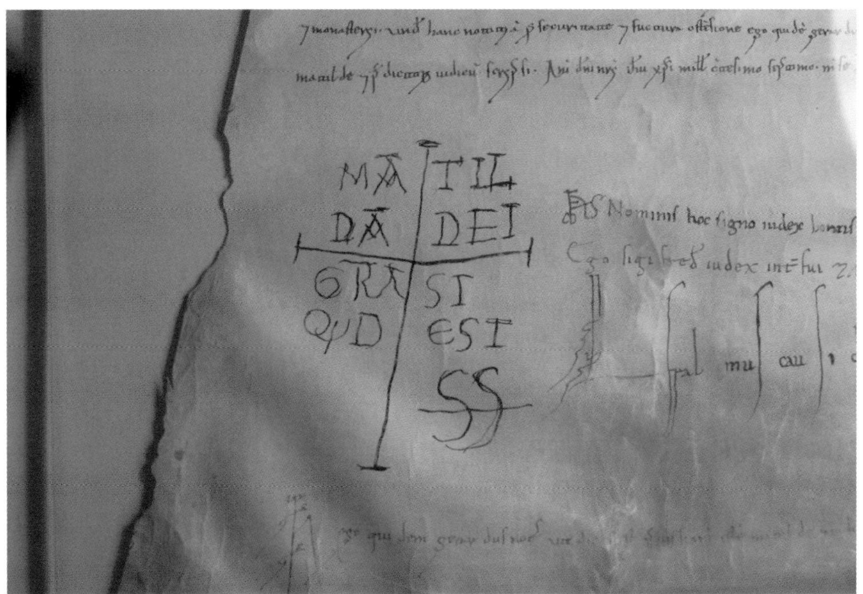

16. Signature of Matilda of Tuscany on Notitia Confirmationis (1107). (*Public domain via Wikimedia Commons*)

Above left: 17. Matilda and Hugh of Cluny interceding for Henry IV. From Vita Mathildis, Codex Vat. lat. 4922 (11th century). (*Public domain via Wikimedia Commons*)

Above right: 18. Joan of Arc in the protocol of the parliament of Paris. Drawing by Clément de Fauquembergue. French National Archives (1429). (*Public domain via Wikimedia Commons*)

19. Joan of Arc, Victorious Over the English, Returns to Orléans and Is Acclaimed by the People, by Jean-Jacques Scherrer (1887). (*Public domain via Wikimedia Commons*)

20. Coronation of Charles VII at Reims, with Joan of Arc present. From Les Vigiles de Charles VII, folio 55v, BnF NAF 4811. Manuscript, Bibliothèque nationale de France (15th century). (*Public domain via Wikimedia Commons*)

21. Christine de Pizan lectures a group of men. The British Library Board, Harley 4431, f.259v. (1413). (*Public domain via Wikimedia Commons*)

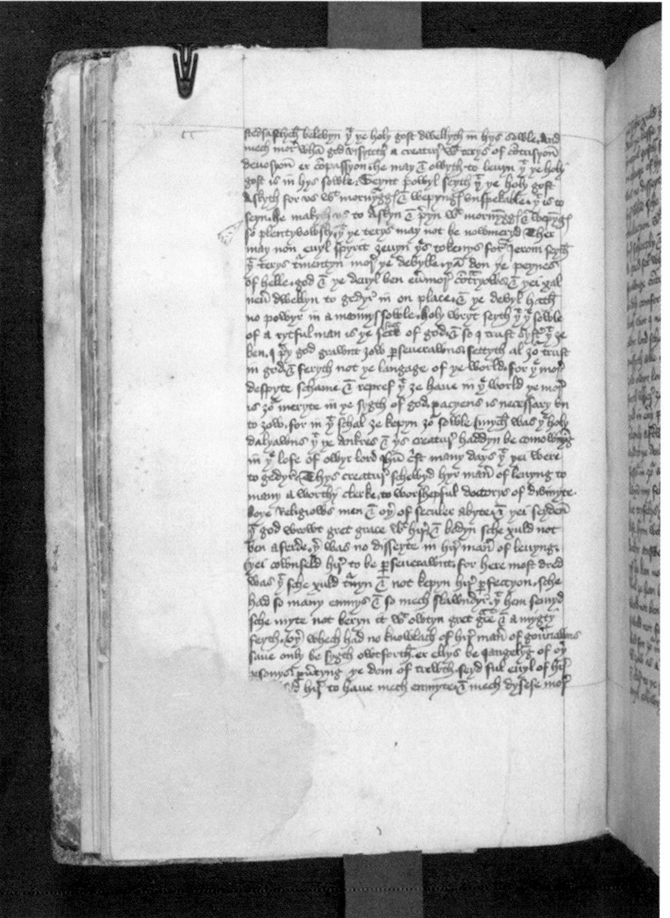

Above: 22. Illumination from *La Cité des Dames*, attributed to the Master of the City of Ladies. Manuscript held by the British Library, Harley MS 4431, fol. 290r (c. 1405–1410). (*Public domain via Wikimedia Commons*)

Left: 23. A page from The *Book of Margery Kempe*, British Library MS Add. 61823 (15th century). (*Public domain via Wikimedia Commons*)

24. Cecily Neville, mother of King Edward IV, depicted in a *Book of Hours* belonging to the Neville family (c.1430). (*Public domain via Wikimedia Commons*)

25. The marriage of Henry VI to Margaret of Anjou. Miniature from *Les Vigiles de la mort de Charles VII* (c.1484). (*Public domain via Wikimedia Commons*)

26. Marriage of Edward IV and Elizabeth Woodville, miniature from *Anciennes Chroniques d'Angleterre* by Jean de Wavrin, Bibliothèque nationale de France (15th century). (*Public domain via Wikimedia Commons*)

27. The tomb effigy of Margaret Beaufort at Westminster Abbey (c.1512). (*Public domain via Wikimedia Commons*) (*CC0 1.0*)

28. The Marriage of Henry VII and Elizabeth of York, after Jan Gossart by H.Cook, Courtesy of the Metropolitan Museum of Art (1826). (*Public domain via Wikimedia Commons*)

Above: 29. The Tudors. Detail from the Whitehall Mural (after Hans Holbein the Younger, 1537), painted by Remigius van Leemput (c.1667). (*Public domain via Wikimedia Commons*). Top left to bottom right: Henry VII, Elizabeth of York, Henry VIII, Jane Seymour

Left: 30. A portrait of Elizabeth of York, Cultural Heritage Agency in the Netherlands Art Collection (c.1530). (*Public domain via Wikimedia Commons*)

spurred her soldiers on to victory.[46] Several towns defected to the Dauphin's side as he travelled northwards with Joan by his side, and the citizens of Reims, occupants of the city held by the Duke of Burgundy, allowed him to enter unopposed in July 1429. This marked the first recorded instance of a legitimate coronation occurring behind enemy lines, and the exceptionality of the situation fits well with the unique nature of Joan's narrative.[47]

The coronation of Charles was conducted hastily and without the traditional grandeur ceremony, but it was a legitimate coronation, nonetheless, held in the cathedral at Reims on 17 July 1429. Once Charles VII had been crowned, Joan's usefulness had run its course. Her determination to pursue an aggressive campaign against the English-Burgundian alliance clashed with the more cautious stance of the king and his advisers, who preferred negotiating peace from a position of strength. This approach was influenced by the fact that the Duke of Burgundy had become receptive to diplomatic overtures.

Making his way to Paris with Joan in August 1429, cities fell to Charles as he continued to negotiate with his adversaries. On 8 September, the Feast of the Nativity of the Virgin Mary, a day on which military engagement was formally prohibited by the Church due to its spiritual significance, Joan initiated her assault on Paris.[48] That evening, after being wounded in the thigh by an arrow and removed from the battlefield, Joan continued to urge her troops to press forward. On the following morning, she rose and ordered the resumption of the offensive. Many who had previously followed her were unwilling to continue to pursue a hopeless assault. Within a day, Charles called off the attack, and Joan retreated in fury.[49] Her refusal to support Charles' pursuit of peace led Joan to embark on a series of unsuccessful private military expeditions, and these failures seemed to suggest God had withdrawn his favour for Joan's cause; consequently, her popularity waned. But Joan was determined to fulfil her mission and drive the English from France.

On 23 May 1430, during an engagement with Burgundian forces at Compiègne, Joan was pulled from her horse by a soldier in the service of John of Luxembourg, a vassal of the Duke of Burgundy, capturing her as a highly prized prisoner of war. After several failed escape attempts, Joan was transferred into English custody in November 1430. As a prisoner of war, Joan was theoretically eligible for ransom. However, Charles had completely abandoned the young woman responsible for his coronation. There was no indication that Charles ever considered negotiating her release or raising her ransom.[50] The 19-year-old Joan was completely alone, discarded and isolated and forced to contend with some of the greatest theologians of her age.

Joan was accused of heresy, but her crime was also dressing as a man and initiating harm to the English cause. This was to be a religious trial, conducted by the Church, seeking to convict the defendant of heresy rather than for war crimes, thereby removing the political dimension of the trial and calling to the universality of the Church. A sentence would be passed, and justice would then be administered by the secular authorities. However, Bedford, King Henry VI's regent in France, made it clear that Joan's fate was predetermined:

> Nevertheless it is our intention to retake and regain possession of this Joan if it comes to pass that she is not convicted or found guilty of the said crimes, or those of them concerning or touching our faith.[51]

If the Church found her innocent, the English secular court would find her guilty. Either way, Joan was condemned.

Joan appeared without a legal representative, forced to speak for and defend herself, completely alone. Unfortunately, her accusers failed to tell Joan precisely what she was accused of, thus she was unaware of the line the questioning would take.[52] Held in Rouen, the capital of English Normandy, Bishop Pierre Cauchon was appointed master of the trial, which took the form of an inquisition. Some of the greatest theologians from the University of Paris had been assembled to assist in the interrogation of the 19-year-old illiterate and theologically ignorant Joan. Of the 131 clerics on the panel, all but 8 were French; thereby, Joan was tried predominantly by her compatriots and not the English.[53]

Although the trial was a foregone conclusion, efforts were made by the tribunal to maintain the appearance of procedural legitimacy.[54] Joan would be questioned by several members of the council, sometimes by a few. The trial initially took place in an open public setting in the royal chapel within the castle at Rouen. Later, to break her spirit, the inquisitors would question her within her cell in the castle as she remained chained. Facing questions from these highly trained scholars, Joan did remarkably well in answering their enquiries. At the beginning of the trial, her interrogators bore witness to the wilful spirit she was famed for in her confidence in some of her flippant answers. 'Asked whether Saint Margaret does not speak English, she answered: "Why would she speak English, when she is not on the English side?"'[55] Unafraid to stand her ground, she refused to answer particular questions, and challenged the requests to repeatedly swear an oath, 'I don't know what you wish to ask me. Perhaps you might ask me things I can't tell you'.[56] However, towards the end, following lengthy interrogations over a five-week period, we bear witness to the breaking of Joan's spirit as her answers became more confused and less coherent. We see the spark fade from Joan as she succumbs to her fate.

The interrogators pursued multiple lines of accusation, notably questioning Joan about Domremy's notorious 'fairy tree', in an effort to implicate her in witchcraft. Joan acknowledged the tree's reputation for healing, yet denied ever seeing fairies there, and prudently conceded that she could not verify any cures, thereby distancing herself from allegations of pagan belief.[57]

Unable to obtain further details about the local superstition, the inquisitors shifted their focus to Joan's assumption of male attire, a central concern throughout the trial. Joan indicated a willingness to wear a dress but maintained that her male clothing had divine sanction, having been instructed by her voice and the saints to dress in this manner.[58] The tribunal viewed her clothing as an indication of moral corruption and a transgression against gender norms, describing it as:

> utterly disregarding the honor due to the female sex, throwing off the bridle of modesty, and forgetting all feminine decency, wore the disgraceful clothing of men, a shocking and vile monstrosity.[59]

Unlike nuns or female transvestite saints who were praised for assuming masculine traits to transcend feminine weakness, Joan's gender nonconformity was seen not as virtuous but as dangerous and illegitimate. Furthermore, Joan did not conform to the accepted models of female sanctity, and thus her perceived holiness had to be discredited to undermine the legitimacy of her cause. Her adoption of male clothing, along with her military activities, was presented by her interrogators as a direct challenge to the patriarchy.[60]

Joan initially told the judges her voices came directly from God. Pressed for further information, Joan included the visitation of saints in her response. Initially reluctant to discuss these visitations in detail, Joan eventually offered up more and more information. She identified the saints as St Michael the Archangel, St Catherine of Alexandria and St Margaret of Antioch. Significantly, the two female saints were also virgins, and despite their youth, like Joan, they became powerful political voices who were also questioned by the leading scholars of their time.[61] Both revered in Joan's region, Joan's sister and niece were named Catherine, and a statue of St Margaret stood in her parish Church of St Remy.[62] St Michael was also venerated in the Lorraine region, and from the fifteenth century, he was associated with the French royal family. Like Joan, Michael was an intermediary between God and man, and as an angel, he transcended gender.[63] If we consider that Joan was pressed for answers on the identity of the angels and her non-descript information in her initial questioning, it would be reasonable to conclude that Joan may have been making up these answers as she went along. In identifying these saints, she may have been trying to identify herself with their legends.[64] But as the questioning regarding these saints progressed and as Joan became more and more willing to discuss them, she unknowingly fell into the trap of her judges.

The interrogators asked Joan to describe the angels; did they appear as spirits or as apparitions in bodily form? Asked if she saw St Michael and the angels corporeally and really, she replied: 'I saw them with the eyes of my body, just as well as I see you'.[65] Joan's visions and voices could have been explained as part of a normal fifteenth-century religious experience.[66] Joan was not the only female visionary or mystic operating in the early fifteenth century. Margery Kempe is a contemporary example, as well as Catherine de la Rochelle, whom Joan met in Autumn 1429. But Joan was no normal visionary; her interrogators were at pains to establish her visions as demonic in nature. Joan, a 19-year-old illiterate peasant girl, was unaware of the deeper theological complexities of her day. Unbeknownst to Joan, visitations from apparitions taking bodily, corporeal form were believed to be demonic in nature, whereas angels and saints were thought to be ethereal.[67] Joan's descriptions of her encounters with the saints, in embracing them, and in touching and kissing their faces and feet, were sufficient to lead to the conclusion that she had conversed with the devil and was a heretic.[68]

To extract an admission of guilt from Joan, she was threatened with torture whilst in her cell; she stoutly refused. But her resolve broke when, on 24 May 1431, Joan was shown the scaffold prepared for her execution, a psychological tactic intended to provoke recantation. Facing death with the executioner present and a crowd gathered, Joan quickly came to the realisation that neither her voices nor King Charles would save her, and she recanted. Joan's decision was likely influenced by fear and a desire to avoid execution. She denied the validity of her apparitions, agreed to submit to the judgment of the Church and confirmed she would abstain from wearing male attire.[69] The following day, her head was shaved as an indication of her repentance, and she was given a woman's dress, which she wore.[70] However, on 28 May, she was found to have once again adopted male clothing. According to some contemporary accounts, Joan resumed male clothing after her dress was removed, possibly as a defence against sexual assault. With no other clothing available, Joan put on the male attire. Other sources suggest the clothing was left in her cell as a form of temptation, knowing Joan was unable to resist.[71] Whether by coercion or choice, her resumption of male attire constituted heresy in the eyes of the Church. Joan was to be executed as a relapsed heretic. When questioned, Joan claimed the decision to resume male clothing was her own, that she did so as a promise to receive the Eucharist had been broken. Moreover, in her fear of the fire, the saints told her: 'that she damned her soul to save her life'.[72] She later asserted that her renunciation of her visions had been made under duress, now admitting she continued to experience divine apparitions. Joan claimed she would rather die than endure prison.[73]

Handed over to the secular powers for her execution, Joan was taken to the marketplace at Rouen on 30 May 1431 to be burned as a relapsed heretic. Joan asked for a crucifix to hold during her execution. A sympathetic Englishman quickly fashioned one from wood and handed it to her. Another crucifix was held before her eyes as she died from smoke inhalation soon after the fire was lit.[74] Her body was destroyed by the fire, and her remains were tossed into the river Seine, removing the possibility of posthumous veneration of any bodily relics.

Charles failed to speak of the maid he had abandoned to the flames until he established an inquiry to investigate the original trial in 1450. The English had now been removed from French lands following their loss of Normandy, and proving Joan's innocence could only strengthen his kingship. Charles' coronation was, after all, a result of Joan's efforts, and if he could associate himself with her legend if she was found innocent, it would not harm his reputation. The record of the Nullification Trial 1455–1456 provides us with some otherwise unknown details of Joan's life, some of which have been used throughout this chapter to offer a much broader depiction of Joan. We hear the voices of Joan's mother, of her childhood friends, of those who fought beside her. The Nullification Trial overturned the previous verdict, declaring the original proceedings corrupt and politically motivated.[75] In 1920, Joan was canonised by the Catholic Church, not as a martyr, but as a Virgin who led an exemplary life.[76] Although the secular authorities were responsible for Joan's execution, the Church had found her guilty, making her recognition as a martyr institutionally problematic. Instead, her execution was framed as the result of a political rather than a religious cause.[77]

The precise nature of Joan's involvement within the army of Charles VII and whether she fought has attracted intense scholarly debate. Some historians have argued she was a mere standard-bearer who did not engage in fighting at all.[78] Others have envisaged a more active role for Joan, who was usually found in the heat of the battle, and therefore cannot be assigned as a mere standard bearer.[79] Although Joan did not engage in hand-to-hand combat, her deployment on the battlefield following rudimentary military training and a bespoke suit of armour indicates that Charles envisaged her playing an active, morale-boosting role rather than serving merely as a figurehead. Her identification with maleness and knighthood, including donning armour and adopting chivalric ideals, became central to her self-conception and public image.[80]

Joan was never in command of Charles' army. Charles' generals offered advice based upon years and sometimes decades of military experience. She did lead a smaller group of soldiers, and others rallied to her standard in the heat of battle. A more appropriate designation for Joan's military status may be 'Captain', given her leadership of small contingents and influence on troop morale. Her aggressive strategy, however, often conflicted with the more measured approach of Charles' seasoned commanders, and this was ultimately her downfall. Whatever her precise military role, Joan's popularity and importance lay in her uniqueness as a woman within the army, and that did enough to reach the popular imagination.[81] She became a beacon of French patriotism and injected a sense of religiosity into the Hundred Years' War. Her legend began to develop within her lifetime, and even when Charles found himself unable to pay the soldiery, many claimed they wished to fight 'in the company of the Maid, saying that they would go wherever she wanted'.[82]

Women Who Wrote

Chapter 9

Anna Comnena (1083–1153)

Anna Comnena is recognised as one of the first female historians of the medieval period. Her epic work, the *Alexiad,* is both a biographical account and a panegyric, written in praise of her father, Emperor Alexius I Comnenus (*c.*1057–1118). It also provides a rare and invaluable perspective on Byzantine politics through the lens of a woman. Anna's decision to undertake the role of a historian was undoubtedly one inspired by the feats of women at the Byzantine court who frequently challenged assumptions about gender and undertook offices traditionally reserved for men. Her own involvement in court intrigue and a succession dispute further underscores the extent to which she challenged contemporary expectations surrounding women's roles in governance and society.

Anna was born in December 1083, the eldest of seven children of the relatively newly crowned Emperor of the Byzantine Empire, Alexius I Comnenus, and his wife, Irene Doukaina (*c.*1066–1138). Alexius, a military general, came to the imperial crown in 1081 following a coup and was considered by contemporaries to have been a generally popular alternative to other potential candidates. Anna proudly proclaimed in the *Alexiad* that she was 'born and bred in the Purple', thus making her a porphyrogeniti.[1] Children born in the Purple, (a phrase derived from the colour of the imperial birthing chamber) or born during the reign of their fathers enjoyed a special status in Byzantine politics and culture. Anna's devotion and obedience to her parents are first alluded to when she was in the womb. Her father was away on campaign when her mother went into labour with Anna. Irene asked Anna to await her father's arrival, and the baby dutifully complied with her mother's request.[2]

Instability and political intrigue made an early betrothal for Anna necessary to secure Alexius' position, and a match was made upon her birth to Constantine Doukas (*c.*1074–1094), a former joint infant emperor from 1074 to 1078, who ruled alongside his father, Michael VII Doukas (*c.*1050–1090), thus further legitimising Alexius' position through his daughter. As was customary in Byzantium, Anna went to live with her future mother-in-law, Maria of Alania (1053–1118). Maria had enjoyed the position of empress twice as the wife of two successive emperors: Constantine's father, Michael VII and his successor Nicephorus III, who ruled

Byzantium for a short time prior to Alexius' coup.[3] Maria was a formidable woman and plotted with Alexius to overthrow her husband and install Alexius as emperor. Alexius was rumoured to have considered making Maria his own wife.[4]

Anna and Constantine were designated as Alexius' heirs and were to rule jointly following his death. However, plans for succession changed once Irene gave Alexius a son, John (1087–1143). John became Alexius' heir, and Anna and Constantine were cast aside.[5] Constantine disappeared from the historical record, perhaps dying around 1094, possibly before or shortly after his formal marriage to Anna.[6]

In the *Alexiad*, Anna tells us in her own words about her remarkable education and thanks her parents for giving her the gift of learning. She was taught Greek, rhetoric, and the sciences and had read Plato and Aristotle.[7] As a teenager, she studied philosophy and, against her parents' wishes, she secretly took lessons in grammar (perceived to be a dangerous pursuit for men, let alone women).[8] The *Alexiad* itself stands as a testament to Anna's excellent education. Throughout her monumental work she references Homer and demonstrates an acute awareness of ancient Greek literature, drawing deliberate parallels between events of her own day and those of the Greek past.[9] Anna's educational journey continued following her marriage to Bryennius who appeared to actively encourage his wife's pursuit of learning. The example of Anna indicates that it was perfectly acceptable for Byzantine women to be highly educated and to follow literary pursuits in Byzantine society.[10]

Anna's second husband was Nikephoros Bryennios (1062–1137), whom she married around 1097. Either his father or grandfather (the sources are unclear as to which) had been captured and blinded by Alexius some years before, but Nikephoros found favour with the Emperor and enjoyed a good relationship with him as his son-in-law.[11] The couple had had two sons, Alexios Comnenus (*c.*1102) and John Doukas (*c.*1103) and two daughters, Irene and Maria, whose dates of birth are unknown and several other children who died in infancy. Significantly, their children were named after members of Anna's family and not Bryennios', indicative of the importance of women within Byzantine society.[12] The marriage appears to have been a happy one with Anna referring to Bryennios as 'my Caesar [who] excelled among all men who live beneath the sun'.[13] Bryennios, an author himself, encouraged his wife's education and became a trusted servant of Alexius, serving the Emperor in military and political missions. Bryennios successfully defended the walls of Constantinople against the aggression of the First Crusaders under the leadership of Godfrey of Bouillon in 1097.[14] Bryennios also accompanied Alexius on military campaigns, who sought the expertise and oratory skills of his well-educated son-in-law in diplomatic and spiritual matters.[15]

The birth of Anna's brother, John in 1087 gave Alexius a clear and definite opportunity for a smooth succession after his death. The Byzantine Empire had experienced tumultuous succession disputes in the eleventh century and a father-to-son transfer of power would offer stability to the Empire, which had lost multiple territories to the Norman incursions from southern Italy as well as the Muslim expansion to the east. Yet Anna still harboured ambitions of the throne, hoping to see her husband crowned instead of John.[16] A strong sense of bitterness runs through the *Alexiad*, and, although he proved to be a worthy successor of their father, Anna cannot conceal her jealousy of John throughout the *Alexiad*. She does not hesitate to undermine John's character, at one point even referring to his 'stupidity'.[17]

Anna's parents were divided in opinion regarding the succession, and as Alexius prepared John for the succession, even producing a handbook on rulership, Irene still hoped to see Anna and Bryennios succeed her husband.[18] Anna tells us that Alexius sought Irene's counsel on the matter throughout his reign; however, according to a later chronicler, Choniatēs, Alexius reminded her that no emperor had set aside a suitable son for his son-in-law.[19] Alexius placed great faith in Irene. When he fell ill in 1112 and was unable to rule, he effectively appointed her as his regent. Irene, in turn placed her faith in Bryennios and handed over administration of the Empire to him.[20]

As Alexius lay on his deathbed in 1118, he confirmed John as his heir. Irene attempted to persuade him to change his mind, but to no avail. Anna describes Alexius' deathbed scene in a dramatic fashion but is careful to present the imperial family as a loving one, with Alexius cared for until the very end by his devoted wife.[21] However, the historical reality was far more turbulent. Irene was actively conspiring to bypass her son John in favour of Anna and Bryennios. According to Choniatēs, John took the signet ring from Alexius' dead finger. Some accused him of theft, and others claimed this was, at the least, inappropriate.[22]

Anna is notably silent on events in which she was implicated immediately following her father's death. Irene continued to uphold her daughter's claim to the throne, but the reason for her preference is unclear. Perhaps she assumed she could wield greater control through Anna than through John. Anna, living in the shadows of a series of powerful Byzantine women who wielded great power and authority, wanted to be empress herself. Her mother was her closest example, and the powerful Maria of Alania undoubtedly helped to shape Anna's character during her formative years, as well as her paternal grandmother and namesake, Anna Dalassene (d.1102). Anna Dalassene was instrumental in securing Alexius' acquisition of the imperial crown and had acted as regent for Alexius during his absence. Although she did not possess the title of empress, Alexius gave his mother remarkable powers throughout his reign.[23]

Before his death, Alexius, aware of his wife's schemes, secretly had his relatives swear to accept only John as their new emperor. John had not been idle and had gathered a significant following. Irene initially won over the support of the Varangians (an elite unit within the Byzantine army, made up mostly of

Anglo-Saxons and Vikings who acted as the emperor's bodyguards). However, when John took the palace by force, support for Irene's cause subsided, and he was declared emperor in August 1118.[24] In the following year, Anna and Irene made another attempt for the throne, but Bryennios's lack of enthusiasm and his failure to make a move against John meant their plans came to nought, and John was left to consolidate his position.[25] Choniatēs claimed that Anna was infuriated with her weak husband and caused her muscles to tense during intercourse, causing Bryennios pain.[26] Bryennios could likely foresee that a coup was an unwise move. He was, after all, a seasoned politician.

Anna's attempts for the throne were unsurprising; Byzantine emperors were no strangers to coups and assassination attempts. What was unusual was a woman's attempt to seize power in this way, and Anna's sex makes her an anomaly in this not uncommon practice. John was surprisingly forgiving, with Anna surviving her brother's wrath with the loss of significant possessions, which were later reinstated. John naturally felt uneasy with the presence of his troublesome mother and sister at the palace and encouraged them both to retire from political life to the convent Kecharitomene, a convent founded by Irene herself.[27] This was not a prison, and Irene and Anna enjoyed a retirement without confines. However, removal from the intellectual and political environment of the palace and its surrounding environs must have felt like a terrible punishment to Anna, a woman of great intellect and a thirst for learning.[28] Anna followed her scholarly interests from her monastic setting, and surrounded herself with some of the most renowned scholars of the day, with whom she discussed the classics, including Plato and Aristotle.[29]

Bryennios continued to serve the imperial throne and was a loyal and dependable military general to John, likely to the great annoyance of his wife, until his death in 1137, and Irene followed him to the grave the following year. Anna's sense of grief at the loss of her father, mother, and husband can be felt through her words, 'But living I died a thousand deaths'.[30] Anna continued to live in the convent Kecharitomene until her own death in 1153, taking the veil on her deathbed.[31]

Anna's removal from political life in the latter years of her life gave her the opportunity to embark on what is considered her greatest achievement, the *Alexiad*. Written in Greek between 1118 and 1148, the significance of the *Alexiad* cannot be overstated. It is the only text of the pre-modern era composed by a woman in Greek. The work is a wonderful insight into political life in eleventh and twelfth-century Byzantium from someone close to the Emperor. Anna was an eyewitness to many of the events she discussed. For those she did not bear witness to, she had access to eyewitnesses; Alexius' generals, Byzantine politicians and significantly, she had access to the imperial archives.

The inclusion of a discussion of detailed military matters has led some historians to speculate that the *Alexiad* was reliant on Bryennius' account and Anna was rather the mere editor of her husband's work.[32] However, most historians have dismissed this claim strongly, advocating that the *Alexiad* is Anna's own composition, whilst acknowledging that Bryennius' work was indeed a useful source for Anna's own work. Indeed, Anna tells us, she wrote her account because her husband had been unable to complete his own version of the history of Alexius, which had been requested of him by Irene.[33]

In the preface to the *Alexiad*, Anna sets out her credentials and the purpose of her book. The term 'historian' is anachronistic; in the Middle Ages, the profession of 'historian' did not exist. However, one could demonstrate their affiliation with other compilers of history (or historians) by following literary convention. Discussing one's credentials, humbling oneself as unfit to the task and setting out the purpose of the text as she does, Anna demonstrates her awareness of these conventions and associates herself with fellow compilers of history. These literary conventions say something about Anna's excellent education – she had read histories and knew how to set out a text in the conventional manner.

The *Alexiad* is, in essence, an epic biography of Alexius, Anna's beloved father. Anna draws upon idealised imagery of a ruler from Biblical sources and classical literature. She points to Alexius' impeccable character and virtues, which make him, in her opinion, the ideal imperial ruler. Anna claims to offer an unbiased account of her father. This is clearly not the case. Her aim was to glorify and honour her father after his death and to present Alexius as a shining example of imperial rule. Alexius and the glorious Byzantine Empire take centre stage; both were the centre of Anna's entire world. Yet despite the obvious exaggerations and biased assessment of her father, historians recognise the value of Anna's work, not only for what it can tell us about Byzantine politics, but also as a rare example of female authorship in the medieval period. Anna refused to adhere to the stereotypical roles expected of medieval women; we can see this in her attempts to overthrow her own brother. Why would she be any less adventurous in her literary pursuits?

One theme that emerges from the *Alexiad* is the close relationship enjoyed between Anna's parents. Irene is presented as an attentive wife and the perfect empress. Saintlike in her deeds and incredibly pious, she would much rather have shunned public life. However, Alexius insisted she accompany him on military expeditions, Anna explains, for she could soothe his gout. But also, to protect her husband from dangerous conspirators who sought to do the Emperor harm.[34] Who better to watch over him than his wife? An alternative reading of Alexius' insistence on Irene's presence during his campaigns is his reluctance to leave a dangerous wife at home in his absence.[35] Anna is at pains to present the ideal nuclear family, children raised by parents devoted to each other and their children. As we have discussed, the reality of the Comnenus family was rather different. Mother and sister plotted against John, but in presenting the family in an ideal way, Anna could further offer praise to Alexius, the ideal father and husband. Perhaps looking back on events in the latter years of her life, Anna remembered a happier time when her father was alive, and an overwhelming sense of nostalgia crept into her work.

The *Alexiad* also comments on wider political events, most notably, the First Crusade (1095–1099), one of the most dramatic and exciting episodes in the *Alexiad*. Indeed, the *Alexiad* is the only contemporary source for the First Crusade from the Byzantine perspective, making it an invaluable source for crusade historians. For Anna, the First Crusade was not solely motivated by a desire to liberate Jerusalem, but also to enact the Latin conquest of the Byzantine Empire. Anna perhaps met some of the First Crusaders as they passed through Constantinople in 1097 when she was a child, and offers some wonderful descriptions of these men from a non-western perspective.[36]

Anna deserves recognition as a pioneering medieval woman for several reasons. Primarily, as an author of an epic biography at a time when almost exclusively such texts were composed by men. Her contribution to historiography is remarkable not only for its literary merit but also for its rare female perspective on Byzantine politics and imperial life. In addition, Anna demonstrated significant political ambition actively encouraged by her mother, another politically astute woman. Anna inserts herself into the *Alexiad* in a seamless way in a narrative strategy rare amongst her contemporaries, but in keeping with her character of pushing beyond established boundaries. In the *Alexiad,* Anna shines a light on a group often excluded from medieval texts – women. Without Anna, information regarding the exploits of women such as Sikelgaita and Empress Irene would be forgotten.

Chapter 10

Christine de Pizan (1364–*c*.1431)

In 1364, in a small town near Venice, Christine de Pizan was born, the first documented woman in history to have made a living solely from her writings. Some have dubbed Christine a 'feminist' and a 'champion of her sex'. However, Christine was very much a product of her time, yet, unusually for a woman, she entered the political fray with the pen, advocating for a female regency during a time of great political upheaval.

Her father, Thomas of Pizan (d.1387), was a well-respected, highly educated physician and astrologer, studying and then lecturing in astrology at the University of Bologna. Christine remembered her father as an incredibly learned man who was 'famous everywhere as a celebrated scholar'.[1] He would have come to know Jean André, the instructor of canon law at the university and his daughter, Novella, whose intellect was so remarkable that she was permitted to lecture her father's classes from behind a screen lest the students be distracted by her beauty.[2] As people sought an explanation for the Black Death that swept across Europe between 1347 and 1353, they turned to science, and in the fourteenth century, astrology was the most advanced branch of the discipline. Astrologers were sought after by rulers who valued their counsel and incorporated their expertise into the courtly decision-making processes.[3] Thomas' services were requested by none other than the French king, Charles V (1338–1380), whose interests in astrology were far more immediate than matters relating to the wonders of the universe. A fragile man who suffered from ill health, he undoubtedly sought answers to the nature of Divine will, considerations which were triggered by French losses during the Hundred Years' War.[4]

Once settled in employment as the king's astrologer at the French court in Paris, Thomas sent for his family in 1368, including his wife, two sons and his 4-year-old daughter, Christine. Christine would never return to her native Venice and self-identified as French as an adult. Received graciously by the king, Christine found his court intellectually stimulating. Charles V was himself highly intelligent and used his royal palace, the Louvre, to create a permanent site for the French royal library. The three-story library contained vernacular translations of popular texts from their original Latin, commissioned by the king.[5] Christine would later

98

recall Charles' love for books, a king who granted his advisers access to his royal collection.[6] Christine herself had access to these books and was incredibly well read, enabling her to draw upon classical literature and more modern treatises in her future literary career. Christine later explained that she resembled her father in all aspects except sex, including intellect. In allegorical form, she described her father's two treasures (medicine and astrology). But because of her sex, Christine was unable to inherit these treasures from her father:

> because I was born a girl, it was not ordained that I should benefit
> in any way from my father's wealth, and I could not inherit, more
> because of custom than justice … and because of this, I lost through
> lack of learning any chance of taking this very rich treasure.[7]

Christine's sex barred her from any formal education, and speaking to the limitations placed on her by her sex, she was instead taught, in her own words, from the 'crumbs I gathered from my father's table'.[8] In later life, she recalled how her father actively encouraged her informal learning.[9]

Christine tells us that her hand in marriage was sought by knights, nobles and clerks on account of her father's position at court as a favourite of the king.[10] In 1380, the 15-year-old Christine made a prestigious match as the bride of Etienne de Castel (d.1389), a well-educated court notary and secretary around ten years her senior. The couple were something of a love match, and whenever Christine wrote of her husband, it was invariably in a positive light, describing him '…without equal in the world; I could not have wished for anyone more wise, prudent, handsome and good than he was, in all respects'.[11] Christine would later write: 'A sweet thing is marriage, I can well prove it by my own experience'.[12] In this ballad, Christine goes on to describe Etienne's gentleness on their wedding night and repeats the line 'the gentle man loves me well'.[13] Etienne encouraged his wife's love of learning, perhaps introducing Christine to royal documents. The couple had three children, two sons and one daughter born between 1381 and 1385, but only two would reach adulthood. Her daughter, Marie, joined the convent at Poissy and her son, Jean, would later join the household of the Earl of Salisbury as a companion for the earl's son, thereby seemingly securing his future.[14]

Christine's early years were marked by happiness, but the late 1380s brought radical change to her world and fortunes. Christine's father and husband were reliant upon the protection and generosity of King Charles V, and when he passed away in 1380, her family found the court of his successor, Charles VI, to be less generous. Charles VI came to the throne as a mere boy of 12, and a regency was formed to rule in his stead. His uncles, Philip II, Duke of Burgundy, Louis I, Duke of Anjou, John, Duke of Berry and Louis II, Duke of Bourbon, served as regents and held on to power until the king reached his early twenties. This was perhaps an early indication of his health issues, which would surface as the years wore on. Thomas and Etienne continued their employment at the French court, but Thomas saw a significant reduction in his income, losing pensions and other income under the new regime.[15]

After eleven years of wedded bliss, Etienne succumbed to the plague in 1389. Christine's father had died shortly before, and Christine was left a widow at the age of 26 with three small children to care for as well as her mother and a niece. Although the loss of the family's two breadwinners was a devastating blow for the family, Christine was left in a relatively secure financial position. She inherited a portion of her father's estate, which she sold to support her family, and was able to draw upon the social and professional connections of her late father and husband. However, Christine encountered considerable challenges in securing a legal claim to her husband's estate, spending the next fourteen years caught up in lawsuits, eventually securing money owed to her from her husband's debtors.[16] Drawing upon her experiences in the court system, speaking to women who might struggle to assert themselves in a man's world, Christine advised 'Speak gently but look out for your rights … she must take on the heart of a man. She must be constant, strong, and wise'.[17]

It is important to note that the deaths of her father and husband did not render Christine or her family destitute. Thomas had been generously compensated by Charles V and had accrued a tidy sum to bequeath to his children. Indeed, Christine did not take a second husband to relieve the financial burden as many young widows did. But for Christine, the loss of the men in her life had a profound effect on her place within the family and her position within the wider world. She would later recall in the form of an allegory, her marriage as a voyage at sea with her husband at the helm. Once he is thrown overboard, Christine grieves and is then transformed and 'had become a true man'.[18] She sets about repairing her ship, and navigates it herself, 'I became a good master, and it was absolutely necessary that I be one in order to help myself and my people, if I did not want to die there'.[19] It was thanks to this transformation that we know the name Christine de Pizan. Assuming financial responsibility for her family as a widow, Christine became the first woman in history to earn an income exclusively from her writings.

Regardless of her sex, Christine was exceptional in her ability to make a career solely from writing. Most writers, who were predominantly male, found employment at the court or within the Church and supplemented their income by writing.[20] Christine's literary career began in grief, composing poetry as a form of therapy as she entered the phase of widowhood. In 1399, she produced a compilation of one hundred poems she had composed entitled *Cent Ballads,* seemingly to attract patronage. Her poetry and her subsequent works were popular amongst the

French Court, and this encouraged the author to continue in her literary pursuits. But Christine did not simply write poetry from grief. As the fifteenth century dawned, she turned her attention to political matters and offered her commentary on contemporary political issues.

Christine's work must be read within the context of the Hundred Years' War (1337–1453), a dynastic conflict between England and France that deeply influenced her themes and shaped her response to political and social instability. This prolonged war witnessed fluctuating fortunes for both France and England; however, during the 1380s, each nation turned its attention internally to address domestic challenges. King Charles VI assumed control of the throne in 1388, but frequent and episodic bouts of madness from 1393 rendered him incapable of ruling. His wife, Isabeau of Bavaria (1370–1435), presided over a regency council; however, Charles's relatives, driven by ambition, sought to exploit the power vacuum created by the king's incapacity, resulting in intense factionalism at the Parisian court. One of these factions was headed by the king's Uncle, Philip the Bold, Duke of Burgundy, and his chief political opponent was Charles' younger brother, Louis, Duke of Orléans. Philip of Burgundy died in 1404, and his son and successor, John the Fearless, the new Duke of Burgundy, continued his father's ambitions and headed his father's faction. In 1407, John orchestrated the assassination of Louis. In response, Louis' son and successor, Charles, allied with his father-in-law, Bernard VII Count of Armagnac, to oppose the Burgundian faction. This alliance marked the beginning of the Armagnac-Burgundian Civil War, which came to dominate French political life until the Treaty of Arras in 1435. This internal strife would cripple France for decades to come and enabled the English to gain the upper hand following Henry V's victory at Agincourt in 1415.[21]

A woman, Isabeau of Bavaria, queen of France, was central to this political dispute, into which Christine directly intervened through her writings. Isabeau has been treated as a villainous, incestuous, adulterous, and traitorous bad mother and wife, largely because of her involvement in the Treaty of Troyes (May 1420), which essentially disinherited her own son by signing over the French monarchy to the English.[22] In 1405, as civil strife continued, the Dauphin, Louis of Guienne, Isabeau's son, was kidnapped by the Duke of Burgundy. In response to the crisis, Christine addressed a letter (intended for public consumption) to the 'excellent, revered and powerful Princess', Isabeau and reminded the queen of her duty as an intercessor amid internal strife.[23] The purpose of the letter was traditionally interpreted as an attack from Christine, who reminded the idle queen of one of her fundamental duties to intercede. However, more recently, the letter has been seen for what it is: a statement intended to support Isabeau as Christine created and defined the queen's authority and commends her for the regency. The letter was designed to instruct the royal council on how to imagine the queen's role, drawing upon her suitability for the role based on her abilities as an intercessor.[24] Christine's letter was written on 5 October, and on 12 October, Isabeau was granted intercessory powers to intervene in the conflict by royal ordinance. Peace was signed between the two factions, and all-out civil war was temporarily averted.[25]

It is no coincidence that Christine produced two additional pieces around the same time, which explicitly challenged conventional clerical views on women and instead promoted the virtues of womanhood. The *Book of the City of Ladies* (1405) and the *Book of the Three Virtues* (1405) were extremely well received, enjoying a wide contemporary readership. An illustrated copy of the *Book of the City of Ladies* was requested by Queen Isabeau in 1414 when arguments once again surfaced regarding the possibility of her rule as regent.[26] In the *Book of the City of Ladies,* Christine, the author (and the protagonist of the story), queries why women are portrayed in such a negative light by male authors. Pondering on this for some time, she concludes that the authors must be right in their assertions, and that those of her sex must be fundamentally bad. She is then visited by three apparitions, Lady Reason, Lady Rectitude and Lady Justice, who point out to her that her own experiences do not support the assertions of these male authors. What Christine creates is a celebration of womanhood and women's achievements throughout history.[27] Within this work, Christine challenges the conventional position against women learning, arguing for their capacity for education and lists various exemplars for women, including the Virgin Mary. Christine links her example to the politics of the day by demonstrating that although the Virgin Mary is second to none, she, by virtue of her sex, cannot usurp the position of her son. Christine does not argue for female independent rule but rather champions Isabeau as a suitable regent possessing intercessory skills akin to the Virgin Mary.[28] But the *Book of the City of Ladies* was not written solely to address contemporary political events; it was a universal defence of the female sex. The inclusion of the word 'City' in the title connects Christine's work to that of St Augustine's *City of God,* another universal history. Like St Augustine's work, it invokes imagery of building, of a community working together for a shared purpose. But more importantly, Christine's title draws attention to women's contribution to civilisation in creating and developing urban centres.[29]

Similarly, the *Book of the Three Virtues* champions the female sex and speaks directly to women. Although intended for a broader readership, the work was addressed to Margaret of Nevers, the child bride of the Dauphin Louis of Guienne, in preparation for her role as future queen. However, she never assumed the role, as her husband passed away in 1415 before succeeding to the throne. This sequel to the *Book of the City of Ladies* offers advice on female survival in a male-dominated world, offering counsel to women of varying social classes and at various stages of womanhood.[30] The three Ladies of Virtue return to Christine and inform her that now the city has been built, she must continue in her work '…so that it will grow even further, we want you to act like the wise bird catcher...' and fill the city with virtuous ladies.[31]

The uniqueness of Christine and her work cannot be overstated. Here we have a fifteenth-century woman challenging conventional misogynistic views and promoting the virtues of the female sex. Her courage is quite remarkable. But her defence of the female sex did not stop there. Christine decided to take her defence of women further and engaged in the fifteenth-century's version of a lengthy Twitter feud.

The *Romance of the Rose* is a French allegorical poem written by Guillaume de Lorris around 1237. Following his death, the poem was continued by Jean de Meun around 1280. It was translated into many different languages, making it accessible to a wider European audience. The poem is built upon the notion of courtly love in which a lover seeks to pick a rose (representing female sexuality). The tale follows the lover's attempts at sexual gratification and throughout is filled with misogynistic and obscene passages, and by the beginning of the fifteenth century, the poem enjoyed something of a cult following.[32] Christine took offence to the poem and its supporters arguing that its interpretation of women was incorrect, and moreover, placed real women in danger from the violence of men. Christine claimed the author's assertions about the sinfulness of women were incorrect, and that he instead had projected his own sexual desires and excesses onto the page and transformed these into accusations about women as sinful and lustful creatures.[33] In her 1399 work entitled *The God of Love's Letter*, Christine first publicly commented on the poem. In the work, Cupid receives a letter from women who complain about the abuses they suffer from men, these '...ladies complain of the great crimes, the accusations, and the many other pains that they receive every day from disloyal men, who blame, defame, and deceive them'.[34] In the same work, Christine further challenges the clerical position on women and the mistreatment of her sex. Addressing why books are full of negative stereotypes about women:

> I answer that women did not write the books ... But if women had written the books, I know for a fact they would have been written differently, for women know when they are wrongly condemned.[35]

In the same year, Christine penned *Moral Teachings* in response to the *Romance of the Rose* and asked the audience to look to their own experiences of women to challenge the misogynistic views of the authors:

> Do not believe all the defamatory statements that some books make about women, for there exist many good women; this, experience shows you.[36]

Christine took on supporters of the *Romance of the Rose* head-on and wrote to Jean de Montreuil, one of its strongest proponents. In her letter of 1401, Christine criticises not only the subject matter, but also the merits of the poem itself writing that the author '…could have produced a much better work, more profitable and with a more elevated sensibility, if he had applied himself to it, so it's a pity he did not do so.'[37] Not understanding why the poem has received such accolades, Christine advocates that it should '…more fittingly be engulfed in a shroud of fire than crowned with laurel'.[38] In a response to Montreuil's defence of the work, Christine wrote:

> …may it not be attributed to folly, arrogance, or presumption that I, a woman, dare to reprimand and refute so subtle an author, and to divest his work of its renown, when he, just one man, dared to undertake to defame and condemn without exception an entire sex.[39]

Christine might have found an ally in her contemporary across the English Channel, Geoffrey Chaucer, had time permitted. Dying in 1400, just as the debate on the *Romance of the Rose* began to take hold, Chaucer translated the poem from French into English. Yet in his translation, he omitted some of the more misogynistic lines that Christine found so intolerable. Consequently, the English audience read a different version from the one circulating in France.[40]

Christine did not solely concern herself with her defence of women and female regency. Her literary activities incorporated the male sphere in equal measure, and she offered explicit political advice to kings, princes and military commanders. In the first French biography of a king written by a woman, Christine explored notions of kingship in the *Book of the Deeds and Good Practices of King Charles V the Wise* completed in 1404. Unusually for the time, Philip, Duke of Burgundy (1342–1404), Charles V's brother, approached Christine and asked her to write the biography. Philip likely had intended the book to be for the consumption of the Dauphin, Louis, but a desire to establish and gain popularity for his own regime had prompted him to request a didactic text from the author.[41] It also reflected a growing nostalgia for the reign of Charles V, and by associating himself with his brother, in choosing the former king's most devout literary supporter, Philip offered himself as a viable alternative to his nephews, one rendered ineffectual by continuous lapses into illness and the other his factional rival.[42] Philip chose Christine for this task because of the illuminating way she had portrayed Charles in an earlier work, the *Book of the Path of Long Study,* written 1402–1403. Philip would die before the work was completed in 1404, and Christine dedicated the biography to Philip's successor, John the Fearless.[43] Much of what we know about the personality of King Charles V comes from Christine's work, and in it, she presents Charles as a wise and chivalrous king.[44] The biography belongs to a genre known as 'Mirror for Princes', prevalent in the Middle Ages. Through Christine's work, Charles' successors and those heading factions at court could look to Charles as an exemplar of ideal kingly behaviour and strive to emulate his virtues.

A general decrease in French morale caused by the lack of progress in the Hundred Years' War caused concerns of a French decay and a decline in chivalry. Christine and some of her contemporary writers offered a re-education to the nobility through military texts and manuals.[45] Christine produced several military and chivalric manuals, including the *Book of the Body Politic* (1407), the *Book of the Deeds of Arms and Chivalry* (1410) and the *Book of Peace* (1413), addressed to the Dauphine. Christine always preferred peace over war, but as a woman of her time, she understood warfare as a necessity of life. In the *Cent Ballads*, Christine called upon her contemporary knights to look to examples from the past for inspiration, to men such as Alexander the Great, Julius Caesar, Charlemagne and Godfrey of Bouillon.[46] In the *Deeds of Arms and Chivalry*, Christine sets out a guide for conducting effective war and outlines the circumstances in which war can be waged justly. These include the defence of the Church, to protect the vulnerable and retribution.[47] In the same text, she offered advice to commanders, suggesting they make rousing speeches only to their captains and not the whole army, as Caesar, one of history's most successful generals, had done.[48] She also focused on the importance of courage as a virtue and recommended that generals ought not to simply tell the tales of battles and victories, but have a variety of stories they could recount of individual acts of heroism and courage from history.[49] Christine also noted that civilians and prisoners ought to be treated with respect and dignity, adding that an escape route should be provided for vanquished armies so the defeated soldiers need not feel compelled to undertake a suicide mission.[50] Christine brought femininity to the subject, writing her *Epistle on the Prison of Human Life* in 1418 to console women who had lost men at the Battle of Agincourt (1415). The loss of much of the aristocracy in this English victory meant there was an appetite for such a work.[51] The sheer number of books Christine produced on military matters is remarkable, and although she had no direct experience of warfare, her proximity to the centres of power gave her authority to comment on such matters.[52]

Christine retired from public life in 1418, removing herself from the French Court and the dangers of the capital as the city plunged into chaos following the flight of the Dauphin (the future King Charles VII) and the massacres in Paris which followed. A demoralised and defeated France was not conducive to writing, and a lack of inspiration likely caused Christine to put down her quill. The author possibly found solace with her daughter at the Convent of Poissy, but a turn of the wheel of fortune brought the famed writer out of retirement.[53]

Joan of Arc reignited the French spirit and inspired her nation to secure its first victory over the English in decades at the Battle of Orléans in 1429. No mere spectator of events, Christine always wrote in response to them, and she created what would be her final work, *The Tale of Joan of Arc,* addressing the politicians she knew so well, instructing them to act in the interests of the French people.[54] In many ways, Joan's career juxtaposed with Christine's own; both women assumed a masculine role and consequently faced significant challenges in establishing themselves within their respective spheres.[55] Christine's literary career ended on a high note with hopes of the restoration of French fortunes in the hands of a prophetic girl. It is unclear whether Christine died before the execution of Joan of Arc in 1431; it would certainly be kinder had she not lived to see French hopes extinguished upon her death.

Christine's literary legacy endured far beyond her death, with over 200 manuscripts of her work in existence today. In comparison, only one manuscript of *Beowulf* survives, and only thirty-two copies of the *Canterbury Tales*, have survived. Several of Christine's surviving manuscripts are in her own hand, a degree of authorial presence which cannot be confirmed in the surviving manuscripts attributed to Chaucer.[56] Of the surviving manuscripts, approximately fifty were created in Christine's own scriptorium and under her supervision.[57] Christine was heavily involved in the creative process and employed the illuminator services of an otherwise unknown illustrator named Anastacia, renowned for her skill in creating manuscript borders and miniature backgrounds.[58] Christine was an excellent promoter of her own brand and included illustrations of herself in her manuscripts, often depicted gifting the work to a patron. Unusual for her time, Christine continually referred to herself throughout her works, identifying herself as the author in an astute marketing strategy. Following her death, her works were enjoyed by a wide audience, translated into English, and in the late fifteenth century, her *Book of Feats of Arms and of Chivalry* was translated and printed by Caxton for King Henry VII. With the advent of the Renaissance, Christine, like many medieval writers, fell out of favour and was not rediscovered until the late eighteenth century, though even then she attracted limited scholarly attention. It was not until the exploration of women's rights in the late nineteenth century and the introduction of feminist and women's history in the twentieth century that Christine's talents and unique status as the first professional female author were fully recognised. In 1886, one article referred to her as 'A Champion of her Sex'.[59] In her discussion of Christine in *The Second Sex,* written in 1949, Simone de Beauvoir writes: 'This is the first time a woman takes up her pen to defend her sex'.[60]

It has often been argued that Christine can be identified as a feminist. This is problematic as no such term existed in Christine's day, therefore making it difficult to identify her with such an anachronistic term.[61] Furthermore, although

Christine extolled the virtues of women and subscribed to the notion that women could, if they possessed the skill set, fulfil roles traditionally performed by men, she was by no means advocating for universal female liberation. Although she did employ a female illuminator, Christine did not offer employment to other women, as far as we know. Christine was no radical reformist; she did not call for the universal education of women, merely advocating for their capacity for learning. Indeed, Sheila Delany considered her to be conservative, loyal first and foremost to her class and not her sex.[62] Even if we cannot convincingly argue for Christine as a proto-feminist, we can most certainly acknowledge her status as an anomaly in her world, as a woman who delved into political issues of her day and uniquely sought to defend the insults and defamations levelled against her sex with the pen.

Chapter 11

Margery Kempe (*c.*1373–1438)

The Book of Margery Kempe is the first autobiography written in English and one of the very few autobiographies we have of a woman prior to the Early Modern era. Margery's book is strongly hagiographical in tone, and some have even referred to it as the first instance of autohagiography.[1] Margery sets herself up as a holy woman and attempts to promote herself as a saint throughout the text.[2] Questioned by Church authorities on several occasions, Margery is mindful that her behaviour could be interpreted as a threat to the official position of the Church; thereby *The Book of Margery Kempe* deliberately establishes her as an admirable figure.[3] The reader suffers with Margery as she endures the scorn of others and her struggle to practice her unique form of piety in an ever-hostile world. Like Margery herself, the book deviates from traditional hagiography and autobiographies in its composition by following a confusing chronology and begins not with her birth and early life, but rather with her entry into womanhood.[4] A deeply personal account, it focuses on Margery's spiritual life rather than her temporal existence, and her spiritual experiences provide the framework of the book. It is an invaluable source for medieval travel, piety and heresy, and significantly an insight into the life of one later medieval woman. Although most information about Margery derives from her book, which presents events solely from her perspective, many of the impersonal aspects it contains can be corroborated by other historical sources. Margery reveals only the aspects of her life she wishes to discuss; nevertheless, *The Book of Margery Kempe* affords the reader a rare glimpse into the life of a middling-class urban woman, what we might call an 'ordinary life'.

Like the tale of Margery Kempe, the book itself suffered a trial of ordeals in the process of its creation. Margery claims that God commanded her to record her story some twenty years after her initial religious experiences. Being illiterate, she employed an amanuensis to write the work as she dictated it, the first of whom was almost certainly her eldest son, John Kempe Junior. Travelling to Danzig, Prussia, where he had met his wife and started a family, John returned to Lynn some years later and agreed to write his mother's autobiography. However, after his death in 1431, attempts to read the text proved futile; a priest remarked it was poorly written and heavily influenced by German.[5] A second scribe, likely her confessor,

Robert Spryngolde, unable to make sense of the original text, agreed to rewrite the text for her, making it legible. *The Book of Margery Kempe* was completed around 1436, shortly before Margery died in around 1438. It remains unclear whether it reached a broad audience immediately after her death or whether she intended it for widespread circulation.

A copy of the manuscript was owned by the Carthusian monks at Mount Grace Priory, North Yorkshire, in the fifteenth century, and extracts from the book were copied in the sixteenth century into a pamphlet. The book then disappeared until a damaged ping pong ball caused William Butler-Bowdon to rifle through the cabinets of his country home in Derbyshire for a replacement in the 1930s, when the manuscript appeared. The manuscript is now housed in the British Library and is frequently displayed for public viewing.[6] Written in Old English, modern English translations have been made throughout the twentieth and twenty-first centuries, bringing it to a wide public audience as a Penguin Classic. The book and Margery herself became the subject of widespread scholarly attention following the advances in the history of women from the 1980s and 1990s, for what it can tell us about the experience of non-royal late medieval women and a glimpse into a hitherto unseen world.

Margery's life began in the prosperous port town of Bishop's Lynn (now known as King's Lynn) in Norfolk, an essential medieval trading point with ships arriving from the Continent to trade their wares throughout England. Margery was born into a rather prosperous merchant family in around 1373, the daughter of John Brunham/Burnham, possibly making his fortune in the wine trade.[7] Brunham became an elite burgess in Lynn and held public office, serving as mayor of Lynn five times, and was elected MP for the town on several occasions. Beyond the commenting of the pride Margery took in her rather affluent origins and her father's status within Lynn, Margery tells us nothing more of her childhood.[8] We know that she married John Kempe at around the age of 20, and the couple had fourteen children.[9] Although John served as a burgess and held the office of chamberlain in 1394, he lacked the social prominence of her father – a detail Margery is careful to emphasise.[10] Margery remarks that when her husband tried to rebuke her for her pride, she replied '…she was come of worthy kindred – he should never have married her'.[11] Theirs may have been a love match of social unequals, thereby forgoing the opportunity for Margery to marry into a gentry family.[12] Margery's accounts of her early marital lust for John substantiate this interpretation.[13]

The Book of Margery Kempe opens with her first pregnancy and childbirth, a physically and psychologically traumatic ordeal that precipitated her initial celestial visions. Ill and terrified of imminent death, Margery wished to confess a long-concealed sin, for the devil warned her if she did not confess it, she would be damned. The confessor was impatient with her, and Margery was unable to confess to this sin.[14] Never describing what the sin was, Margery alludes to it throughout the book as a cause of great shame and guilt. Margery claims she was then tormented by devils, and she began to self-harm, tearing at her own skin with her nails, leaving scars that were visible for the rest of her life. Eventually, she was tied up for her own safety.[15] Despairing for her life, Christ appeared to Margery in a vision, and this experience healed her ailments.[16] More visions would later follow, but until then, it seems Margery continued her life as before, and the vision did not alter her behaviour.

Margery enjoyed a healthy sex life with her husband (judging by their extensive number of children) and was even tempted into adultery by a friend who rejected her after making an advance.[17] Margery prayed to be delivered from these temptations and even began to wear a hair shirt and began to fast. Margery expressed her desire to live a chaste life, but her husband initially refused until Margery eventually agreed to pay off John's debts in exchange for her chastity; thereafter, they lived separately.[18] While Margery's payment underscores her superior socioeconomic standing relative to her husband, it simultaneously reveals her subordinate legal status as his property, obliging her to purchase her own autonomy.[19] Margery later enters into a mystical marriage with God in the presence of the Virgin Mary, the twelve apostles and a throng of saints and holy persons.[20] This marriage was something of a foretaste of heaven, and in her soul, God offered to reveal all his secrets and counsels. From then on, Margery conducted herself as if she were the bride of God on par with Mary Magdalene, and even the Virgin Mary, whom she experienced in her visions as a comforter and friend.[21]

Margery was part of a trend of late medieval holy women who experienced visions and communicated with the divine and then had their experiences committed to paper, thereby moving away from traditional notions of virginity as the exclusive route to female sanctity.[22] A catch-all label for these women who expressed their devotion in a variety of forms is 'mystic', and this descriptor is often attributed to Margery. Margery's married and motherly status was not a bar to sanctity, as models such as St Bridget of Sweden had shown. Bridget, a wife with eight children who died around the year Margery was born (1373), rejected the traditional feminine roles of wife and motherhood for a life of pilgrimage and mysticism, devoting her life to the divine. Margery would have known *The Life of St Bridget,* which was translated into English in the fifteenth century and became popular among women in English secular and religious societies.[23] Margery certainly took Bridget as a model for her own path to holiness and even sought out the saint's maid while in Rome and conversed with a man who knew her.[24] Similar to St Bridget, Margery had a mystical marriage to the Godhead, placed herself in voluntary poverty as Bridget had done, and Margery refers to the saint on multiple occasions throughout her book.[25] *The Book of Margery Kempe* is in many ways her struggle to emulate St Bridget and other near-contemporary holy women, and Margery's own attempts to attain sanctity.

Margery is best remembered for her weeping as an expression of her piety, which transformed her devotion from private prayer to public display. Margery identifies her weeping with her entrance into the mystical experience, 'sometimes continuing weeping for two hours and often longer without ceasing'.[26] Margery faced her first experience of weeping during her pilgrimage to the Holy Land, and this intense religious expression continued on the return journey and remained with her for the rest of her life. Weeping for herself, souls in purgatory, for her sin and that of others, Christ reassured Margery that the devil 'is angry with you, because you torment him more with your weeping than all the fire in hell does; you win many souls from him with your weeping'.[27] This visitation offers Margery some comfort and validation for her weeping and is intended to reassure the validity of Margery's experience to the reader. The loud and continuous weeping frustrated those who recognised it for what it was, as an attempt to draw attention to herself.

During a vision, Christ instructs Margery to wear white clothing and a wedding ring as part of her private form of devotion to the divine. When Margery was questioned by the Archbishop of York, he queried, 'Why do you go about in white clothes? Are you a virgin?'[28] Although white clothing was not exclusive to virgins, it was certainly associated with virginity by Margery's contemporaries, and she wore this colour to evoke precisely this reaction.[29] Margery herself never confirms why she wore white clothing, nor its symbolism, but it is clear that Margery was creating a unique public identity for herself as a married woman with fourteen children who had taken a vow of chastity, clad in the symbols of virginity.[30] The white clothing and the ring she wore were visual representations of her love for Christ and the unique private rule created for her by Christ, and her contemporaries understood she wore the colour to signify her holiness.[31] Margery wore white clothing for the explicit purpose of drawing attention to herself, to attract ridicule and to create controversy.[32]

Another aspect of Margery's piety, which forms a large part of her book, is pilgrimage and travel. Just as Jerusalem was considered to be the centre of the world, so Jerusalem occupies a central place within Margery's book, and her experiences on pilgrimage to this most holy of places affected the rest of her life.[33] Margery set out for Jerusalem in 1413 and experienced intense visions and weeping when she came into contact with the places most strongly associated with Christ's life and death. As per the norm, Margery travelled in the company of others for safety and guidance. Margery's continual weeping and her continual rebuking greatly angered her companions.[34] On the way to Jerusalem,

> They cut her gown so short that it only came a little below her knee, and made her put on some white canvas in a kind of sacking apron, so that she would be taken for a fool, and people would not make much of her or hold her in any repute. They made her sit at the end of the table below all the others, so that she scarcely dared speak a word.[35]

Mealtimes were social events and an opportunity to exhibit a sense of community, particularly important when travelling abroad and alone, as Margery did.[36] In excluding Margery from communal eating, it is they, not Margery, who break the harmony of the community (as Margery is so often accused throughout the book) and Margery is portrayed as morally superior.[37] Margery's pilgrimages were intended to inform the reader less about the destinations and more about her relationships with her fellow travellers.[38]

Pilgrimages were intended to be gruelling, to bring the pilgrim even closer to the sufferings of Christ, and, presumably for this reason, Christ instructed Margery to give away all of her money when on pilgrimage in Rome. Margery dutifully obeyed, becoming dependent on the hospitality of strangers for sustenance, shelter, and travel home. In Rome, Margery provoked mixed responses; scorned by her companions, others convinced of her holiness offered hospitality in exchange for prayers, as she developed the persona of a holy person paid to pray for the sick and the dead.[39]

Margery undertook a pilgrimage to Santiago de Compostella in 1417 and embarked on a final pilgrimage in 1433–1434, a woman now in her sixties with a bad foot. As a 'woman of great age' she was advised not to board the ship at Ipswich that would bear her daughter-in-law to Prussia. Even her daughter-in-law was against the idea, but Margery ignored various pleas and boarded the ship. Severe weather blew them off course to Norway, and from there they travelled some 1000 miles to Danzig, Prussia.[40] Margery then made her way to Aachen, a centre for pilgrimage, before returning to England. Her record of international travel is remarkable for a late medieval woman, visiting the three main centres for pilgrimage of her era: Jerusalem, Rome and Santiago de Compostella.

Margery undertook various pilgrimages within the British Isles, visiting the Shrine of Our Lady of Walsingham and Canterbury Cathedral. She travelled extensively throughout England, visiting York, Beverley, Lincoln and Norwich. In her travels and pilgrimages, Margery defied conventional gender norms that prescribed a domestic role for women, centred on child-rearing and home life.[41] Margery's husband did not accompany her on her international travels, but he did on occasion travel with her throughout England, such as her pilgrimage to Canterbury Cathedral. However, Margery made a spectacle of herself in pontificating to the monks, which enraged them. John fled the scene, and she was rescued by two young men who returned her to her husband, embarrassed by her behaviour.[42]

Margery's travels to Canterbury offer but one instance of many in which she was accused of heresy. After admonishing the monks at Canterbury, they threaten to burn her as a Lollard, a particular brand of heresy initiated by Oxford theologian John Wyclif (*c.*1328–1384) in the late fourteenth century.[43] Lollards rejected some of the Church's fundamental teachings, including denying the Pope's authority, challenging the Church's position on the Eucharist and the Sacraments, denouncing pilgrimages and condemning the veneration of images as idolatry. Wyclif and his followers were condemned by the Papacy in 1377, and in 1401, the English Parliament passed a bill, *Contra Lollardos,* which set out provisions for the arrest, incarceration, and even burning of Lollards. Nevertheless, the Lollard movement received support from some high-status individuals, such as Sir John Oldcastle, who led a rebellion against Henry V in 1414 and was executed following its collapse. The authorities were actively seeking out Lollards through the surveillance and interrogation of suspected individuals during Margery's lifetime. William Sawtry, the sometime parish priest of St Margaret's in Lynn, a parish church Margery attended, was the first to be burnt as a Lollard in 1401. Even though his name is not mentioned in her book, he must have been known to Margery.[44] Eighty-three suspects were questioned by Bishop Alnwick of Norwich on suspicion of Lollardy between 1428 and 1431. Lollardy was not an intangible fear; those suspected were interrogated, and some paid with their lives within her very town. Margery's pushing of the boundaries of orthodox Christianity raised suspicions within her community.[45] Her expression of religious devotion, in her weeping, pontificating and her clothing was peculiarly unique and difficult to categorise by the authorities, which raised their suspicions during the time of Lollard persecutions.

Margery was arrested on suspicion of Lollardy on several occasions, notably in the summer of 1417 by the mayor of the city of Leicester and appeared before the abbot of the abbey of the Augustinian canons, Leicester. Margery was questioned on the articles of faith and was found to be orthodox in her beliefs.[46] But the mayor asked her why she wore white clothes and claimed, 'I believe you have come here to lure away our wives from us, and lead them off with you'.[47] The mayor, and doubtless countless others, feared that Margery set a bad example of womanhood, rejecting the restraints of marriage and motherhood and might have encouraged other women to do the same.[48] Thus, the threat Margery posed to societal cohesion was not necessarily religious in nature.

A month or so later, in September 1417, Margery travelled to York and was again arrested and summoned to appear before the Archbishop of York, Henry Bowet, who was also concerned with her clothing.[49] The authorities were seemingly unable to categorise Margery's peculiar private devotion and were confused by her visual expression of her religiosity. There was also a concern with Margery's public speaking; Lollards promoted the notion of female preachers, prohibited by St Paul, of which she was reminded during her interrogation.[50] Although she denied ever preaching, Margery did indeed walk a fine line between preaching and teaching, especially in her admonition of clerics. Again, Margery was questioned on the articles of faith and found to be orthodox before reprimanding the archbishop.[51] Margery expressed her desire to remain in York, but there was a concern in the Archbishop's household once again regarding her influence; 'the people have great faith in her talk, and perhaps she might lead some of them astray'.[52]

Margery was permitted to stay in York but was again arrested a brief time afterwards. On this occasion, she had attracted the attention of John of Lancaster, Duke of Bedford (1389–1435), who ordered her arrest and instructed that she be brought again before the Archbishop of York. Bedford was serving as lieutenant whilst his brother, King Henry V, was in France. Bedford was deeply concerned with heresy, and at the time of Margery's arrest, Sir John Oldcastle was still at large, and his capture was a primary concern.[53] It is against this wider historical context which we must consider Margery's arrest. But Bedford's interest in Margery was not solely motivated by Oldcastle's rebellion. Margery had made the acquaintance of Bedford's aunt, Joan de Beaufort, who expressed favourable regard for Margery. However, Bedford accused Margery of attempting to compel Joan de Beaufort's daughter, Lady Elizabeth Greystoke, to leave her husband. Margery denied the charge, which carried heretical implications, as one of the tenets of Lollardy rejected the Sacraments as invalid, thereby allowing for the easy dissolution of marriage.[54] Wherever she travelled, both Church and secular authorities were alarmed by Margery's influence over other women; like Lollardy, her teachings were seen as potentially contagious and in need of suppression.

Her rejection of gender norms was voiced by both men and women who heckled Margery as she entered the town shouting, 'Woman, give up this life that you lead, and go and spin, and card wool, as other women do, and do not suffer so much shame and unhappiness'.[55] The authorities and the public were unsure of what to make of her; she was a wife and mother but acted the part of a widow or a virgin.[56] She conformed to the notion of dissent in rejecting her proper gendered role, yet she did adhere to the teachings of the orthodox Catholic faith. She was a regular pilgrim and an avid confessor, two tenets of the Christian faith rejected by Lollards. Her teaching could at times be considered preaching, but her conformity to other doctrines of the Catholic faith doubtless saved her from any serious repercussions of blurring the lines in this regard. Her arrests were more indicative of a determination to silence her rather than any genuine belief she was a Lollard.[57] Always theologically correct when questioned, Margery nonetheless was a danger to the Christian community, and, as we see with each arrest, the prevailing opinion of Church authorities was to expel her or silence her.[58] Margery is repeatedly silenced throughout *The Book of Margery Kempe*; her confessor initially refuses to hear her troubling confession, the authorities' persistent interrogations were likely aimed at intimidating her into submission, and the very difficulties she faced in composing her book may themselves be seen as attempts to suppress her voice.[59] The attempts to eradicate her voice form part of her suffering, which is a central theme of the book.

For the purposes of the book, and undoubtedly on a personal level, Margery needed people to stand against her and to actively criticise her, for this was part of her attempts to imitate the sufferings of Christ and ultimately part of her attempts at sanctity.[60] The hecklers, the accusations of heresy, the fellow pilgrims who rejected her, all those who mock her throughout the book serve to emphasise her holiness. Margery deliberately made a scene to gain attention and attract persecution by making a spectacle of herself through her tears, her appearance and her insistence on rebuking people. As Christ was rejected and mocked, suffering became part of Margery's persona and her route to holiness.

Margery the mystic, the traveller, the subverter of her society's gendered values, created a new identity for herself which challenged conventional expressions of religious devotion for a lay woman. Her trailblazing activities took her across the Continent and beyond, accepting the perilous risks for a woman travelling alone. When at home, she was not afraid to stand up to Church officials who examined or criticised her, questioning their own religiosity in turn. She infuriated many with her tears and piety but found friends and supporters wherever she went. Unafraid to challenge the authorities in pursuit of her piety and committing her experiences to paper, Margery Kempe was an incredible woman.

Women of the Wars
of the Roses

Margaret of Anjou (1430–1482)

One of the most prominent political figures in the Wars of the Roses, Margaret of Anjou was cast as the murderess of Richard, Duke of York (1411–1460) by Shakespeare in an entirely fictional scene. He referred to her as: 'She-wolf of France, but worse than wolves of France'.[1] Shakespeare's Margaret was a ruthless figurehead for the Lancastrian party, navigating her way through a male-dominated political world. Like Isabella of France, over a century before her, Margaret was dubbed 'She-wolf of France', reflecting yet another instance of history shaped by the perspective of the victors as her Yorkist rivals besmirched her name through their propaganda.[2] Like Isabella of France, Margaret was vilified for her strength of character and sheer determination to protect the rights of her son.

Life began well for Margaret, born in 1430 to René, Duke of Anjou and his wife, Isabella. Her paternal aunt was married to Charles VII of France, and her paternal grandparents were Louis II, Duke of Anjou and king of Naples, and Yolande, daughter of the king of Aragon. Margaret spent much of her youth in the company of either her mother, Isabella, daughter of Charles II, Duke of Lorraine or with her paternal grandmother, Yolande. Both were formidable women, acutely aware of their privilege, and appear to have exerted considerable influence over the formation of Margaret's character. Women on the Continent experienced greater freedom of power, often acting independently as regents for their husbands and sons, an opportunity rarely offered to women in England.[3] The ongoing troubles between England and France saw Margaret wed Henry VI of England (1421–1471) to secure peace between the two rival kingdoms.

King Henry VI of England was the only legitimate son of the illustrious Henry V (1386–1422) and Catherine of Valois (1401–1437), daughter of the French King Charles VI. The hero of Agincourt, Henry V died unexpectedly, likely of dysentery, in September 1422 at the age of 35. His 9-month-old son was declared his successor, Henry VI, and a council of noblemen ruled as regents for the minor king. With the lack of a strong monarch, the nobility was left unchecked and created their own mini kingdoms within the realm. Two rival factions emerged from the king's minority; one of these factions, known as the Yorkist faction, came to be dominated by Richard, Duke of York and Henry's uncle, Humphrey, Duke of

Gloucester. Richard had the strongest claim to the English throne, even stronger than Henry's. On his mother's side, he was the direct descendant of Lionel, Duke of Clarence, the third son of King Edward III and on his father's side, he was the heir of Edmund, Edward III's fifth son. York's rivals comprised the Lancastrian faction headed by Henry's great-uncle, Bishop Henry Beaufort, the Earl of Suffolk and his nephew, Edmund Beaufort, Earl of Somerset. The Beauforts were descendants of the union between John of Gaunt (1340–1399), Edward III's fourth son and his mistress Kathryn Swynford, to whom Gaunt was later married (1396), and his children were declared legitimate. Henry VI was also a descendant of John of Gaunt, his great-grandfather, a result of his first marriage to Blanche of Lancaster. These two factions held opposing opinions regarding the French war, with Humphrey and York wishing to continue to fight for English interests and Beaufort, Suffolk and Somerset considering the war an unnecessary waste of English finances. Each rival group vied for control of the king. Henry favoured the approach of Beaufort and wished to seek more diplomatic methods to bring the war in France to a conclusion. From 1437, Henry ruled himself, at least in name. As he began to take more control of the government, the factions continued their feuds. It was into this situation that Margaret, as a young woman of 15 years of age, was thrust.

William de la Pole, Earl of Suffolk (1396–1450), came to France to negotiate the marriage of Henry and Margaret and stood as proxy for Henry on 24 March 1444 when the marriage was celebrated at St Martin, Tours.[4] The seeds of the lasting friendship between Margaret and Suffolk were seemingly planted at this time. The terms of the marriage were of little profit to the English; Margaret brought with her a small dowry of 20,000 francs, and a mere two-year truce between France and England was agreed. In return, Henry would relinquish his control of Maine and Anjou.[5] Considering Henry's mother brought to her marriage the French throne, Henry VI's marriage to Margaret was met with disappointment as many believed he had sold himself short and could have attained either a more profitable bride or extracted more from the marriage treaty.

As Margaret landed upon English soil, Henry disguised himself as a squire delivering a letter to peek at his young bride. In this episode, playing into notions of chivalric performance, Margaret pays little attention to Henry, and when his true identity is revealed, Margaret is said to be distressed that she kept the king on his knees for so long.[6] Margaret celebrated her marriage to Henry at Titchfield Abbey on 22 April 1445, where the king presented his new wife with the gift of a lion.[7] Margaret was crowned at Westminster Abbey on 30 May 1445. Represented as the dove of peace, it was hoped she would bring accord between her natal and marital kingdoms.[8] The royal couple were young and seemingly in good physical health; it was hoped the union would bring many children, and in particular strong sons to end the dynastic troubles of the previous century.

Leaving aside her later involvement in the Wars of the Roses (1455–1487), which has in many ways tarnished Margaret's reputation, in the day-to-day business of queenship, Margaret appears to have been rather successful. She was sufficiently pious and ran the royal household. Margaret had no public role in the early years of her marriage; her role was likely limited thanks to the efforts of Henry's political enemies.[9] However, Margaret's influence can be detected in some of Henry's early policies, as she sought to advance her natal family's interests, a practice that quickly earned her unpopularity in England.[10] In a letter from Henry to Charles VII of December 1445, Henry acknowledged Margaret's role in ensuring England's surrender of Maine and Anjou to French control as per the marriage treaty.[11] As a French bride living in a kingdom recently defeated in the lengthy Hundred Years' War, Margaret was inevitably suspected of favouring French interests, and her involvement in such policies drew criticism. Coupled with this, Henry was a weak, pliable king, leading one contemporary to remark: 'that the king was fitter for a cloister than a throne'.[12] Contenders continued to vie for control of the king even once he reached adulthood, with his wife now joining the fray as an ardent supporter of the Lancastrian cause.

At the encouragement of Suffolk and Margaret, Henry had Humphrey arrested for treason in 1447, convinced that Humphrey was vying for the throne. Humphrey died in prison, leaving Richard of York as the main contender to Henry's throne and, given that Henry had sired no children, Henry's now heir presumptive. He was sent to govern Ireland to neutralise the threat he posed to the Lancastrian faction.[13] But the wheel of fortune was about to turn for Suffolk. The ultimately unpopular marriage treaty he had arranged for his king was to be his downfall. In 1450, Suffolk was impeached by parliament, arrested and imprisoned in the Tower of London. Henry attempted to spare the life of his trusted advisor by exiling him for five years. As Suffolk made his way to Calais, he was captured by a group of wayward sailors manning the 'Nicholas of the Tower' vessel, who violently executed the king's favourite.[14] It was now the turn of Suffolk's ally, Edmund Beaufort, Earl of Somerset (1406–1455), to rise to ascendancy and head the Lancastrian faction, and it was in Somerset that Margaret found her new ally.[15]

Cade's rebellion sprang up in Kent in April 1450, in response to English losses in France and local economic issues. Henry's lack of control during the rebellion revealed the shortcomings of not only his character but also his kingship.[16] Margaret, on the other hand, took an active political role and offered pardons to the rebels in exchange for dispersal, fulfilling her queenly duty as peacemaker.[17] However, Margaret seems to go beyond the bounds of queenship and, rather than acting as an intercessor pleading for mercy on the rebels' behalf, appears to act as the king's representative, directly working to end the conflict.[18] York returned from Ireland in September 1450 and skilfully turned the rebellion to his advantage, portraying himself as the champion of the rebels' cause and a reformer.[19] York, as a claimant to the English throne, was a serious threat to Henry and Margaret; Margaret had yet to provide Henry with a son and heir to secure his own lineage. Margaret felt increasing pressure to conceive a child under the circumstances.

Henry did not appear to have suffered from any physical impairments that would have prevented him from siring a child with Margaret. Some have pointed to Henry's later sanctity and suggested his pious nature may have played a part; however, there is little evidence to indicate that Henry was particularly pious during his lifetime.[20] It appears that the couple perhaps simply suffered from misfortune in their failure to conceive a child in the early years of their marriage. Their marriage appears to have been a happy one. Henry was attentive to his wife's interests, and Margaret's founding of Queen's College, Cambridge, after Henry's foundation of King's College indicates some shared interests.[21] Blame for a lack of children usually lay with the wife. However, given Henry's later lapses into madness and his over-reliance on the counsel of others, contemporaries were able to portray his inability to father children early on as another dimension to his dysfunctionality and his incapacity for rulership.[22]

After eight years of marriage, Margaret gave birth to a son named Edward on 13 October 1453. Henry was informed of the safe arrival of his son, but he did not indicate that he understood. For in August of that year, news had reached Henry of the English defeat at Castillo, Gascony. In the battle, many Englishmen had perished, including Henry's commanders. Within days, Henry seemingly had some sort of mental breakdown and fell into a malady which some modern historians have suggested was catatonic schizophrenia. Henry's grandfather, King Charles VI, experienced psychotic episodes, and a hereditary illness may have been the cause. Remedies were sought for Henry, who could not speak, walk and was totally unresponsive.[23]

Emboldened by the birth of Prince Edward, Margaret placed a bid for regency in January 1454, presenting herself as a mother and a peacemaker by ensuring no one faction, either York or Somerset, gained control of governance.[24] It was a rather bold request and without exact precedent in England. Had Margaret not been the mother of the heir to the throne, it is unlikely she would have made such a courageous move.[25] Margaret's upbringing had taught her that women on the Continent could and often did wield power on behalf of their husbands and sons when necessary. Margaret's grandmother, Yolande of Aragon and her mother, Isabella, both acted as regents for Margaret's father during his absence from Anjou. And Isabella even took command of her husband's military forces during his imprisonment.[26] Unfortunately for Margaret, this was not Anjou and her request was rejected. Instead, a Protectorate was established in March 1454, headed by her rival, Richard of York, and Margaret was completely excluded from governance. In a move to neutralise his opposition, York had Somerset, one of

Margaret's closest allies, arrested and confined to the Tower of London for treason in November 1453. Despite Margaret's misgivings regarding York, her son was publicly declared heir to the throne by parliament, which offered her some comfort in a precarious moment.[27]

Henry made a recovery on Christmas Day, 1454, much to the relief of his wife, and was delighted to learn he had finally fathered a son. York promptly relinquished his post, and Henry ordered the release of Somerset from the Tower without charge, who resumed his position as close ally of the king and queen as before.[28] Fearful of royal retaliation for the imprisonment of Somerset and in an attempt to regain a prime place at court, York claimed he intended to purge Henry's corrupt advisers and raised a military force.[29] Henry, along with his Lancastrian supporters, met York's forces at St Albans on 22 May 1455, and the first battle of the Wars of the Roses was fought. In the ensuing fight, Somerset was killed, and Henry received a minor wound to the neck but was safely escorted from the battlefield. Following this clash, York was reconciled with the king and swore fealty to him. York had demonstrated his strength and removed one of his most dangerous rivals in the process.[30] With the loss of Somerset as the leader of the Lancastrian faction, Margaret took his place, and her incomparable access to the king made her a formidable adversary to York.

In November 1455, Henry was once again reported to be ill, and York was again appointed Protector. York directly threatened Margaret's finances when he ordered an audit into royal household expenses with the view to taking some control of the royal expenditures and achieving solvency. Margaret strongly opposed York's reforms, and she received backing from the Lords.[31] It was only once York resigned from this position in February 1456, compelled to do so by the Lords and possibly Henry himself, who had now recovered, that Margaret emerged as a serious political player.[32] Still feeling the looming threat of York, Margaret took Prince Edward to the Midlands and his future patrimony in Chester, likely in an effort to secure support for the Lancastrian cause.[33] In August 1456, Henry joined his wife and son at Coventry, and the intention of Margaret appears to have been to establish another power base within the kingdom from which to rule.[34]

The king attempted to reconcile the York and Lancastrian factions on 25 March 1458 through a celebration known as 'Loveday' – a time-honoured medieval celebration used to settle public and private quarrels in a very public way. Members of the opposing factions entered St Paul's Cathedral together, walking hand in hand. Henry VI appeared in his crown and royal robes; crown-wearing was an opportunity for a king to demonstrate his imperial majesty and authority, and the symbolism here would not have been missed. Behind Henry walked Margaret and York hand in hand. For their audience, the rival pair put on a show of familiarity and friendliness. Although the Loveday reconciliation did little to quell tensions in the long term, the position of Margaret, as the focus of the parade alongside the head of her rival faction, signified her role as the figurehead of the Lancastrian cause and her central role in Henry's regime.[35]

Significantly, questions regarding Prince Edward's legitimacy arose at the time of Margaret's increased political power. In 1456, John Helton was executed for questioning Prince Edward's parentage, even alleging that Margaret was not the child's mother.[36] The Yorkists were said to have considered Edward a bastard, which therefore barred him from inheriting his father's throne.[37] Accusations regarding Edward's parentage were driven by a desire to exclude him from the throne, but they were also a way of challenging Margaret's authority. Allegations regarding Margaret's sexual misconduct suggested she was degenerate in other aspects of her life; she was unqueenly, a subverter of the natural order and essentially unfit for the office of consort.[38] Francesco Coppini reported to Pope Pius II in 1460 that York's nephew, Warwick, had claimed the king's power lay 'in the hands of his wife and those who defile the king's chamber'.[39] The implication was clear: Margaret's promiscuity and Henry's inability to control his wife had caused disorder not only on a private level but also in the kingdom more widely.[40] A queen's chastity was fundamental; questions regarding the paternity of a prince could destabilise the monarchy and throw the kingdom into political turmoil, coincidentally, just the sort of chaos York desired to seize the throne for himself. Rumours of Margaret's alleged infidelity not only questioned her character but also served to criticise the king as a weak cuckold, an ineffective man and king. This conclusion was given more authority by Henry's health issues at the time of the birth of his son and his inability to acknowledge him as his own in the early months of the boy's life.

Tensions were brewing once again in 1459, to such an extent that Margaret, along with Henry, completely withdrew from London to the safety of Coventry in the spring. It was from Coventry that a meeting of the great council was called in June 1459, with only members of the Lancastrian faction in attendance. The purpose of the gathering was to ensure the destruction of the Yorkist faction once and for all. The Yorkists were indicted for treason as Henry believed York was about the seize his throne, and their attempts to raise a force to acquire a hearing from Henry were presented as evidence by their enemies for their treasonous intentions.[41] In accusing York and his allies of treason, Henry and the Lancastrian faction in effect goaded the Yorkists into military action. The Yorkists, led by York, Salisbury and his son, the rising star, Warwick, met the Lancastrian forces at Blore Heath on 23 September 1459. It was a resounding victory for the Yorkists, but the jubilation was short-lived. In October 1459, Henry and Margaret gathered a larger force in their defeat and met the Yorkists at The Rout of Ludford Bridge, where the Lancastrians were the victors. York, Salisbury and Warwick slipped away and evaded capture.[42]

In the aftermath of these military conflicts, Henry and the Lancastrian faction sought to assert their authority in response to this now-open threat to Henry's crown. Calling a parliament at Coventry in December, dubbed 'The Parliament of Devils', sixty-six attending lords swore their allegiance to Henry, Margaret and Prince Edward as his father's designated heir.[43] The Yorkists returned with force once again and challenged Henry at Northampton, where the king was captured and taken to London as a prisoner. In October 1460, York made a formal claim to the English throne based on lineage without any reference to Henry's incapacity and inability to rule. A compromise was made, and Henry agreed to acknowledge York as his heir, thereby excluding Prince Edward from the throne. This left Margaret absolutely furious. Henry's capitulation made it increasingly difficult to attract support for his cause, for Henry had already accepted defeat.[44] But Margaret was not so easily cast aside and took up the mantle, fighting for her son's rightful position as heir to his father's throne.

Having fled to Scotland, Margaret gathered support from the Scots and her northern allies, confronting York's forces at the Battle of Wakefield on 30 December 1460. Margaret's forces secured a much-needed victory for her cause, and by the battle's end, York and his son Edmund lay dead. Shakespeare falsely claimed Margaret offered a captive York a handkerchief soaked in his own son's blood, a description designed to portray her not only as cruel but as the very worst example of womanhood.[45] Indeed, Margaret did not even witness the battle but remained in Scotland.[46]

The Yorkist cause was now taken up by York's son, Edward, Earl of March (1442–1483) and his cousin, Richard Neville, Earl of Warwick (1428–1471). Elated by her success, Margaret marched south and defeated the Yorkists at the Second Battle of St Albans in February 1461. Margaret regained control of Henry and marched to London. However, the citizens feared an army marching from the north and would not permit Margaret entry into the city. They sent a delegation of ladies, which included the Duchesses of Bedford and Buckingham, to negotiate with Margaret.[47] Faced with the threat of one powerful woman, it seemed natural and necessary to send other women to negotiate with her. But the negotiations did not achieve the desired effect for Margaret, and lacking control of the city made the Lancastrian cause incredibly difficult. Margaret was forced to retreat and march north. Margaret's failure to gain control of London was pivotal, and her involvement in this campaign damaged her reputation at a crucial moment.[48] From a position of strength, controlling the City of London, York's son, the Earl of March, proclaimed himself king on 4 March 1461 and was crowned King Edward IV at Westminster on 28 June 1461. With a new, young and vigorous king installed on the throne, a man in complete contrast to the weak Henry VI, much of the kingdom lost faith in the Lancastrian cause now represented by Margaret and her son.[49] Edward IV won a resounding victory at the Battle of Towton on 29 March 1461, which forced Henry, Margaret and their son into exile.

The former royal family now retreated to Scotland, and from there, Margaret sought to muster support for the dying Lancastrian cause. She travelled to France in 1462 seeking assistance from the new French king, Louis XI (1423–1483), her cousin. Although Louis was not warm to her cause, Margaret used her diplomatic skills to secure 20,000 francs from Louis in exchange for the surrender of Calais to the French Crown. Margaret set sail for Scotland in October with a mere 800 soldiers provided by Louis. Joining her husband, her French-sponsored expedition achieved little. Margaret once again returned to the Continent with Prince Edward in August 1463, leaving her husband at Bamburgh. She would never see Henry again.[50]

The longer Edward IV remained king, the more difficult it was for Margaret to muster support for what now seemed more like a lost cause. However, Margaret's fortunes changed in 1470 when Warwick and Edward's younger brother, Clarence, rebelled against the new king. The rebels made their way to France seeking an alliance with Margaret. Having trouble forgetting Warwick's involvement in the overthrow of her husband, Margaret initially refused to work with Warwick. Until, in a powerful public display of submission that underscored Margaret's dominance, 'With great reverence Warwick went on his knees and asked her pardon'.[51] Margaret eventually recognised the importance of Warwick to her cause, and to mark this new alliance, Prince Edward was betrothed to Warwick's daughter, Anne Neville, on 25 July 1470. Warwick promised Margaret that in exchange for her support, he would see Henry restored to the throne and her son reinstated as his heir. Warwick earned the epithet 'Kingmaker' for his pivotal role in the Wars of the Roses and his remarkable power to both make and unmake kings.

Warwick sailed for England with sixty ships secured from Louis XI in September 1470, while Margaret waited on the Continent for news. On 6 October, Warwick had secured London and released Henry from his imprisonment and declared him king once again. However, Warwick struggled to gain control of England, a testament to the popularity of Edward IV. To harness support, Henry VI, along with Warwick's brother, Archbishop George Neville, ventured out in public along the streets of London. However, Henry's appearance, dressed rather shabbily in a blue robe, did little to muster enthusiasm for his cause. Edward returned to London on 11 April 1471 and once again imprisoned Henry in the Tower of London and declared himself king once again.[52]

Margaret set sail for England and arrived at Weymouth in April 1471, but Edward was far from ready to relinquish the crown he had taken from Henry for a second time, and proved to be a far more resolute defender of his cause than Henry had been. He mustered a force and confronted the Lancastrians, now headed by his cousin, Warwick, at Barnet on 14 April 1471. Here, Warwick was killed, and the Lancastrian cause dwindled. But Margaret was not ready to relinquish the claims of her son just yet.

Margaret out-manoeuvred Edward, and he pursued her as she travelled west to meet up with the Welsh contingent mustered by Jasper Tudor, half-brother of Henry VI and one of the strongest proponents for her cause.[53] It was 4 May 1471, and Margaret, along with her daughter-in-law, Anne Neville, had taken shelter in a religious house situated close to the site of the forthcoming battle at Tewkesbury, while her son, Prince Edward, mustered the Lancastrian troops.[54] Edward soon engaged, and the day that had started so full of hope for Margaret ended when her 17-year-old son was killed. Edward had Margaret brought to Coventry, her former power base and then paraded her through the streets of London on 21 May 1471 in a humiliating spectacle, treating her as the spoils of victory. That same night, Henry was murdered, a prisoner in the Tower of London, likely at Edward's behest.[55]

The Lancastrian cause, at least for now, was lost, and Margaret relinquished all claims to the English throne. From 1471 until 1475, she was held in the custody of Alice de la Pole, granddaughter of Geoffrey Chaucer and the widow of Suffolk, her friend, the man whom Margaret first met in France, as he arranged for her marriage to Henry.[56] Edward was desperate to rid himself of his predecessor's widow, but sadly, few cared for her fate, not even her own father. Louis XI agreed to take Margaret in 1476 and gave Edward 50,000 francs for her ransom. In exchange, Margaret was to relinquish all her claims to her father's and her mother's ancestral lands to Louis. This once majestic queen of England was forced to live in quiet retirement, financially reliant on the king of France.[57] Margaret died on 25 August 1482, just three years before Henry Tudor would re-instate the Lancastrians as kings of England once more.

Margaret's unusual role in English politics left her open to accusations of unqueenly conduct and ultimately unfeminine behaviour. Margaret played no direct military role, yet critics cast her as a militant figure to tarnish her reputation and scapegoat her for the failures of Henry's reign.[58] Of French origin, marrying into a kingdom which had recently lost much of its territory in France, Margaret would always be treated with suspicion. Margaret exhibited the courage and fortitude that her husband lacked, and thus the royal couple subverted conventional gendered norms and structures of royal authority. Margaret's reputation suffered further at the hands of those hostile to the Lancastrian cause, cast as a usurper who took advantage of her sick husband and plunged the kingdom into chaos. More recently, we have a clearer and more accurate portrait of this remarkable queen as we move away from Shakespeare and Yorkist propaganda. Her courage and willingness to challenge the barriers of her sex are remarkable, and few other queens could boast such an eventful life as that of Margaret of Anjou.

Chapter 13

Elizabeth Woodville (*c.*1437–1492)

In many ways, Elizabeth Woodville's story ran parallel to Margaret of Anjou's. Both were queen consorts of England, twice. Both women were crucial to their respective husbands' kingships. Like Margaret, Elizabeth's fate was inextricably linked to the course of the Wars of the Roses and the reputation of both consorts was besmirched by their political adversaries. Both women eventually fell afoul of the Yorkist regime, and this was undoubtedly particularly painful for Elizabeth as she became the victim of a propaganda campaign initiated by her brother-in-law. While parallels exist between the two women, Elizabeth remains an anomaly in medieval queenship due to her relatively modest origins, which set her apart from all other consorts of the period.

Elizabeth's mother, Jacquetta of Luxembourg (*c.*1416–1472), was born into a prestigious European family. Jacquetta's brother was Peter I, Count of St Pol, and she could count Margaret of Anjou amongst her relatives as well as emperors of the Holy Roman Empire. Jacquetta's first husband, the brother of King Henry V, John of Lancaster, Duke of Bedford, died in 1435 after just two years of marriage, leaving Jacquetta a wealthy, childless teenage widow and an attractive bride. To the outrage of her family, Jacquetta married Richard Woodville (1405–1469) in 1437, evidently for love, for he was a mere English gentry man and household knight, a former chamberlain to Bedford. Despite this mismatched marriage of social unequals, Jacquetta and Richard had a seemingly happy marriage and twelve children were born from their union, the eldest of which was Elizabeth Woodville, born around 1437 shortly after their marriage.

Assumingly raised at the family home at Grafton, Northamptonshire, we know little of Elizabeth's upbringing. She probably received an education befitting her status with an emphasis on piety and learning to read in both English and French. Elizabeth would have been taught how to run a household of her own in preparation for her eventual marriage. Yet given Jacquetta's noble origins, Elizabeth may have received a relatively good education, as suggested by surviving evidence. One of the Stonor letters, for instance, notes Elizabeth wrote 'with her awn hand'.[1] Furthermore, Elizabeth's ownership of a copy of Caxton's first English book, in addition to her brother Anthony's patronage of Caxton in later years, suggests a love of literature that was fostered and developed from an early age. Jacquetta bequeathed many of the books from her first husband's French library, including a book of poems written by Christine de Pizan. Works of literature such as these would have made for perfect educational tools for the young Elizabeth and would have offered Jacquetta the opportunity to impress upon her children a similar cultural milieu she had no doubt enjoyed as a child.[2]

Her mother's status offered Elizabeth connections to the nobility and even the royal family. Jacquetta was one of the noble ladies who escorted the young Margaret of Anjou from Rouen to her new home in England in 1445.[3] Elizabeth may have been with her mother on this auspicious occasion. Cecily Neville, Duchess of York (1415–1495) and her husband, Richard, Duke of York, were also in the city, presumably accompanied by their sons, most notably Edward, Elizabeth's future husband. It is intriguing to think that many of the key players responsible for Margaret's downfall, some decades later, were potentially gathered at Rouen to welcome her as the new queen of England in 1445.[4] Before the arrival of Margaret of Anjou, Jacquetta was the highest-ranking noblewoman in England.[5] It could be argued that Elizabeth inherited her mother's social status, as she would have inherited her father's had he been the social superior.[6]

Elizabeth was at the relatively mature age of 19 or 20 before she married her first husband, Sir John Grey, the son and heir of Lord Ferrers of Groby, around 1455. Elizabeth bore him two sons, Thomas Grey (*c.*1455–1501) and Richard Grey (*c.*1457–1483), before Sir John died as a staunch supporter of the Lancastrian cause at the Second Battle of St Albans in February 1461. Although this was a decisive victory for the Lancastrians, unable to build upon their success, the Yorkist leader was able to declare himself King Edward IV on 4 March. The balance of power had quickly shifted. Elizabeth now found herself a vulnerable widow and on the losing side of a civil war. Her parents had always supported the Lancastrian cause, Jacquetta as a relative of the queen, and her father had fought the Yorkists at Towton in June 1461. Henry VI had given Woodville the title 'Earl Rivers' in 1448 and bestowed upon him a series of honours, including enrolment as a Knight of the Garter in 1450. Following Edward's acquisition of the throne, Woodville and his eldest son, Anthony (*c.*1440–1483), were for a brief time Edward's prisoners in the Tower until July 1461.

Domestic issues would bring Elizabeth into King Edward's orbit. Following her husband's death, Elizabeth was unable to secure the manors assigned to her dower, as the Grey family obstructed her claims.[7] Not content to let the matter settle, Elizabeth used all her connections to seek the king's intervention on the matter and petitioned him in person. It is possible that Elizabeth was known to Edward for many years prior to their marriage, but the evidence is unclear. What we do have is a traditional story to preface the marriage: Elizabeth met Edward under a tree while he was hunting near her home at Grafton and pleaded for his help in her dispute with the Greys. Edward, a known womaniser, asked her to be his mistress. She refused, reportedly threatening her own life to protect her honour, which only fuelled Edward's desire, prompting his proposal. A short time after, on 1 May 1464, he wed the widow in a secret ceremony on the Woodville family property. The only witnesses to the marriage were the priest, Jacquetta, an unnamed gentlewoman and a young man who sang at the ceremony. Edward's decision to keep the marriage a secret for several months indicates he was acutely aware of the social and political implications of the marriage.[8]

Edward was eventually forced to reveal his marriage at the Council of Reading in September 1464. The council were pressing Edward to marry. He had already turned down Isabella, daughter of the King of Castile (she would become the mother of Katherine of Aragon). When Edward revealed his marriage to Elizabeth, Warwick the Kingmaker, in particular, was furious and humiliated. Since April of that year, he had been working to secure a profitable and politically beneficial marriage for Edward with the French king's sister-in-law, Bona of Savoy; ironically, Edward had been married for the majority of this time.[9] Moreover, Edwards' failure to confide in Warwick, the man responsible for his seizure of the throne, must have intensified his anger.[10] In marrying Elizabeth for love, Edward had thrown away an important diplomatic opportunity, one which could have strengthened his throne. Edward's position remained precarious; as a usurper, he faced the constant risk that Henry VI might reclaim the throne and depose him (as did eventually occur in 1470).

However, Edward's seemingly impulsive behaviour might not have been all that impetuous at all. The young king may have seen his marriage to Elizabeth as a step towards independence from Warwick, and making his own decision on such a pivotal matter was an obvious demonstration that he, not Warwick, was the king of England.[11] Edward's marriage into a family of Lancastrian supporters, with connections to the most respected of Lancastrians (Bedford, Jacquetta's first husband), may have softened the most ardent Lancastrians. However, this was likely more a consequence of the union than a deliberate strategic consideration.[12]

The marriage sent shock waves throughout the nation, an English king taking one of his subjects for his queen had not occurred since 1066 when Harold Godwinson wed Edith of Mercia. The council voiced their disapproval of the marriage: 'They told him that she was not his match; however good and fair she'.[13] Warwick never did soften toward Elizabeth, and neither did Cecily of York, Edward's mother, who reportedly continued to disapprove of the marriage into the 1480s.[14] Thomas More, writing in the sixteenth century, claimed that Cecily initially tried to have the marriage annulled.[15] While the veracity of this account is unsubstantiated, it nonetheless reflects her disapproval of the marriage as recounted some fifty years later.

Disapproval of Elizabeth also stemmed from her status as a widow, albeit she had proven her fertility as the mother of two healthy sons; the consensus was that a king ought to marry a virgin.[16] Caspar Weinreich of Danzig gives us some contemporary commentary on this matter:

> although royal custom in England demands that a king should marry a virgin, whoever she may be, legitimately born and not a widow, yet the King took this one against the wish of all his lords.[17]

Fifteenth-century canonists considered second marriages to be borne out of a desire for continued sexual relations, and, as one of the fundamental virtues of queenship was chastity, this called her ability to fulfil this function into question.[18] Elizabeth's coronation was tailored to reflect her unusual status as a widow. Biblical mothers, such as Mary Cleophas, reportedly married twice, and St Elizabeth were portrayed by actors at the celebration to shift the focus to an alternative acceptable queenly characteristic, that of motherhood, thus amplifying her fertility in place of her virginity.[19]

Elizabeth's coronation, which took place in May 1465, was attended by Jacquetta's brother, Jacques de Luxembourg, along with a large retinue. Edward's insistence on the attendance of his new foreign in-laws suggests his awareness of the need to showcase Elizabeth's foreign connections, thus strengthening her position at court.[20] As part of the celebrations, a tournament was held in which several of Jacques' knights participated.[21]

Elizabeth brought a large immediate family into her marriage: six sisters, five brothers, and two younger sons. Luchino Dalleghiexia wrote in his correspondence to the Duke of Milan: 'Since her coronation she has always exerted herself to aggrandise her relations'.[22] Elizabeth arranged advantageous marriages for her siblings and sons and secured court positions for them, often at the expense of established nobility. Elizabeth's father was perhaps the greatest benefactor of Edward's favour. From relatively humble origins, Woodville was appointed treasurer of England in 1466 and the following year constable of the realm.[23] His daughters became some of the most eligible maids in England, securing prestigious marriages. The Woodvilles were engulfing an already limited supply of the marriage market and benefited from Edward's generous distribution of lands and titles, many taken from disgraced Lancastrians.[24] In a further annoyance to the nobility, Elizabeth brought no dowry to the marriage, meaning Edward provided dower lands for his new queen from the crown.[25]

Elizabeth performed her fundamental duty as queen by providing Edward with an impressive number of children. The first child of the union was named Elizabeth, the future consort of Henry VII, born in February 1466. Bohemian visitors Tetzel and Rozmital bore witness to Elizabeth's churching and were impressed by the pomp and ceremony of the festivities. A banquet followed the ceremony, where Elizabeth was seated upon a golden chair. Her mother and sister-in-law knelt on either side of her until she had completed the first course. The other ladies in attendance remained kneeling for three hours. Jacquetta again knelt before her daughter following the banquet as Elizabeth watched on as her guests enjoyed the dancing. Jacquetta only rose occasionally to soothe her aching knees.[26] Some historians, such as Scofield, have noted this as evidence for Elizabeth's haughtiness, yet Elizabeth was merely conforming to contemporary conventions and adhering to proper queenly conduct.[27]

The couple were blessed with fertility, and many more children followed. A second daughter, Mary (1467–1482), joined her sister, and then a third daughter, Cecily (1469–1507), was born. A report claimed the news: 'rejoiced the king and all the nobles exceedingly, though they would have preferred a son'.[28] A son did soon follow, the future King Edward V (1470–c.1483). The prince was given his own household at Ludlow Castle, and Elizabeth's brother, Anthony, was appointed as his tutor and governor. More children followed: Margaret (1472–1472), Richard (1473–c.1483), Anne (1475–1511), George (1477–1479), Catherine (1479–1527), and Bridget (1480–1507). The royal couple's decision to have so many children may have stemmed from Edward's desire to strongly contrast himself with Henry VI, his Lancastrian opponent, who managed to father only one child. Children were highly valued as a way to secure one's dynasty, and Elizabeth earned the praise of her contemporaries for her fertility. Like her contemporary and opponent in the enduring Wars of the Roses, Margaret of Anjou, Elizabeth would have to fight to secure the rights of her children. But whereas Margaret took an active part in politics and was visibly doing so, the extent of Elizabeth's involvement in politics is far from clear. Her power seemingly operated in the private rather than the public sphere, and her numerous relations served as advisors to the king. Elizabeth was blessed with a capable and militarily active and successful husband, in contrast to Margaret, whose husband's failing health forced her to take the lead, or at least attempt to, in matters of state.

Warwick, formerly a close companion and advisor to Edward, his cousin, had earned the epithet 'Kingmaker' for his instrumental role in Edward's seizure of the throne. Warwick believed he could as easily undo a king as make one. Tensions had been brewing between Edward and Warwick ever since Edward's secret marriage to Elizabeth in 1464 and the subsequent rise of the Woodville family. By the late 1460s, a power struggle in Europe centred on disputes between France and Burgundy. Warwick advised an alliance with the French, but the king rejected this advice and decided to back Burgundy. Warwick felt increasingly excluded from the increasingly large circle of influence surrounding Edward and was now but one voice of many and a diminishing one at that.

The Woodvilles' rapid rise disrupted the aristocratic marriage market, offending Warwick, who at the time was seeking suitable husbands for his daughters Isabel and Anne Neville. Warwick was the wealthiest magnate in England, and an obvious match was Warwick's eldest daughter, Isabel, to Edward's brother, George, Duke of Clarence (1449–1478), with whom Warwick began to ally himself from 1467. Fearing a strong coalition between his brother and Warwick, Edward's refusal to ratify the match was another personal affront to Warwick.[29] Against the king's wishes, Isabel and George were duly wed at Calais in July 1469, and the alliance between Warwick and his son-in-law was formalised. Warwick and George accused the Woodvilles of forcing up taxes to satisfy their insatiable greed and requested that the king return to the taking of counsel from the other nobles.[30] The pair gained support for a rebellion against the king and met Edward's forces at the Battle of Edgecote on 24 July 1469. Edward was defeated, captured and imprisoned in Middleham Castle. Shortly afterwards, Elizabeth was informed that her father and her brother John had been executed.[31]

Warwick's regime proved unpopular, and eventually, king and kingmaker were reconciled in September 1469, and Edward resumed the throne once more. Peace was short-lived, and Warwick sought to install his son-in-law, George, on the throne in early 1470 by staging a rebellion in Lincolnshire. The rebellion failed, and in March 1470, Warwick, along with his son-in-law, escaped to France. There, they conspired with Margaret of Anjou to launch an invasion of England and to install Henry VI once again on the throne. To seal this new alliance, Warwick's daughter, Anne, was wed to Margaret's son, Prince Edward. The invasion force landed on English shores in September 1470.[32] In preparation for the birth of her fourth child, Elizabeth had retired to the Tower of London. But upon hearing the news that Edward had fled the kingdom for Burgundy, Elizabeth sought the sanctuary of Westminster Abbey and took residence there with her three daughters and her mother. Warwick dispatched his ally, Lady Scrope, to attend to the queen (or to spy on her).[33]

Elizabeth gave birth to a son, Prince Edward, the future King Edward V, on 1 November 1470, the first son born to the royal couple. The child was duly baptised in the abbey, and Lady Scrope stood as godmother, likely a goodwill gesture on the part of Elizabeth to protect Edward's newborn heir, a threat to Henry VI's newly restored regime.[34] By March 1471, Edward had returned to England and was delighted at the news of a newborn son and heir. He marched on London and was restored as king. By April of that year, Elizabeth was rescued from her sanctuary, and the royal family was reunited.[35] Elizabeth's strife during this time won her the admiration of Londoners, with whom she seemingly suffered alongside during this tumultuous time. A contemporary poem praises her and reflects something of the mood of the growing adoration of the brave queen:

> O queen Elizabeth, of blessed creature,
> O glorious God, what pain had she?
> What languor and anguish did she endure?
> When her lord and sovereign was in adversity.
> To hear of her weeping it was a great pity,
> When she remembered the King, she was woo,
> Thus in every thing the will of God is doo.[36]

Edward met Warwick, his once-close friend and confidant, now his greatest threat, at the Battle of Barnet in April 1471, where Warwick was killed. Edward soon defeated Margaret at Tewkesbury (4 May 1471), and with Henry VI dead and his son and heir killed in battle, Edward IV could enjoy his second reign alongside his wife once more, and the kingdom prospered in relative peace for the next twelve years.

On 9 April 1483, Edward died suddenly, merely 40 years of age. The cause of his death was unrecorded; however, his excessive consumption of food and drink in his later years has led some to speculate that it adversely affected his health.[37] The following day, in the presence of his mother, the 12-year-old prince was declared King Edward V, without debate. Ascending to the throne in a century marked by both foreign and internal strife, he lacked military and political achievements, and Elizabeth was acutely aware of her son's precarious grip on the throne. Rather than appointing Richard of Gloucester (1452–1485), (hereafter referred to as Gloucester), Edward's younger brother as Protectorate, as per the dying king's wishes, the Woodvilles planned to crown Edward V immediately. They invoked the precedent of Henry VI's 1429 coronation, which had effectively ended his minority, recognising him as a sovereign and eliminating the requirement of a Protector. The kingdom would then be run by a minority government over which Gloucester could preside, and the Woodvilles could influence the king informally.[38]

Before 1483, Elizabeth's relationship with Gloucester appears to have been cordial, and there is nothing to suggest that Gloucester harboured any personal animosity towards the Woodvilles. Elizabeth's decision to sideline Gloucester did not cause her any distress; she did not fear her brother-in-law, as she should have done.[39] The evidence does not necessarily suggest that Gloucester had ambitions for the throne before 1483, although whatever his personal feelings were is unknown. Perhaps Gloucester seized an opportunity created by the Woodvilles' ambitions, or they gave him an excuse to carry out his long-planned designs.

King Edward V made his way towards London in preparation for his coronation, planned for 4 May 1483, accompanied by his uncle, Anthony Woodville and his half-brother, Richard Grey. The latter two met with Gloucester at Northampton, who seized them and incarcerated them at Pontefract Castle.[40] Gloucester then moved swiftly to Stony Stratford to meet the king, falsely accusing Anthony and

Richard Grey of plotting to kill him.[41] The young king's defence of his maternal uncle and half-brother was dismissed, and Gloucester took possession of Edward and sent him to the Tower of London in preparation for his coronation, as was customary. Gloucester portrayed himself as the dutiful uncle and loyal servant, obtaining oaths of allegiance to the new king, oaths he himself gave to his nephew. Edward was not hidden away but kept in plain sight, coming to no harm.[42] Taking possession of Edward was fundamental to power, which had swiftly passed from the Woodvilles to Gloucester. In a fatal miscalculation, which removed any sign of resistance to Gloucester's potential plans at this stage, Elizabeth left London along with her children (those who were not in Gloucester's custody) and fled to the sanctuary of Westminster Abbey.[43] Although Westminster did not offer complete protection from her enemies, Elizabeth deemed it less likely that Gloucester would seize her sons Thomas of Dorset and Richard, Duke of York, whilst his mother and their sisters were present within the confines of the abbey.[44]

With the Woodvilles removed from London, Gloucester dominated the council and was appointed Lord Protector on 8 May 1483. The king's coronation had been postponed until 24 June, when the Protectorate would come to an end. Gloucester's actions did not overtly suggest usurpation, but Elizabeth's guarded response to Gloucester's entry into London and the arrest of her eldest son and brother indicates that she had already anticipated his intentions. Elizabeth found herself in a quandary, two of her sons were in the custody of Gloucester. Her elder son, Richard Grey, was accused by Gloucester of treason and faced the gallows. From the sanctuary of Westminster, Elizabeth looked to fulfil her maternal duty by attempting to secure Richard Grey's release. Her retreat to Westminster in the year 1470 projected the image of the ideal mother and queen, giving birth amidst turmoil and ensuring the safety of her growing brood. However, on this occasion, Gloucester used Elizabeth's femininity against her and tried to cast her as a scheming sorceress and seductress.[45]

On 15 June, Gloucester wrote to the Mayor of York requesting military aid from the north. Within this letter, we find some perhaps predictable assertions that Elizabeth and her Woodville relations threatened 'the old royal blood'. Gloucester also accused Elizabeth and her relations of plotting to kill him, adding that Elizabeth did so by 'subtle and damnable ways' and that she had 'forecast' Gloucester's death.[46] Similar accusations had previously been made against Eleanor Cobham and Queen Joan of Navarre earlier in the century. Accusations of witchcraft were often used to silence women and remove their authority.[47] However, it is also possible that Gloucester genuinely believed his own claims.[48]

Gloucester rekindled old accusations of witchcraft levelled against Jacquetta, who had died in 1472. In 1469–1470 during Warwick's rebellion and reinstatement of Henry VI, Thomas Wake, a squire, had claimed that Jacquetta owned a lead image of a man with its limbs broken (presumably intended to represent Warwick).

In 1469, it was also claimed that Jacquetta had images of a man and a woman (taken to be Elizabeth and Edward IV). It was suggested that these images were used in some sort of sorcery to bring about the marriage of Edward to Elizabeth.[49] It was considered plausible that Jacquetta's daughter might also engage in these practices. Moreover, given Elizabeth's vulnerable position, it seemed natural she might turn to such practices in 1483 to harm Gloucester.[50] In a petition from parliament (orchestrated by Gloucester) which would invite him to take the crown, it was alleged that the marriage between Elizabeth and Edward was made:

> by sorcery and witchcraft committed by the said Elizabeth and her mother, Jacquetta, duchess of Bedford, as the common opinion of the people and the public voice and fame is through all this land.[51]

It is unclear whether the marriage could have been declared invalid on the basis of sorcery, but it did serve to damage Elizabeth's reputation.[52] Gloucester, therefore, sought other means to render Elizabeth's marriage invalid, and he struck hard.

Edward and Elizabeth's clandestine marriage was a constant source of controversy, leaving Elizabeth vulnerable to challenges regarding its validity. Gloucester alleged Edward had been legally bound in marriage before his union with Elizabeth to Lady Eleanor Butler (conveniently deceased since 1468). But the Bishop of Bath and Wells claimed to have witnessed this earlier secret marriage.[53] Consequently, in January 1484, a Statute of Parliament known as *Titulus Regius* declared Elizabeth's children by Edward illegitimate as their marriage was invalid.

On 25 June 1483, Elizabeth's brother, Anthony, and her son, Richard Grey, were executed for treason. The following day, Gloucester took the throne as King Richard III. Elizabeth had earlier been coerced into surrendering her youngest son, Richard, Duke of York, to Gloucester under the pretence of preparing for his brother's coronation, a ceremony that never took place. After the summer of 1483, Edward and Richard were never seen again. They have become known as 'The Princes in the Tower' and much speculation has surrounded their fate. Some have argued that the brothers escaped, but a more plausible explanation is that they were murdered on the orders of their uncle, eliminating their potential as figureheads for opposition to Gloucester's rule.

As her marriage was declared invalid, Elizabeth did not enjoy the privileges accorded to a dowager queen. Her lands were removed from her and given to the Crown. Her eldest son, Thomas of Dorset, who had accompanied her into the sanctuary of Westminster, escaped and fled to Brittany to join the resistance headed by Henry Tudor. In autumn 1483, Elizabeth conspired with Margaret Beaufort's physician, Lewis Caerleon, lending support to an uprising to overthrow Gloucester, known as Buckingham's Rebellion.[54] Gloucester commanded significant support; without it, he could not have seized the throne, but not all were comfortable with the removal of a child, the son of an anointed king and presumably the murder of these royal princes. Ultimately, the uprising failed, and to prevent any future trouble from the former queen, Gloucester ordered a heavy guard to surround Westminster Abbey.[55] Unable to help her sons, Elizabeth focused on securing her daughters' futures. In March 1484, she arranged their release and was assured they would receive husbands befitting their status. Once a powerful consort, Elizabeth was now retired on a modest income, yet from this setback, one of her daughters would rise to glory.

The Battle of Bosworth, 22 August 1485, marked the end of the Yorkist dynasty when Gloucester was killed, and Henry Tudor claimed the throne. Henry repealed *Titulus Regius* and married Elizabeth's eldest daughter, Elizabeth of York, in January 1486. Henry VII restored Elizabeth to the status of dowager queen, returning her dowager lands and granting her a handsome annual income of 400 marks.[56] There were now too many royal ladies at court, and it would be easy to see how Elizabeth would be put out by the dominant Margaret Beaufort. Elizabeth Woodville quietly slipped into retirement at Bermondsey Abbey, undoubtedly grieved by the loss of so many of her male relatives, not least of all, three of her sons. Elizabeth died on 8 June 1492 and was buried with her beloved husband, Edward, in a quiet ceremony four days later at St George's Chapel, Windsor.

Historians have judged Elizabeth Woodville varyingly, as a scheming, ambitious woman or even as a victim of her own success. However, her ambitions appear driven by genuine love for her children and not by a lust for personal power. The sources are sympathetic to her plight when discussions centre around the fate of her sons, particularly the Princes in the Tower. Elizabeth is portrayed most positively when seen as a mother acting in the best interests of her children, desperately striving to save her sons from their tragic and terrifying fate.[57] From her glory days as the wife of the handsome Edward IV, to cowering in the abbey with her daughters, Elizabeth's anguish in surrendering her youngest son to Gloucester evokes deep sympathy. Elizabeth's care and devotion to her children are no clearer than in her will. Written in her final days with few material possessions to leave, the former queen says goodbye to her beloved children. In these sorrowful words, Elizabeth steps out from the inanimate pages of history and comes alive, her devotion as a mother, the role in which she most excelled, is powerfully evident:

> Where I have no worldly goods to do the Queen's Grace, my dearest daughter, a pleasure with, neither to reward any of my children, according to my heart and mind, I beseech God Almighty to bless her Grace, with all her noble issue, and with as good heart and mind as is possible to me, I give her Grace my blessing, and all the foresaid my children.[58]

Chapter 14

Margaret Beaufort (1443–1509)

While Richard Neville, Earl of Warwick, earned the epithet 'Kingmaker,' it could equally be applied to Lady Margaret Beaufort, given her pivotal role in the establishment of the Tudor dynasty. Margaret's will, determination, and political skill, surpassing that of many of her male contemporaries, reshaped the course of English politics and history. Margaret exemplified that women could, in certain circumstances, exercise power and influence on par with their male counterparts. These were valuable lessons to leave and the most precious legacy she could bequeath to her great-granddaughters, the first queens of England, Mary I and Elizabeth I.

Margaret was born on 31 May 1443, the daughter of John Beaufort, Duke of Somerset (1404–1444) and Margaret Beauchamp (c.1410–1482). John Beaufort was the grandson of John of Gaunt on his father's side, giving Margaret a dynastic link to Edward III and making her the kin of Henry VI. John's mother, Margaret Holland (1385–1439), a great-granddaughter of Edward I, was a powerful, wealthy landowner, and the estates she had accumulated in her life would later make her granddaughter, Margaret, an incredibly wealthy woman in her own right.[1] Margaret's mother, Margaret Beauchamp, was the widow of Sir Oliver St John (d.1437) by whom she had five children, giving Margaret an extensive half-blood family whom she was incredibly close to throughout her life.

Margaret would not have remembered her father, for John Beaufort was to die at the age of 40, likely by suicide as a disgraced captain following a disastrous campaign in France as part of the Hundred Years' War.[2] This left Margaret the sole heiress of his estates in 1444 before her first birthday. Her father's lands were substantial, with estates in Kent, Worcestershire, Lincolnshire, Norfolk, Somerset, Essex, and Sussex, and these were now bequeathed to the young Margaret. Margaret's substantial inheritance rendered her and her mother vulnerable, necessitating male protection through wardship.[3] Henry VI awarded Margaret's wardship to William de la Pole, the Earl of Suffolk, who, in contrast to her father, had distinguished himself fighting in France.[4] Presumably, Margaret spent much of her early life with her mother at the Castle of Maxey in the Fenlands.[5] Like her daughter, Margaret's mother would marry a succession of husbands, and her third and final marriage was to Lionel de Wells, by whom she had one son, John Wells, who would eventually marry Cecily, the sister of Elizabeth of York.

At the age of 6, Margaret was wed to the 8-year-old John de la Pole, the son of her ward, whom she married, by word only, in 1450. However, the marriage was voidable given that both spouses were below the age of consent on the occasion of their wedding.[6] Henry VI had Margaret brought to his court in 1453, and, as Margaret tried to make sense of this event in later years that occurred when she was 9 years old, she recalled she was presented with two suitors, John de la Pole and Edmund Tudor Earl of Richmond (*c.*1430–1456), half-brother to King Henry VI. In reality, Margaret's fate was already sealed; Henry aimed to reward Edmund and secure his future with a marriage to a wealthy heiress. But Margaret recalled the event differently. Unsure of which suitor to choose, an old lady advised her to pray to St Nicholas, the patron saint of maidens, for guidance. Later that evening, the saint put into her mind Edmund Tudor, and so Margaret chose him as her future husband.[7] It is indicative of Margaret's character that she recalled the event in such a way, suggesting that she possessed agency in the matter at such a young age. Henry gave her wardship to Edmund and his other half-brother, Jasper Tudor (*c.*1431–1495). The 26-year-old Edmund married Margaret, his 12-year-old bride, in 1455. It could have been Henry's intention to make Edmund his heir, for he was still childless in 1453, and his marriage to Margaret, with her own dynastic links, would have placed Edmund in a much stronger position.[8]

It was customary and advised to wait to consummate the marriage until the bride was at least 14 years old. Unfortunately for Margaret, Edmund, with a blatant disregard for his bride's health, did not wait and impregnated his wife when she was 13. His haste was likely driven by greed, for the law of the land permitted a husband to enjoy his wife's estates until he died if the union had been consummated and a child was born, even if that child, or for that matter, the wife, did not survive childbirth.[9] Margaret's estates received a handsome income of over £1000 annually, and evidently, the temptation was too much for the man twice her age. In November 1456, Edmund died from the plague, leaving his 13-year-old wife six months pregnant and extremely vulnerable. Indeed, Margaret and her unborn child were at risk of contracting the plague from Edmund.[10] Alone and afraid, Margaret took refuge with her brother-in-law, Jasper Tudor, who offered her and her unborn baby his protection.

Margaret gave birth to a healthy boy, Henry Tudor, Earl of Richmond, on 28 January 1457 at Pembroke Castle, the stronghold of Jasper Tudor. Henry would be her only child. Unsurprisingly, the birth was a difficult one. Margaret was a small child of a slight frame, as John Fisher reflected, 'It seemed a miracle that of so little a personage anyone should have been born at all'.[11] The traumatic experience left Margaret with deep psychological and undoubtedly physical scars as well. In fourteen years of marriage to her third husband, the couple did not produce any children. Indeed, in her fourth marriage, no provision was made for any potential children, suggesting that Margaret was incapable or unwilling to bear any more children.[12] It is telling that as a grandmother, along with her daughter-in-law, Margaret interceded with the king to ensure that her 9-year-old granddaughter and namesake, Margaret, betrothed to the king of Scotland was not sent to the Scottish court as a child, in fear that the king would not wait until she was near adulthood to consummate the marriage.[13]

It is assumed that Henry remained under the protection of Jasper when his mother left Pembroke in 1458 to marry her third husband and her second cousin, Sir Henry Stafford (*c*.1425–1471), a fellow supporter of the Lancastrian cause. The 14-year-old Margaret, determined to choose her own destiny, had opted for a match that would further and protect her own interests and those of her son. More importantly, Margaret did not want a husband to be forced upon her once again. Stafford was the second son of Henry, Duke of Buckingham and was the only man in England as powerful as Richard, Duke of York.[14]

Margaret's union with Stafford appears to have been a happy one, and the sources suggest the couple spent little time apart. Stafford took his wife with him when he toured their estates, and he even brought Margaret with him to parliament.[15] Margaret's wealth afforded the couple a luxurious lifestyle, and they maintained close contact with Henry, often visiting him at Pembroke. But the world Henry was born into and the one Margaret moved through was a turbulent one, and subject to frequent radical royal change. Margaret was a Lancastrian, devoted to the cause of Henry VI, her kin, as was her husband. In March 1461, the Lancastrian forces were defeated by the Yorkists at the Battle of Towton, led by the charismatic 18-year-old Duke of York, who was crowned King Edward IV three months later.

Despite her ultimate loyalty to Henry VI, Margaret was pragmatic and accepted Edward as the new king, and in return he pardoned Margaret and Stafford (who had fought against the new king at Towton) ensuring Margaret would keep all her lands from her father's inheritance and her dower lands from her marriage to Edmund.[16] Stafford would demonstrate his loyalty to the new Yorkist dynasty in March 1470 when he joined Edward's army to put down the Lincolnshire Rising. The decision was undoubtedly challenging, given that members of Margaret's own family were involved in the rebellion.[17]

Margaret seized upon the opportunity to take Henry, who had been under the wardship of William Lord Herbert, to meet his uncle, King Henry VI, following his brief restoration to the throne in October 1470 and mother and son were reunited for a brief time. It was at this meeting that Polydore Vergil and Bernard André recounted Henry VI's alleged prophecy in which he predicted that Henry Tudor would one day become king and recognised him as his heir.[18] With a son of his own to succeed him, it seems unlikely Henry VI would have made such a prediction; however, this alleged conversation was later used to full effect by Tudor propagandists to further legitimise Henry VII's kingship.[19]

In May 1471, King Henry VI died a prisoner in the Tower of London. His son, Prince Edward, had been killed by Edward IV at the Battle of Tewkesbury earlier that month. Henry was now a significant potential threat to Edward, now an even stronger Lancastrian claimant to the throne. Consequently, Margaret asked Jasper to take Henry to the Continent.[20] In 1475, Edward requested that Henry return from his exile in Brittany for the purpose of marrying one of his daughters. Likely a ploy to have him killed, Henry sensed the danger, narrowly escaping by feigning illness.[21] Throughout Henry's fourteen-year exile, Margaret corresponded frequently with her son, sending money and secretly plotting his return.

Upon Stafford's death in October 1471, the now 28-year-old Margaret once again demonstrated her pragmatism and sought to continue favourable relations with Edward IV. She married for a fourth time in October 1473, Thomas Lord Stanley (1435–1504), eight years her senior and steward of the king's household. Stanley had fathered eleven children with his first wife, three of whom survived into adulthood. If Margaret had made a conscious decision not to have children, or was unable to bear them, this may have played a part in Margaret's decision to marry him, for his dynasty was secure.[22] Her marriage to Stanley brought Margaret into close contact with the Woodvilles. Her prominence at court was acknowledged by her involvement in the celebrations of the birth of Princess Bridget, Edward's daughter, as Margaret carried the newborn to her baptism. Margaret had even successfully negotiated with the royal family for the return of her son from exile, with Edward drafting a pardon for him.[23] However, these negotiations came to nothing for Edward died suddenly in 1483, and English politics was once again flung into chaos.

Margaret's relations with the new king, Richard III (Gloucester), appear to have been initially amicable, and she even participated in his coronation, bearing Queen Anne's train.[24] However, to Margaret's disappointment, Gloucester did not ratify Edward's previous agreement with her to permit Henry to return from exile, which caused Margaret to look to alternative means to restore her son.[25] Margaret's involvement in Buckingham's Rebellion is treated by some historians as marginal, whereas others recognise her as its central instigator, seeking to restore Edward V and facilitate an invasion force led by Henry and Jasper.[26] Although the rebellion, planned for 18 October 1483, bears his name and is attributed to him, Buckingham, once a close friend and conspirator of Gloucester, had very little involvement in its organisation and the course of events.[27] While held captive in Buckingham's stronghold at Brecon Castle, Bishop Morton was regularly visited by Margaret's estate manager, Reginald Bray, who appears to have been tasked with recruiting support for her cause.[28] It appears that Bray conveyed plans of a rebellion to Morton, and eventually Buckingham was brought into their confidence.[29] Buckingham duly wrote to Henry in September 1483 about the planned rebellion and invited the exiled Tudor to join him.[30] An alternative narrative is offered by Edward Hall, writing in the mid-sixteenth century. He claimed that Margaret herself informed Buckingham of the planned rebellion in a chance encounter on the road between Worcester and Bridgnorth, thus giving her a more centralised role in the plot.[31] Margaret and her conspirators may have even suggested that Buckingham, as a potential candidate for the throne, would become king as a means of gaining his support.[32] Little evidence survives relating to the rebellion, their demands and their intended course of action. Despite garnering substantial support, especially from the Woodvilles, the rebellion ultimately failed.[33] The 'Princes in the Tower' were taken into the inner chambers of the Tower and were never seen again.[34]

Buckingham was executed along with several other rebels for treason. Facing charges of treason herself, it was Stanley's loyalty that spared Margaret's attainment or, even worse, the noose. She was, however, forced to forfeit her lands, which were transferred to her husband along with her titles.[35] Margaret was barred from inheriting lands from her mother, and lands set aside for her son were distributed among others. To restrict her movements, she was placed under house arrest; her husband, her jailer and her household servants were removed.[36]

Edward V and his brother, Richard, were now presumed dead, and from this time, the focus of resistance to Gloucester shifted from the release of Edward V to a new potential claimant, Henry Tudor. Although nothing legally barred women from the throne, Margaret had not even been considered as a contender, just as Elizabeth of York would be dismissed as a possible queen regnant.[37] England would not be ready for a queen regnant until Margaret's great-granddaughters ruled seven decades later.

Margaret attempted to secure her son's return by resurrecting an old notion of marrying Henry to Elizabeth of York, now the eldest of Edward's successors following the disappearance of her brothers. The marriage between the rightful Yorkist heir and the sole surviving Lancastrian heir would offer Henry's kingship legitimacy and bring an end to the bitter fighting of the Wars of the Roses. Margaret plotted with Elizabeth Woodville to unite their houses and see their children wed and ultimately remove Gloucester in favour of the couple. Messages were passed to and from the ladies via Margaret's physician, Lewis Caerleon, a frequent visitor to Elizabeth Woodville, who had taken sanctuary in Westminster Abbey.[38] Henry swore to marry Elizabeth of York in December 1483 and waited for his moment.

Henry's energies between 1483 and 1485 were spent gathering support from Brittany and France and assembling a force large enough to offer some resistance to Gloucester and his supporters. Bray, Margaret's close confidant, collected money on her behalf to send to Henry to fund his invasion fleet.[39] In summer 1485, he set sail for England and landed in Pembrokeshire. From there, Henry marched towards Bosworth, increasing his army as he went. Stanley had been summoned to Gloucester's side for fear that Margaret 'might induce her husband to go over to the party of her son'.[40] Stanley refused the summons, feigned illness and instead marched south, awaiting the arrival of his stepson and in a quandary as to what action to take.

Henry's forces engaged Gloucester's at the Battle of Bosworth on 22 August 1485, and famously, Stanley's inaction helped to secure his stepson's victory. Loyalty to Margaret undoubtedly played a decisive factor in his decision, and he was rewarded with the title of Earl of Derby, the first of many honours Henry bestowed upon his stepfather.[41] Against all odds, Henry was now the king of England. Margaret emerged from the fruits of victory as the king's mother. She had enjoyed a life of power, influence and prestige, but it was as the king's mother that she reached the pinnacle of power as Henry repaid his mother for her unwavering devotion. Henry had spent fourteen years in exile and had found himself a king in an unfamiliar land; he was not acquainted with its customs and court. He turned to his mother for support and guidance, and Margaret, possibly preparing for this moment for at least the past couple of years, relished the role.

Margaret was reunited with her son in September 1485, and the pair spent a considerable amount of time together in Woking, Margaret's luxurious manor house. From there, Henry ordered that Coldharbour, a magnificent London royal residence on the Thames, be prepared for '*my lady the Kinges moder*' and was fitted with a window bearing her arms.[42] Significantly, it had once belonged to one of Margaret's ancestors, John Holland.[43] The residence became a centre of Tudor hospitality, and Margaret entertained many royal guests there over many happy years.[44] Henry had his future consort, Elizabeth of York, along with her cousin, Edward of Warwick (1475–1499), sent to Margaret at Coldharbour. Not only was Margaret afforded the opportunity to become better acquainted with her future daughter-in-law, but she could also keep a watchful eye on Edward, who was now a potential contender for the throne as the son of George, Duke of Clarence.[45] Margaret would spend the latter months of 1485 busily preparing for her son's coronation, quite possibly the proudest moment in her entire life. John Fisher noted in her month's mind that when her son was crowned in triumph and glory, she wept for joy.[46]

Among Henry's earliest proclamations was the restoration of Margaret's lands and titles seized by Gloucester, followed by granting her the legal autonomy of a *femme sole*. The status of *femme sole* was usually reserved for single women and identified them as having an independent legal and economic status.[47] For Margaret, a married woman, this rendered her financially independent from her husband, giving her full control of her own estates and financial interests. In practice, this meant that Margaret could establish her own household distinct from that of her husband.[48] Margaret established her base of operation at Collyweston, Northamptonshire, in 1487 and transformed this medieval manor house into a sumptuous Tudor palace.

Margaret used the palace as a display of Tudor magnificence and in 1503 hosted the wedding celebrations for her granddaughter and namesake, Princess Margaret, before she made her way to Scotland to take her place there as queen consort.[49] Margaret had hundreds of servants in her employment at her various residences and was said to have been an affable employer. Henry Parker, a member of her household, later recalled that Margaret remembered all the names of her servants and even visited them when they were sick.[50]

Henry formalised Margaret's authority in the East Midlands by delegating to her conciliar powers at Collyweston, where she established a court of equity operating in the name of the king, complete with its own prison. Her council was often asked to intervene in cases formally reserved for ecclesiastical courts, such was her moral standing. One case she heard related to John Stokesley, later Bishop of London, who was accused of baptising a cat.[51] She also heard treasonable cases and dealt with challenges to her son's legitimacy as king, and thus became an important protector and defender of the Tudor dynasty.[52] A woman presiding over such a court was unique and a testament to Margaret's authority and the respect she had earned. A further indication of the great honour Henry bestowed upon his mother was in granting her the wardships of various aristocrats, including Edward Stafford, the 5-year-old son of the Duke of Buckingham and the 10-year-old Edward of Warwick. Margaret was given £500 annually for their expenses.[53] Several other aristocratic and gentry children were also placed in her care, including three of Elizabeth of York's sisters, two children of the Earl of Northumberland and future Bishop of London, Hugh Oldham. By raising a multitude of influential children, Margaret made significant connections which would be to the benefit of herself and the Tudor dynasty in the years that followed.[54]

From 1499, Margaret began to sign her name 'Margaret R' as opposed to the 'M Richmond' she had used since the 1460s. This seems to mirror the adoption of the signatures 'HR' used by Henry and 'Elizabeth R' used by the queen.[55] Her use of this signature has been hotly debated; the R could potentially refer to her title Lady Richmond, a title she had held on account of her marriage to Edmund Tudor and had used since her teens. Alternatively, it could stand for 'regina', or queen.[56] The use of Margaret R does appear to have been a deliberate attempt on the part of Margaret to associate herself with her son and convey the well-known fact that without her blood, and indeed her help, Henry would not have been king at all.

Continuing a close relationship with her son as his family grew, Margaret had rooms reserved for her use at every royal residence; often, these rooms would be linked to the chambers of her son.[57] Mother and son were very close in age and evidently got along rather well. It has been suggested that Margaret's overbearing personality pushed Elizabeth from the limelight, and Henry chose to listen to the advice of his mother rather than his wife.[58] Certainly, Margaret spent a lot of time with the royal couple, especially in the early years of Henry's reign. Margaret walked merely half a step behind Elizabeth, and while the royal couple wore crowns, Margaret wore a coronet.[59] Indeed, her status at court was described as 'semi-regal'.

John Hewick, a yeoman of the crown was accused of Treasonable Language in February 1500 when upon returning from conversing with the king and queen it was alleged that he exclaimed: 'he had spoken with the Queen's Grace, and should have spoken more with her said Grace had not been for that strong whore the King's mother'.[60] Perhaps Margaret was trying to save Elizabeth the trouble of conversing with an opportunistic servant, or perhaps she was overstepping the mark and interfering in Elizabeth's business.[61] The sub-prior of Santa Cruz wrote to King Ferdinand and Isabella, parents of Katherine of Aragon (1485–1536), in 1498, during the negotiations for the marriage of Katherine of Aragon and Prince Arthur (1486–1502), writing of Elizabeth 'She is kept in subjection by the mother of the King.'[62] There are similar passages which portray Margaret taking precedence over Elizabeth; however, all of these comments are made by Spanish ambassadors, recent arrivals with little knowledge of the English court, and are not substantiated by other evidence.[63] As argued elsewhere, it is also possible that Elizabeth purposely removed herself from the limelight and allowed Margaret to take a leading role in Tudor politics.[64] Elizabeth benefited from her mother-in-law's assistance during the preparations for the arrival of Katherine of Aragon, as the pair assisted the princess into her new home.[65] Margaret did enjoy a seemingly good relationship with her daughter-in-law and grandchildren, and had rooms reserved for Elizabeth at Collyweston.[66]

Margaret was renowned for her piety and led a life of prayer, abstinence and charity. As a married woman in her fifties, she took a vow of chastity with the consent of her fourth husband, Stanley. Margaret provided for twelve poor people at her manor of Hatfield, feeding them, clothing them and offering shelter. They were cared for by a nurse, and Margaret covered all expenses for their care.[67] Margaret understood the importance of education and the training of secular priests to disseminate the word of God to the masses. Created at the encouragement of John Fisher, Humanist scholar and later her confessor, she founded two colleges at Cambridge, Christ College in 1505 and St John's College, which was completed after her death.[68] Margaret was not only a patron of John Fisher, but also two early printers, William Caxton and Wynkyn de Worde. Margaret's life extended beyond politics, education and piety. She enjoyed entertainment, and her accounts show she paid for clothes and shoes for her fool named Skip. Following Skip's death, another fool named 'Reginald the Idiot' was to replace him. Margaret also enjoyed chess and even gambled on the outcome of these games. She once sent a man named Buckden to go on pilgrimage in her stead while she enjoyed a game of cards.[69]

In the latter years of her life, Margaret would experience the loss of many of her nearest and dearest. In 1502, her eldest grandson, Prince Arthur, died, followed by his mother, Elizabeth, the following year. Margaret was widowed upon the death of Stanley in 1504, and in 1508, she experienced her greatest grief as her son's health began to fail, and he called his mother to his side. Margaret spent the last months of Henry's life in almost constant attendance on her 52-year-old son, who finally succumbed to illness, probably Tuberculosis, and slipped into death on 21 April 1509. A testament to the trust he placed in his mother, Henry designated her the executrix of his will.[70] Setting aside her personal grief, Margaret's priority was ensuring the survival of the Tudor dynasty. Margaret headed the council, which met to arrange Henry VII's funeral and led the selection of members of the council to govern until her grandson's coronation.[71]

The coronation of Henry VIII and his new wife, and his brother's widow, Katherine of Aragon, took place on 24 June 1509, marking the last time Margaret would see her grandson. Henry VIII's reign ushered in a new age, at the beginning of a new century, one that left behind the pains of the Wars of the Roses as Henry, born of the Houses of York and Lancaster, took the throne at the threshold of manhood. Margaret must have felt a mixture of pride and sorrow as she stood, the last Lancastrian survivor of the tumultuous previous century, knowing she would not live to see this new age. Margaret, the ultimate survivor of the fifteenth century, now a frail woman of 66 years, died at Westminster on 29 June 1509. Pious until death, Margaret's legacy would not only be that of the Tudor dynasty but also her generosity as a foundress of educational institutions, as well as furthering her faith within the kingdom. She was laid to rest in Westminster Abbey in the Henry VII chapel.

Margaret's friend and confessor, Bishop John Fisher, preached a sermon at her month's mind and recalled that, in moments of pure joy, Margaret would dread adversity that she felt would surely follow.[72] Undoubtedly, Margaret's tumultuous childhood, the trauma of childbirth and the separation from her son during his childhood and early adult life left Margaret with emotional scars from which she never did quite recover. Fisher's portrayal of the vulnerable Margaret is a stark contrast to her later reputation as an invincible matriarch, a rare example of a strong and independent woman exerting political authority in a man's world. Although undoubtedly a formidable woman, there was a hidden vulnerability to her character that she permitted few to see.

Chapter 15

Elizabeth of York (1466–1503)

Elizabeth of York takes this book to the very end of the medieval period. A true survivor of the Wars of the Roses, her fate and the establishment of the Tudor dynasty were largely shaped by the political acumen of her mother, Elizabeth Woodville, and her mother-in-law, Margaret Beaufort. An essential component of her husband's kingship, Elizabeth deliberately avoided public political involvement. Instead, she offered an example of the ideal queen consort and worked to exert her influence in the private sphere.

Elizabeth of York was born in February 1466 to King Edward IV and Elizabeth Woodville, soon after her parents' marriage. Her father had been assured by his physician, Dominic de Sergio, that 'the queen was conceived with a Prince'. The birth of a son would have gone some way to securing Edward's throne amid the dynastic struggles of the Wars of the Roses. Waiting outside the birthing chamber at Westminster Palace, Dominic heard the cries of the newborn and inquired as to the sex of the child. The queen's maids replied mockingly: 'Whatsoever the queen's grace hath here within, sure it is that a fool stands there without'.[1]

Elizabeth would be joined by more siblings, six sisters and three brothers (although not all reached adulthood), in addition to her two half-brothers on her mother's side. Bernard Andreas wrote of Elizabeth: 'the love she bore her brothers and sisters was unheard of and almost incredible'.[2] Elizabeth was kept under the watchful eye of her mother in her early years. We know the 3-year-old Elizabeth, along with her two younger sisters, accompanied her mother to Norwich in June 1469 and from there witnessed a grand pageant. It was perhaps this occasion which ignited her love for pageantry, which would continue throughout her life.[3] This visit to Norwich was interrupted by news that her godfather, Warwick, had rebelled against her father. The pregnant Elizabeth Woodville fled with her young daughters, not to a fortified place but to the sanctuary of Westminster Abbey, suggesting the queen and her children faced real and significant danger.[4] Elizabeth would once again return to the safety of the abbey as a teenager, but she was rescued on this occasion once her father returned from exile and again resumed the throne in March 1470. Elizabeth had entered the abbey as the heir of her father, but would emerge with a baby brother who had replaced her in this regard.

Edward used his daughter as a political pawn to heal his ongoing rift with Warwick. Elizabeth was betrothed to Warwick's nephew and heir presumptive, George Neville. However, this engagement was short-lived as the father of Elizabeth's betrothed, John Neville, betrayed the king and clashed with him at the Battle of Barnet in 1471.[5] Elizabeth once again entered the marriage market and, in August 1475, became betrothed to Charles, the Dauphin, the son and heir of King Louis XI of France, as part of a treaty signed with her father at Picquigny. Elizabeth was thereafter referred to as Madam le Dauphine, even by her father. In preparation for her future role as queen of France, an emphasis was placed upon an education in French and Spanish to ensure she was fluent in both languages.[6] Significantly, Elizabeth was to be the first English princess destined to become the queen of France and from the age of 9, she prepared for this role in her homeland.[7] Elizabeth's betrothal to Charles was broken in 1482 when Louis had his son betrothed to the daughter of Maximilian of Austria, and Edward's treaty with France was broken. His anxiety about the security of his kingdom, considering the breaking of this truce, was allegedly cited as a cause for the illness from which he died the following year.[8]

Elizabeth enjoyed a seemingly good relationship with her father. In a rare insight into royal relations, she was noted to have danced with him and the Duke of Buckingham at the age of 6 at one of her mother's banquets.[9] She had a great love for dancing and music throughout her life, pastimes which she would pass on to her son, Henry.[10] A love of literature was presumably cultivated from her Woodville roots. Among the many signatures belonging to members of the Woodville family on a French Manuscript *Romances of the Saint Graal* appears the signature '*Elysabeth, the kyngys dowther*', alongside the mark of her sister, Cecily. Judging by the many signatures on this manuscript, including that of Elizabeth Woodville, we can assume that literature was important to Elizabeth's maternal family, with books treasured and shared.[11] The ability to read was expected for a fifteenth-century princess, but writing was an altogether different skill, and one deemed of lesser importance to aristocratic women. However, a curious contemporary ballad credits Elizabeth with excellent writing skills, going as far as to pen letters for Thomas Stanley before Bosworth. Although likely a work of fiction, the ballad gives some indication of the contemporary perception of the young Princess Elizabeth.[12]

As a young princess, Elizabeth enjoyed all the pomp and ceremony of the court. As a small child, she witnessed the amazing spectacle of the colourful procession of her paternal aunt, Margaret, as she left London to marry Charles, Duke of Burgundy, in an exhibition of the splendour of the English Court.[13] Alongside another paternal aunt, also named Elizabeth, the honour of the title Lady of the Garter was bestowed upon the young princess in 1477.[14] The Woodvilles had a natural talent for jousting, and her maternal uncle, Anthony Woodville, was the embodiment of chivalry and masculinity, a splendid jouster, reportedly the best in the realm.[15] As an 11-year-old girl, she witnessed the jousting festivities held to celebrate the marriage of her 4-year-old brother, Richard, to Anne Mowbray. The event was made all the more memorable for Elizabeth, who was given the honour of selecting the winning team.[16]

Yet all this splendour and grandeur that had characterised Elizabeth's early years would be no more than a distant memory when, on 3 April 1483, Elizabeth's father suddenly died at the age of 40. Elizabeth's younger brother, the 12-year-old Edward, was next in line, and her status quickly shifted from that of daughter of the king to that of the king's sister. As the family mourned, young Edward V was seized by his uncle, Richard of Gloucester. Gloucester also arrested Elizabeth's half-brother, Richard Grey and her maternal uncle, Anthony Woodville. Once again, fearing for the safety of herself and of her children, Elizabeth Woodville fled with the young Elizabeth and the rest of her siblings (who were not in the custody of their uncle) to Westminster Abbey.

The royal children were confined to the abbey, and in June 1483, Elizabeth Woodville was persuaded to hand over her youngest son, Richard, Duke of York, to join his brother, Edward, in the Tower in preparation for the latter's coronation.[17] After the summer of 1483, Elizabeth's two brothers, known to history as 'The Prince in the Tower', were never seen again.

Gloucester moved swiftly to consolidate his claim to the throne and eliminate potential challenges from Edward IV's other children by having Princess Elizabeth and her siblings declared illegitimate through the parliamentary statute *Titulus Regius*. Gloucester came to an agreement with Elizabeth Woodville that no harm would come to her daughters; he also promised to find 'Gentlemen born' husbands for them and offered them a small annual income of 200 marks each.[18] As the king's daughter, Princess Elizabeth was destined for a prestigious marriage, but now her illegitimate status potentially dashed all hopes for a suitable marriage. There were talks of her marriage to William Stillington, an illegitimate son of the Bishop of Bath and Wells.[19] Yet nothing came of these discussions, for Princess Elizabeth was destined for a far greater marriage, and the selection of a spouse for her eldest daughter was something Elizabeth Woodville was not prepared to relinquish.

Following the presumed deaths of her younger brothers, Elizabeth was thrust into the spotlight; she embodied all that remained of Yorkist legitimacy.[20] Although Gloucester had declared his niece illegitimate, this was not accepted by all. Indeed, during her sanctuary within the abbey in summer 1483, some recommended to Elizabeth Woodville:

> that some of the king's daughters should leave Westminster, and go
> in disguise to the parts beyond the sea; in order that … the kingdom
> might still, in consequence of the safety of the daughters, some day
> fall again into the hands of the rightful heir.[21]

England was not quite ready for a female ruler in the late fifteenth century; that experiment would first be undertaken by Elizabeth of York's granddaughter, Mary, some seventy years later. However, it was acknowledged that women were conduits for power. Henry I had attempted to pass the throne onto his daughter, but it was only her cousin, Stephen's, more successful bid that prevented her succession. In any event, she transmitted the throne to her son, Henry II. In 1404, Henry IV (1367–1413) had the nobility swear an oath regarding his succession to 'his eldest son, my lord the prince, and to the heirs of his body'.[22] The 'heirs of his body' did not specify the sex of the children whom the king expected to succeed him, therefore leaving open the possibility of his succession by a daughter who could potentially transmit the kingship to a husband or a son. Fifteenth-century women could transmit sovereign power, even if they themselves were not considered capable of possessing it.[23]

The newly crowned king kept his niece close and under surveillance, thereby hoping to negate the chances of Princess Elizabeth becoming a figurehead for any challenge to his throne. Elizabeth joined the court of Gloucester and his consort, Anne, sometime around March 1484, and her beauty was noted by courtiers.[24] Around a month after Elizabeth arrived at court, the king's son, Edward, died aged 18 months old. His wife, Anne, became ill shortly thereafter, and her illness was said to have increased 'because the king entirely shunned her bed'.[25] At the Christmas Court of 1484, the Croyland Chronicler noted that Elizabeth and Anne were dressed in gowns:

> being of similar colour and shape, a thing that caused the people to murmur and the nobles and prelates greatly to wonder thereat; while it was said by many that the king was bent, either on the anticipated death of the queen taking place, or else, by means of divorce . . . on contracting a marriage with the said Elizabeth. For it appeared that in no other way could his kingly power be established, or the hopes of his rival be put an end to.[26]

This choice of clothing was symbolic and intended to signify harmony between Elizabeth and her uncle's immediate family, in a visual display indicative of the former princess ingratiating herself with Gloucester's new regime. In a display of kinship, Elizabeth would appear at court dressed similarly to her mother-in-law in later years.[27] However, the Croyland Chronicler instead suggested the symbolic spectacle in 1484 was indicative of Gloucester's intention to marry his niece.

Sir George Buck, writing in the early seventeenth century, claimed to have read and included in his work a letter allegedly written by Elizabeth of York to the Duke of Norfolk relating to Gloucester. Buck's original manuscript was damaged by a fire, and his great-nephew undertook the task of filling in the missing words from his uncle's account of the letter. The additions made by the original editor, Buck's great-nephew, are in brackets:

> First she thanked him for his many courtesies and friendly [offices, an]d then she prayed him as before to be a mediator for her in the cause of [the marriage] to the k[i]ng, who, as she wrote, was her only joy and maker in [this] world, and that she was his in heart and in thoughts, in [body,] and in all. And then she intimated that the better half of Fe[bruary] was past, and that she feared the queen would nev[er die].[28]

Altering the words within the brackets fundamentally changes the tone and meaning of the letter. In the unedited version of the letter, there was no reference to marriage at all.[29] If marriage was the subject of the letter, Elizabeth could have been requesting the king's assistance in a nuptial to another; perhaps she was asking the king to find her a husband. The final sentence portrays Elizabeth as a cold-hearted, selfish young woman, in direct contrast to all other knowledge we have of her as a kind, compassionate individual.[30]

Even if these were Buck's intended words, his testimony has been called into doubt by modern historians; the original letter quickly disappeared, and Buck, a Gloucester apologist, was not beyond tampering with sources to make them fit his narrative.[31] However, there is evidence to suggest rumours were circulating regarding the prospect of this incestuous marriage among Elizabeth's contemporaries. As the Croyland Chronicler remarked, nobles from the north told the king that in no uncertain terms would they support his plans to marry Elizabeth and 'they brought to him more than twelve Doctors of Divinity, who asserted that the pope could grant no dispensation in the case of such a degree of consanguinity'.[32]

It is unclear whether Pope Innocent VIII would have granted papal dispensation for such a union. In a similar case, Innocent's predecessor, Alexander VI, gave dispensation permitting Ferdinand II, King of Naples, to marry Joanna, his aunt.[33] An English king entering an incestuous marriage with his niece was a step too far for the English nobility, who had already turned a blind eye to the murder of the intended bride's teenage brothers not two years prior.[34] The king's thoughts regarding this proposed union are unknown, but the rumours were sufficient enough for Gloucester to publicly deny them. Shortly before Easter 1485, Gloucester stood before the mayor and citizens of London in the great hall of the Hospital of St John and denied that he had ever planned to marry his niece 'in a loud and distinct voice'.[35] Gloucester also sent a letter to his power base in York ordering these rumours to be dismissed.[36] Gloucester then attempted to distance himself from his niece by sending Elizabeth to Sheriff Hutton in Yorkshire, where she joined her cousin, Edward, the son of the Duke of Clarence, another potential claimant to the throne. Gloucester felt safe in the knowledge that his biggest rival claimants were now virtual prisoners. Powerless as she was, the 19-year-old Elizabeth was about to play a monumental role in the downfall of her uncle and change English politics forever. For whilst rumours of a potential marriage to her uncle were abound, Elizabeth was already engaged, betrothed to the 28-year-old exile, Henry Tudor, Earl of Richmond. And rumours had reached him in Brittany of Gloucester's intention to marry his betrothed.

From within the confines of Westminster Abbey, Elizabeth Woodville did not sit idle. Ever the devoted mother, she sought to secure some sort of future for her eldest daughter. As such, she plotted with Margaret Beaufort via the physician Lewis Caerleon, who had access to the dowager queen, to marry Elizabeth to Henry Tudor and end not only Gloucester's reign but also the Wars of the Roses.

Henry Tudor, born in 1457, was a Lancastrian claimant to the English crown. His deceased father, Edmund Tudor, half-brother of King Henry VI, had died before he was born. Henry also claimed kingship through his mother, Margaret Beaufort, who, herself, was the great-granddaughter of John of Gaunt and Kathryn Swynford. From 1471, following the death of Henry VI, Henry Tudor became the head of the Lancastrian house, and for the boy's safety, he fled into exile in Brittany, where he would spend the next fourteen years.[37] Henry bided his time, and an opportunity to claim the throne for the Lancastrian cause came in 1483 when Buckingham rebelled against the newly crowned Gloucester. Henry launched an invasion force to support the rebellion, but after hearing news of Buckingham's execution, Henry abandoned his mission and returned to the Continent.[38] Henry was joined in exile by male members of the Woodville family and disaffected Yorkists and Lancastrians fleeing the clutches of Gloucester. According to Polydore Vergil, in 1483, it was decided between Elizabeth Woodville and Margaret Beaufort that the dowager queen would support Henry's bid for the throne, and once king, he would take Elizabeth as his bride.[39] In December 1483 at Rennes Cathedral in France, Henry swore an oath to marry Elizabeth once he became king.[40] The head of the Yorkist house was to wed Henry, the head of the House of Lancaster, which would bring an end to decades of fighting brought on by the Wars of the Roses.[41] Papal dispensation was required since the pair shared a common ancestor in King Edward III, and this was swiftly granted in the hopes of reconciling the two warring factions.[42] In 1483, the chances of Henry's success were slim. And from the bleak sanctuary of Westminster, it is unclear whether Elizabeth believed the betrothal would ever come to fruition. She had been engaged twice before, and much of her teenage years were devoted to preparing her for her role as queen of France, but this came to nought. With expectations of a grand marriage, such as that to the Dauphin during her father's lifetime, her proposed marriage to a Lancastrian exile was likely met with little enthusiasm by Elizabeth.

Henry Tudor landed at Milford Haven, Pembrokeshire, in August 1485 and made his way to Bosworth, mustering troops as he marched. The chances of Henry's success on the face of it were slim; he was fighting on unfamiliar territory, in a kingdom he had not visited for fourteen years. Henry was an alien to the English nobility, and his claim to the throne was questionable, resting partly on his mother's ancestry as a product of the love affair between John of Gaunt and Kathryn Swynford. The children of this union were only declared legitimate by the Pope in 1396, and although their legitimacy was legally accepted, Henry IV added a stipulation 'except the royal dignity', thus barring them from inheriting the throne.[43] Henry's father, Edmund Tudor, was the product of the scandalous union of Henry V's widow, Catherine of Valois, daughter of King Charles VI of France and a Welsh squire, Owen Tudor (d.1461).

But legitimacy to the throne rested not on lineage alone, but on winning battles, and Henry proved himself king-worthy by killing Gloucester at the Battle of Bosworth Field on 22 August 1485 and taking the crown. Henry released his betrothed from her captivity at Sheriff Hutton and placed her in the care of her mother in London. Henry rescinded *Titulus Regius,* thereby restoring Elizabeth's legitimacy. Elizabeth represented the House of York and offered much-needed legitimacy to Henry's kingship.[44] As the Croyland continuator commented, Elizabeth would offer whatever appeared to be missing in the king's title.[45] However, Henry wanted to ensure that it was his rule, his reign, and not that of his future wife.

Henry celebrated his coronation on 30 October 1485 in a sumptuous ceremony. The following month, he called his first parliament, which declared:

> the inheritance of the crown of this realm … shall rest, remain and
> abide, in the most royal person of our now sovereign lord King Henry,
> the Seventh, and in the heirs of his body … and in none other.[46]

Henry appears to have deliberately delayed his marriage to Elizabeth until January 1486. Some have suggested there were rumours that Elizabeth was pregnant with Gloucester's child, and Henry's forestalling of his marriage would ensure that any children produced from the union were biologically his own.[47] However, the delay was a purely political move for Henry desired to establish his own legitimacy that was separate from that of his wife. Yet Henry had to strike a careful balance; it was his wife's claim that would satisfy Yorkist supporters, and Elizabeth had a better claim to the throne than Henry. Henry wrote to the Pope and claimed he had selected Elizabeth for his bride because 'the beauty and chastity of this lady are indeed so great that Lucretia nor Diana herself were ever either more beautiful or more chaste'.[48] Henry was careful to create an image in which Elizabeth's claim to the throne did not surpass his own and chose instead to focus on his new wife's virtues, which made her consort worthy, and not her blood.

Yet Henry could not afford to overly underplay Elizabeth's status, and the delayed wedding caused some concerns with Yorkists and their sympathisers. The matter was raised in parliament on 10 December 1485 as Thomas Lovell, speaker of the Commons, requested that Henry marry Elizabeth, to which he assented. However, the tone of the statement lacks confrontation suggesting this was a staged event designed to illustrate public enthusiasm for the union.[49] It also demonstrated parliament and monarchy working in close partnership to bring about the end of the Wars of the Roses by joining the two warring houses together in matrimony.[50] The fifteenth century was a turbulent time for the monarchy; four kings had ruled since 1429, two were removed only to regain their thrones for a second time, two had died the prisoners of their usurpers, and a usurper himself had been killed in battle. Henry was a shrewd politician and understood that to do what so many in the previous five decades before him had failed to do, he needed to use all political tools at his disposal to validate his kingship and win the hearts and minds of his subjects. Far from stemming from Henry's indecision, the deferment of the marriage allowed him to strengthen his political position.

By January 1486, Henry felt established enough in his own kingship to celebrate his wedding. Papal dispensation had been granted in March 1484 for Henry, Earl of Richmond and Elizabeth Plantagenet, but Henry wanted to ensure the validity of his marriage could never be questioned and obtained a second dispensation which referred to his new status as king.[51] The wedding ceremony took place on 18 January 1486 at Westminster with much pomp and ceremony; however, the specific details of the celebration have not survived. The newly invented printing press was used to full effect to disseminate Tudor propaganda, and Henry ordered English translations of the Papal dispensation to be printed and distributed throughout the kingdom.[52]

The emblem most associated with this union, and the greatest piece of propaganda conceived by Henry, was the creation of the Tudor Rose. Edward IV had used a white rose for dynastic symbolism, but the red rose was associated with Lancaster before Henry, but its symbolic merging was his invention. The single red rose carved into the bed Henry shared with his wife was a symbolic reminder of his heritage, which grew in importance for him personally.[53] The merging of these two roses of the Lancastrian red petals surrounding those of the white Yorkist rose is now synonymous with the Tudors and the end of the Wars of the Roses.[54] But nothing better demonstrated the unity of the two families and secured dynastic stability than the birth of Elizabeth and Henry's first child, Prince Arthur, on 19 September 1486.

Arthur, named to create a dynastic link back to the mythical first king of the Britons, was born eight months following the marriage of his parents. Arthur was either premature, or Henry and Elizabeth had consummated their union prior to their official marriage. Elizabeth proved to be a fertile consort, as her mother had been before her, and gave Henry several spares to accompany his heir. Three of these additional children survived infancy: Margaret (1489–1541), queen of Scotland. Henry, the future King Henry VIII (1491–1547) and Mary (1496–1533), queen of France. Several other children died in infancy or were stillborn, including Elizabeth (1492), Edmund (1499) and Katherine (1503). The couple seem to have had a loving relationship, and unlike her father, who is known to have had several mistresses, there is no evidence that Henry strayed from his wife.[55] Elizabeth took an interest in her children's education, ensuring Arthur and Henry received a good grounding in classical humanism. Henry and Margaret developed a fondness for music, and given Elizabeth's interest in this pastime, we can assume that she was involved in their education on this subject too and spent a significant amount of time with her children.[56] Henry VIII, in particular, appears to have enjoyed a close relationship with his mother, in whose company he was kept in his early years. This may explain why he chose to favour some of those in her service in his own reign.[57]

Whilst Elizabeth settled into the role of motherhood, Henry dealt with threats to his throne. He defeated a series of pretenders to his throne, and these challenges undoubtedly stirred up memories of grief for Elizabeth and her mother. One pretender was Lambert Simnel. In 1487, Simnel emerged and gained support, first claiming to be Elizabeth's youngest brother, Richard of York, and then, when rumours abounded claiming Edward, Earl of Warwick, had died, Simnel switched his impersonation and took on the persona of Edward.[58] Edward was Elizabeth's cousin with whom she shared her imprisonment in the custody of their uncle. Edward of Warwick was the son of George, Duke of Clarence, brother of Edward IV and Gloucester, thereby giving him a strong claim to the throne. Looking for an excuse to remove Henry VII from the throne, some Yorkists, including Elizabeth's aunt, Margaret, the Dowager Duchess of Burgundy, threw their support behind this imposter. The rebellion was put down by Henry, who showed mercy to Simnel, a puppet of the Yorkists. Simnel was put to work in the royal household and eventually rose to the rank of falconer for the king.[59]

The appearance of Perkin Warbeck in 1492, claiming to be Richard, Duke of York, Elizabeth's youngest brother, undoubtedly resurfaced many memories of grief and sorrow for Elizabeth and her mother. Given a lack of evidence for Elizabeth's reactions, historians have concluded that Elizabeth must have denied that either Perkin Warbeck or Lambert Simnel were her relation. Warbeck's execution in 1499 must have been all the more distressful for Elizabeth, for Warbeck had implicated her cousin, the real Edward of Warwick, in his attempt to escape the Tower of London and Edward, too, was executed for treason. New evidence has suggested that Perkin Warbeck may in fact have been Richard of York, but this theory has been contested.[60] It is interesting to consider whether Elizabeth would have identified Perkin as her youngest brother. If Richard had survived, his claim to the throne as the only surviving son of Edward IV was stronger than hers and her husband's. Yet, given what we know about Elizabeth's gentle and compassionate character, it seems unlikely she would have permitted her lost younger brother to be confined to the Tower once more. Or was she powerless to intervene, even if Perkin was indeed Richard? Perhaps, if she did recognise him as her brother, the threat to her husband and her son was so great that it was best to let sleeping dogs lie and those presumed dead to remain that way.

The rebellions Henry faced during his early reign can partially explain why Elizabeth's coronation, like her marriage, was delayed. Or it could also be part of Henry's policy to downplay his wife's status as a legitimate heir to the throne. But by November 1487, Elizabeth had proven her worth as a consort. Moreover, her popularity amongst her subjects only grew on account of her caring disposition, and she reminded them of her father, of happy memory, who ruled over a prosperous kingdom.[61]

In contrast to the perception of Henry the miser that developed over the centuries, the king spared no expense on his wife's coronation. The occasion took place on 25 November 1487 when parliament was sitting, thereby permitting the optimum number of attendees, including leading nobles and clergy.[62] It was an opportunity for Henry to show off not only his queen but the splendour of the Tudor dynasty. People lined the streets to get a glimpse of Elizabeth, who wore purple velvet trimmed with ermine fur. Her sister, Cecily, carried Elizabeth's train as she made her way towards Westminster Hall. The procession was headed by knights, monks and bishops, and Elizabeth was followed by duchesses and countesses.[63] The crowds were so eager to take home the memento of the day in a time-honoured tradition of seizing a piece of the cloth upon which the queen had walked, that a stampede occurred and some within the crowd were killed.[64]

Only following her coronation did Henry provide his wife with formal lands by gifting to Elizabeth lands formerly held by her mother, who had by this time retired from court to Bermondsey Abbey.[65] Elizabeth led a luxurious lifestyle befitting her station on this income. The cost of clothing for herself and her servants was paid for by the king, who even paid off her debts.[66] Elizabeth was generous, and perhaps her family were the greatest beneficiaries of her generosity.[67] The queen filled her court with dancing and music, and the king paid handsomely for entertainers, including dancers, wrestlers, jugglers and acrobats.[68] Like every ideal consort, Elizabeth was pious, and her generosity extended to the Church, to whom she granted numerous gifts, and like her mother before her, gave frequent gifts to the Carthusian House of Jesus of Bethlehem in Sheen.[69]

Following her coronation, little is known of Elizabeth's political activity, suggesting she played a limited role in politics, wielding little political power; this is in contrast to her mother, the daughter of a knight with no claim to power, but through her marriage to the king. During her husband's lifetime, Elizabeth Woodville enjoyed power that far surpassed that of her daughter.[70] This may have been a personal choice on Elizabeth's part and not a deliberate attempt by her husband to sideline her. Quite often, those queens who did become politically involved, like Elizabeth's own mother, were depicted in a negative light. A queen's absence from the sources was a compliment to her character. As one Spanish ambassador, Don Pedro de Ayala, observed, 'the Queen [is] beloved, because she is powerless'.[71] Rather, Elizabeth's political involvement was likely conventional, taking place in the private sphere, as opposed to taking part in politics publicly.[72] Elizabeth was heavily involved with the negotiations regarding the marriage of her eldest son to Katherine of Aragon, as discussed below. However, De Ayala also noted, 'The King is much influenced by his mother'.[73] Some historians have suggested that Elizabeth's role as consort was restricted by her dominant mother-in-law, Margaret Beaufort.

In preparation for the birth of her first grandchild, Margaret issued several ordinances which dictated the arrangements for Elizabeth's birthing chamber. They specified the cloths covering the windows, the furniture and even the size of the bed sheets.[74] These ordinances have often been cited as evidence for Margaret's control over the royal household and Elizabeth's diminishing role. However, there is evidence of the king's mother and her daughter-in-law working side by side rather than in competition. For instance, the pair sponsored Caxton's edition of *Fifteen Oes and Other Prayers* in 1491, and both influenced the king to delay the marriage of Princess Margaret to James IV of Scotland.[75] Elizabeth may have been willing to allow her mother-in-law to take the lead in some aspects of royal life, thereby allowing Elizabeth to remove herself from the limelight, to retain the image of the ideal consort and remove herself from any accusations of the scheming and ambitious woman that her mother had received. Perhaps Elizabeth Woodville's greatest gift to her daughter was as a lesson in how not to conduct oneself as queen.

Elizabeth was continually praised as a queen and a future mother-in-law during the negotiations of Prince Arthur's marriage to Katherine of Aragon. In one of the few letters written by Elizabeth to have survived (1497), she wrote to Queen Isabella describing Katherine as 'our common daughter'.[76] Elizabeth corresponded frequently with the family of her future daughter-in-law, and her ability to alleviate their concerns and her sincerity feature strongly in the correspondence. Elizabeth requested that Katherine learn to speak French, for the ladies of the English court knew little Latin or Spanish. She also suggested that Katherine develop a taste for wine, for English water was unsuitable for drinking.[77] These requests transcend any political negotiations and show a genuine concern for Katherine's well-being. Previous experience had taught Elizabeth how daunting preparation for the role of a consort to a foreign prince could be.

Elizabeth was overjoyed when Katherine finally arrived in England in November 1501, celebrating the marriage of her eldest son to the daughter of two powerful Spanish rulers. The marriage, however, would be short-lived as Arthur contracted an illness and died on 2 April 1502, aged just 15. It is when learning of this horrific news that we see something of the relationship between Elizabeth and Henry and the close bond they shared that went beyond the conventions of royal marriage for political gain. When the news was broken to Henry, 'he sent for the Queen, saying that he and his Queen would take the painful sorrows together'.[78] Elizabeth comforted the king and reassured him that his line would still survive, for they had other surviving children, a Prince and two daughters. In a rather stoic manner, not allowing her husband to see her true sorrow, she told Henry they 'are both young enough' to parent more children. Returning to her chamber, Elizabeth broke down into inconsolable grief. Her ladies requested the king come to comfort her 'Then his Grace of true gentle and faithful love, in good haste came and relieved her'.[79]

True to her words, Elizabeth became pregnant for the eighth and final time and delivered a girl whom the couple named Katherine for their lately widowed daughter-in-law on 2 February 1503. The baby would live for only sixteen days, but a worse fate had befallen her father. It is unclear how Elizabeth became ill following the birth of Katherine; likely, she contracted puerperal fever, but she became ill and passed away on 11 February 1503, on her thirty-seventh birthday.[80] Henry retreated into his private chambers and gave himself over to grief. Elizabeth's funeral was an extremely lavish affair at a cost of around £2800 (around £1.8 million today), whereas Edward IV's funeral totalled just under £1500 in comparison.[81]

Unlike many other queens consorts we have discussed within this book, there is no difference of opinion regarding Elizabeth's personality; she was universally loved. Elizabeth's blood made her a trailblazing woman. Although she was not afforded the privilege of taking the throne herself (the thought probably never even entered her head), her blood gave her husband legitimacy and, despite his downplaying of the importance of her bloodline, Henry would have found it difficult to establish himself as king without her. Elizabeth's personality made her the ideal queen consort and a model for subsequent queens to follow, in particular, her many daughters-in-law through her son, Henry VIII. Elizabeth helped to establish the Tudor dynasty, and her own granddaughters, Mary I and her namesake, Elizabeth I, would eventually become the first queens of England. Elizabeth was devoted to her son, the future Henry VIII, and it is worth considering what sort of king he would have become if his mother had not died so prematurely. Would the Reformation have even occurred, or would Elizabeth have encouraged Henry to remain devoted to Katherine of Aragon as his father had been devoted to her?

Notes

Abbreviations

Alexiad   *The Alexiad of Anna Comnena*, Sewter, E.R.A. (trans.) (Penguin Books, Baltimore, 1969) .

ASC   *The Anglo-Saxon Chronicle*, Garmonsway, G.N. (ed. and trans.) (J.M. Dent & Sons, London, 1972).

ASSER   Asser, *Alfred the Great: Asser's Life of King Alfred and Other Contemporary Sources*, Keynes, S. and Lapidge, M. (ed. and trans.), (Penguin Books, Harmondsworth, 1983).

BMK   *The Book of Margery Kempe*, Windeatt, B.A. (trans.), (Penguin Classics, London, 2004).

Croyland   *Ingulph's Chronicle of the Abbey of Croyland*, Riley, H.T. (trans.), (H. G. Bohn, London, 1854).

EEC   *Encomium Emmae Reginae*, Campbell, A. (ed. and trans.), (Cambridge University Press, Cambridge, 1998).

Trial   *The Trial of Joan of Arc*, Hobbins, D. (ed. and trans.), (Harvard University Press, London, 2005).

Introduction

1. Earenfight, T., *Queenship in Medieval Europe*, (Palgrave Macmillan, Basingstoke, 2013), p. 6.
2. Poulet, A., 'Capetian Women and the Regency: The Genesis of a Vocation', in Parsons, J.C. (ed.), *Medieval Queenship*, (Alan Sutton Publishing, Stroud, 1994), pp. 103–104.
3. Huneycutt, L.L., 'Intercession and the High-Medieval Queen: The Esther Topos', in Carpenter, J. and MacLean, S.B. (eds.), *Power of the Weak: Studies on Medieval Women*, (University of Illinois Press, Urbana and Chicago, 1995), p. 131.
4. Earenfight, T., *Queenship*, pp. 11–12; Lewis, K.J., *Kingship and Masculinity in Late Medieval England*, (Routledge, New Haven and London, 2013), pp. 9–10.
5. Stafford, P., 'Sons and Mothers: Family Politics in the Early Middle Ages', in Baker, D. (ed.) *Medieval Women*, (The Ecclesiastical History Society, Oxford, 1978), p. 80.
6. Hodgson, N.R., *Women, Crusading and the Holy Land in Historical Narrative*, (Boydell & Brewer, Woodbridge, 2007), p. 49.

Chapter 1: Æthelflæd

1. Henry, Archdeacon of Huntingdon, *Historia Anglorum: The History of the English People,* Greenway, D. (ed. and trans.), (Oxford: Clarendon Press, 1996), p. 309.

2. *ASSER,* p. 77.

3. *ASSER,* p. 77.

4. Traves, A., 'Genealogy and Royal Women in Asser's *Life of King Alfred*: Politics, Prestige, and Maternal Kinship in Early Medieval England', *Early Medieval Europe*, Vol. 30, No. 1, (2022), p. 109 .

5. Anlezark, D., *Alfred the Great*, (Arc Humanities Press, Kalamazoo, 2017), p.33.

6. Carver, M., 'Living in a Material World: Æthelflæd's Archaeology', in Hardie, R. (ed.), *Æthelflæd, Lady of the Mercians, and Women in Tenth-Century England,* (Medieval Institute Publications, Boston, 2023), pp. 32–33.

7. Anlezark, D., *Alfred the Great*, p.34.

8. Firth, M., *Early English Queens, 850–1000: Potestas Reginae,* (Routledge, New Haven and London, 2013), p. 228.

9. *ASSER,* p. 90.

10. Arman, J., *The Warrior Queen: The Life and Legend of Æthelflæd, Daughter of Alfred the Great,* (Amberley, Stroud, 2017), p. 20.

11. Rabin, A., 'The Charters of Æthelflæd', in Hardie, R. (ed.), *Æthelflæd, Lady of the Mercians, and Women in Tenth-Century England,* (Medieval Institute Publications, Boston, 2023), p. 126.

12. Blake, M. and Sargent, A., '"For the Protection of All the People": Æthelflæd and Her Burhs in Northwest Mercia', *Midland History,* Vol. 43, No. 2, (2018), p. 149.

13. Bailey, M., 'Ælfwynn, Second Lady of the Mercians', in Higham, N.J. and Hill, D.H. (eds.), *Edward the Elder: 899–924,* (Routledge, New Haven and London, 2001), p. 113.

14. Carver, M., 'Living in a Material World', p. 33.

15. Bailey, M., 'Ælfwynn, Second Lady of the Mercians', pp. 112–113.

16. Rabin, A., 'The Charters of Æthelflæd', pp. 118–119.

17. Carver, M., 'Living in a Material World', p. 35.

18. Rabin, A., 'The Charters of Æthelflæd', pp. 126–127.

19. Stafford, P., 'The King's Wife in Wessex 800–1066', *Past & Present*, No. 91, (1981), p. 4.

20. *ASC*, p. 82; Stafford, P., 'The King's Wife in Wessex 800–1066', p.4.

21. Stafford, P., 'The King's Wife in Wessex 800–1066', p. 3.

22. Ibid., p. 4.

23. *ASSER*, pp. 71–72.

24. Stafford, P., 'The King's Wife in Wessex 800–1066', p. 4.

25. Klimek, K., 'Æthelflæd: History and Legend', *Quidditas,* 34, (2013), p. 15.

26. Wood, M., 'The Annals of Æthelflæd: Notes towards an Attempted Reconstruction', in Hardie, R. (ed.), *Æthelflæd, Lady of the Mercians, and Women in Tenth-Century England*, (Medieval Institute Publications, Boston, 2023), p. 62.

27. Banham, D., 'Did the Lady of the Mercians Make Her Own Bread? Gender, Status, and Food Production in Early Medieval England', in Hardie, R. (ed.), *Æthelflæd,*

Lady of the Mercians, and Women in Tenth-Century England, (Medieval Institute Publications, Boston, 2023), pp. 165–166.

28. Ibid., pp. 165–167.
29. Insley, C., 'Collapse, Reconfiguration or Renegotiation? The Strange End of the Mercian Kingdom, 850–924', *Reti Medievali Rivista,* Vol. 17, No. 2, (2016), p. 9.
30. Stafford, P., 'Political Women in Mercia, Eighth to Early Tenth Centuries', in Brown, M.P., Farr, C.A. (eds.), *Mercia: An Anglo-Saxon Kingdom in Europe,* (Bloomsbury Publishing, London, 2005), p. 47.
31. Wood, M., 'The Annals of Æthelflæd: Notes towards an Attempted Reconstruction', p. 62.
32. Carver, M., 'Living in a Material World', p. 38.
33. Hardie, R., 'Æthelflæd Then and Now: Introduction', in Hardie, R. (ed.), *Æthelflæd, Lady of the Mercians, and Women in Tenth-Century England,* (Medieval Institute Publications, Boston, 2023), p. 2.
34. Carver, M., 'Living in a Material World', p. 36; Blake, M. and Sargent, A., 'For the Protection of All the People', p. 121.
35. Insley, C., 'Collapse, Reconfiguration or Renegotiation? The Strange End of the Mercian Kingdom, 850–924', p. 9.
36. Bailey, M., 'Ælfwynn, Second Lady of the Mercians', p. 113.
37. *Annals of Ireland, Three Fragments, Copied from Ancient Sources by Dubhaltach MacFirbisigh; and Edited, with a Translation and Notes, from a Manuscript Preserved in the Burgundian Library at Brussels,* (Dublin Irish Archaeological and Celtic Society, Dublin, 1860), pp. 227–229.
38. *Annals of Ireland,* pp. 226–227.
39. Firth, M., 'On the Dating of the Norse Siege of Chester' *Notes and Queries,* Vol. 69 No. 1, (2022), p. 1.
40. *Annals of Ireland,* pp. 235–237.
41. Carver, M., 'Living in a Material World', pp. 38–39.
42. Ibid., p. 53.
43. Ibid., p. 41; Wood, M., 'The Annals of Æthelflæd: Notes towards an Attempted Reconstruction', pp. 66–67.
44. Ryan, M.J., 'Conquest, Reform and the Making of England', in Higham, N. and Ryan, M.J. (eds.), *The Anglo-Saxon World,* (Yale University Press, New Haven and London, 2013), p. 299.
45. *ASC,* p. 96.
46. Wood, M., 'The Annals of Æthelflæd: Notes towards an Attempted Reconstruction', p. 66.
47. *ASC,* p. 97.
48. Arman, J., *The Warrior Queen: The Life and Legend of Æthelflæd, Daughter of Alfred the Great,* (Amberley, Stroud, 2017), pp. 57–58.
49. *ASC,* p. 96.
50. Carver, M., 'Living in a Material World', p. 41.
51. Costambeys, M., 'Æthelflæd', *Oxford Dictionary of National Biography,* (2018), p. 2.
52. Carver, M., 'Living in a Material World', p. 50.

53. Hicklin, A., 'Æthelflaed and Female Power in Tenth-Century Europe', in Hardie, R. (ed.), *Æthelflæd, Lady of the Mercians, and Women in Tenth-Century England*, (Medieval Institute Publications, Boston, 2023), p. 93.
54. *ASC*, p. 100.
55. Hicklin, A., 'Æthelflaed and Female Power in Tenth-Century Europe', p. 94.
56. Ibid., p. 94 .
57. *ASC*, p. 101; Thompson Smith, S., 'Remembering the Lady of Mercia', in Norris, R., Stephenson, R. and Trilling, R.R. (eds.), *Feminist Approaches to Early Medieval English Studies*, (Amsterdam University Press, Amsterdam, 2023), p. 88.
58. Costambeys, M., 'Æthelflæd', *Oxford Dictionary of National Biography*, (2018), p. 2.
59. *ASC*, p. 105.
60. Carver, M., 'Living in a Material World', p. 42.
61. *ASC*, p. 105.
62. *ASC*, p. 105.
63. *ASC*, p. 105.
64. Bailey, M., 'Ælfwynn, Second Lady of the Mercians', p. 122.
65. Ibid., pp. 115–116.
66. Ibid., p. 117.
67. *Irish Annals*, p. 247.
68. *ASC*, p. 42.
69. Snook, B., 'Women in the Anglo-Saxon Chronicle Before AD 800', in Dresvina, J., and Sparks, N. (eds.), *Authority and Gender in Medieval and Renaissance Chronicles*, (Cambridge Scholars Publishing, Newcastle-upon-Tyne, 2012), p. 48.
70. *ASC*, p. 105.
71. Foot, S., *Æthelstan: The First King of England*, (Yale University Press, New Haven and London, 2011), p. 73.
72. Ibid., pp. 12–13.
73. Foot, S., 'Æthelstan', Oxford Dictionary of National Biography, (2011), p. 1.
74. Ibid., p. 3.

Chapter 2: Emma of Normandy

1. Roach, L., *Æthelred: The Unready*, (Yale University Press, New Haven and London, 2016), pp. 6–7.
2. Keynes, S., 'A Tale of Two Kings: Alfred the Great and Æthelred the Unready', *Transactions of the Royal Historical Society*, Vol. 36, No. 12, (1986), p. 217.
3. *Encomium Emmae Reginae*, Campbell, A. (ed. and trans.), (Cambridge University Press, Cambridge, 1998).
4. Van Houts, E., *The Normans in Europe*, (Manchester University Press, Manchester, 2013), pp. 58–59 and 92.
5. Tyler, E.M., 'Talking about History in Eleventh-Century England: the *Encomium Emmae Reginae* and the Court of Harthacnut', p. 375.
6. Stafford, P., *Queen Emma and Queen Edith, Queenship and Power in Eleventh-Century England*, (Blackwell Publishing, Oxford, 1997), pp. 212–213.

7. Keynes, S., 'Emma [Ælfgifu]', *Oxford Dictionary of National Biography*, (2014), pp. 1–2.

8. Stafford, P., *Queen Emma and Queen Edith*, p. 211.

9. Kibbee, D.A., *For to Speke Frenche Trewely: The French Language in England, 1000–1600. Its Status, Description and Instruction*, (John Benjamins Publishing Company, Philadelphia, 1991), p. 8.

10. Earenfight, T., *Queenship*, p. 104; For further discussion of the role of women at the court of Wessex, see chapter on *Æthelflaed*.

11. Stafford, P., *Queen Emma and Queen Edith*, p. 217.

12. Ibid., pp. 221–222.

13. Ibid., p. 216.

14. Ryan, M.J., 'Conquest, Reform and the Making of England', in Higham, N. and Ryan, M.J. (eds.), *The Anglo-Saxon World*, (Yale University Press, New Haven and London, 2013), p. 348.

15. Cavendish, R., 'The St Brice's Day Massacre', *History Today*, Vol. 52, (2002), pp. 62–63.

16. Stenton, F.M., *Anglo-Saxon England*, (The Clarendon Press, Oxford, 1975), p. 380.

17. Stafford, P., *Queen Emma and Queen Edith*, p. 223.

18. Roach, L., *Æthelred: The Unready*, p. 309.

19. *ASC*, p. 187.

20. Keynes, S., 'Emma [Ælfgifu]', p. 2.

21. Stafford, P., 'Emma: The Powers of the Queen in the Eleventh Century', in Duggan, A. (ed.), *Queens and Queenship in Medieval Europe*, (Boydell & Brewer, Woodbridge, 1997), p. 7.

22. *ASC*, p. 155.

23. *EEC*, p. 33.

24. Bolton, T., 'Ælfgifu of Northampton: Cnut the Great's "Other Woman"', *Nottingham Medieval Studies*, Vol. 51, No. 1, (2007), p. 252.

25. *EEC*, p. 41.

26. Bolton, T., 'Ælfgifu of Northampton: Cnut the Great's "Other Woman"', p. 258.

27. *EEC.*, p. 33.

28. Van Houts, E., 'Queens in the Anglo-Norman/Angevin Realm 1066–1216', in Zey, C. (ed.), *Mächtige Frauen? Königinnen und Fürstinnen im Europäischen Mittelalter*, (Verlagsgruppe Patmos, Düsseldorf, 2015), p. 201.

29. *ASC*, p. 188.

30. Van Houts, E., 'Queens in the Anglo-Norman/Angevin realm 1066–1216', p. 201.

31. Bolton, T., 'Ælfgifu of Northampton: Cnut the Great's "Other Woman"', p.263.

32. Van Houts, E., 'Queens in the Anglo-Norman/Angevin realm 1066–1216', p. 201.

33. Stafford, P., 'Emma: The Powers of the Queen in the Eleventh Century', pp. 7–8.

34. Keynes, S., 'Emma [Ælfgifu]', p. 2.

35. Ibid., p. 2.

36. Stafford, P., *Queen Emma and Queen Edith*, pp. 232–233; Howard, I., *Harthacnut: The Last Danish King of England*, (The History Press, Cheltenham, 2008), pp. 15 and 27.

37. *ASC*, p. 158.
38. *ASC*, p. 159.
39. Stafford, P., *Queen Emma and Queen Edith*, pp. 237–238.
40. *ASC*, p. 159.
41. *EEC*, p. 41.
42. *EEC*, p. 43.
43. Marafioti, N., *The King's Body: Burial and Succession in Late Anglo-Saxon England*, (University of Toronto Press, Toronto, 2014), p. 128.
44. Ibid., p. 133.
45. *ASC*, p. 158.
46. *EEC*, p. 43.
47. *ASC*, p. 160.
48. *ASC*, p. 160.
49. Stafford, P., *Queen Emma and Queen Edith*, p. 247.
50. Tyler, E.M., 'Talking about History in Eleventh-Century England: the *Encomium Emmae Reginae* and the Court of Harthacnut', p. 361.
51. *ASC*, p. 162.
52. Marafioti, N., *The King's Body: Burial and Succession in Late Anglo-Saxon England*, p. 126.
53. *ASC*, pp. 160 and 162.
54. Orchard, A., 'The Literary Background to the "Encomium Emmae Reginae"', *The Journal of Medieval Latin*, Vol. 11, (2001), p. 165.
55. *EEC*, p. xxxix.
56. Butler, E., 'Authority and Language in the Encomium Emmae Reginae', *English Studies*, Vol. 101, No. 1, (2020), p. 8.
57. Tyler, E.M., 'Talking about History in Eleventh-Century England: the *Encomium Emmae Reginae* and the Court of Harthacnut', p. 364.
58. *EEC*, p. 53.
59. Stafford, P., *Queen Emma and Queen Edith*, p. 249.
60. *ASC*, p. 163.
61. Stafford, P., *Queen Emma and Queen Edith*, pp. 249–250.
62. Ibid., p. 251.
63. *ASC*, p. 162.
64. Stafford, P., *Queen Emma and Queen Edith*, p. 250.
65. Keynes, S., 'Emma [Ælfgifu]', p. 3.

Chapter 3: Empress Matilda

1. Beem, C., '"Greater by Marriage": The Matrimonial Career of the Empress Matilda', in Levin, C. and Bucholz, R. (eds.), *Queens and Power in Medieval and Early Modern England*, (University of Nebraska Press, Nebraska, 2009), p. 1.
2. Hanley, C., *Matilda: Empress, Queen, Warrior*, (Yale University Press, New Haven and London, 2019), p. 1.

3. Chibnall, M., 'Matilda [Matilda of England]', *Oxford Dictionary of National Biography*, (2004), p. 1.

4. Huneycutt, L.L., *Matilda of Scotland: A Study in Medieval Queenship*, (Boydell & Brewer, Woodbridge, 2003), pp. 88–89.

5. Castor, H., *She-Wolves: The Women Who Ruled England Before Elizabeth*, (HarperCollins, New York, 2012), pp. 51–52.

6. Chibnall, M., *The Empress Matilda, Queen Consort, Queen Mother and Lady of the English*, (Blackwell Publishing, Oxford, 1992), p. 23.

7. Ibid., p. 24.

8. Ibid., p. 25.

9. Tolhurst, F., *Geoffrey of Monmouth and the Translation of Female Kingship*, (Palgrave Macmillan, Basingstoke, 2013), p. 33.

10. Hanley, C., *Matilda: Empress, Queen, Warrior*, p. 24.

11. Ibid., p. 24.

12. Chibnall, M., 'Matilda [Matilda of England]', p. 2.

13. For a discussion of this dispute, see chapter on *Matilda of Tuscany*.

14. Chibnall, M., *The Empress Matilda*, pp. 31–32.

15. Castor, H., *She-Wolves*, p. 62.

16. Van Houts, E., 'Queens in the Anglo-Norman/Angevin realm 1066–1216', p. 214.

17. Castor, H., *She-Wolves*, p. 33.

18. Strahl, H.C., '"Compassion Alone Moved Me to Tell This Story": Orderic Vitalis on the Wreck of the White Ship', *Journal of Medieval History*, Vol. 51, No. 1, (2025), p. 57.

19. Huneycutt, L.L., 'Female Succession and the Language of Power in the Writings of Twelfth-Century Churchmen', in Parsons, J.C. (ed.), *Medieval Queenship*, (Alan Sutton Publishing, Stroud, 1994), p. 195.

20. Firth, A.S., *The Creation of the Jerusalemite Dynasty in the Twelfth Century: Kingship, Military Masculinity and Fatherhood in William of Tyre's Historia*, (Unpublished Ph.D. Dissertation, University of Huddersfield, 2016).

21. Beem, C., '"Greater by Marriage": The Matrimonial Career of the Empress Matilda', pp. 3–4.

22. Hanley, C., *Matilda: Empress, Queen, Warrior*, pp. 57–58.

23. Tolhurst, F., *Geoffrey of Monmouth*, p. 32.

24. Huneycutt, L.L., 'Female Succession', p. 195.

25. Chibnall, M., *The Empress Matilda*, pp. 51–53.

26. Gillingham, J., *The Angevin Empire*, (Oxford University Press, New York, 2001), pp. 8–9; Lewis, M., *Stephen and Matilda's Civil War*, (Pen & Sword Books, Barnsley, 2020), p. 11.

27. Castor, H., *She-Wolves*, pp. 68–69.

28. Chibnall, M., *The Empress Matilda*, p. 60.

29. Hollister, W.C. and Keefe, T.K., 'The Making of the Angevin Empire', *Journal of British Studies*, Vol. 12, No. 2, (1973), pp. 15–16.

30. Beem, C., '"Greater by Marriage": The Matrimonial Career of the Empress Matilda', p. 5.

31. Beem, C., 'The Virtuous Virago: The Empress Matilda and the Politics of Womanhood in Twelfth-Century England', in Levin, C. and Stewart-Nuz, C. (eds.), *Scholars and Poets Talk about Queens,* (Palgrave Macmillan, Basingstoke, 2015), p. 88.

32. Chibnall, M., *The Empress Matilda,* pp. 57–58.

33. Castor, H., *She-Wolves,* p. 70.

34. Chibnall, M., *The Empress Matilda,* pp. 59–60.

35. Castor, H., *She-Wolves,* pp. 71–72.

36. Forester, T. (ed. and trans.), *The Chronicle of Henry of Huntingdon,* (Henry G. Bohn, London, 1853), p. 259.

37. Castor, H., *She-Wolves,* p. 72.

38. Carpenter, D.A., *The Struggle for Mastery: Britain, 1066–1284,* (Oxford University Press, Oxford, 2003), p. 161 .

39. King, E., *King Stephen,* (Yale University Press, New Haven and London, 2011), p. 43.

40. Beem, C., '"Greater by Marriage": The Matrimonial Career of the Empress Matilda', p. 7.

41. Hanley, C., *Matilda: Empress, Queen, Warrior,* p. 92.

42. Ibid., p. 85.

43. Beem, C., '"Greater by Marriage": The Matrimonial Career of the Empress Matilda', p. 7.

44. Chibnall, M., *The Empress Matilda,* p. 67.

45. Hanley, C., *Matilda: Empress, Queen, Warrior,* p. 88.

46. Beem, C., '"Greater by Marriage": The Matrimonial Career of the Empress Matilda', p. 6.

47. Huneycutt, L.L., 'Female Succession', p. 195.

48. Castor, H., *She-Wolves,* p. 86.

49. Thompson, K., 'Affairs of State: The Illegitimate Children of Henry I', *Journal of Medieval History,* Vol. 29, No. 2, (2003), pp. 129–151.

50. Couch, D., 'Robert, First Earl of Gloucester', *Oxford Dictionary of National Biography,* (2006), p. 3.

51. Chibnall, M., *The Empress Matilda,* p. 82.

52. Tolhurst, F., *Geoffrey of Monmouth,* p. 37.

53. Castor, H., *She-Wolves,* p. 89.

54. Ibid., p. 90.

55. Chibnall, M., *The Empress Matilda,* p. 81.

56. Bradbury, J., *Stephen and Matilda: The Civil War of 1139–53,* (Alan Sutton Publishing, Stroud, 1996), p. 45.

57. Tolhurst, F., *Geoffrey of Monmouth,* p. 35.

58. Chibnall, M., *The Empress Matilda,* pp. 93–95.

59. Ibid., pp. 97–8.

60. Beem, C., '"Greater by Marriage": The Matrimonial Career of the Empress Matilda', pp. 10–11.

61. Ibid., p. 11.

62. Ibid.
63. *Gesta Stephani,* Potter, K.R. and Davis, R.H.C. (eds. and trans.), (Clarendon Press, Oxford, 1976), p. 123.
64. Ibid., p.119.
65. Huneycutt, L.L., 'Female Succession', p. 200.
66. Chibnall, M., *The Empress Matilda,* p. 115.
67. Beem, C., 'The Virtuous Virago', p. 95.
68. Chibnall, M., *The Empress Matilda,* pp. 116–117.
69. Lewis, M., *Stephen and Matilda's Civil War,* p. 150.
70. Beem, C., '"Greater by Marriage": The Matrimonial Career of the Empress Matilda', p. 13.
71. Chibnall, M., *The Empress Matilda,* p. 206.
72. Hosler, J.D., *Henry II: A Medieval Soldier at War, 1147–1189,* (Brill, Leiden, 2007), p.5.
73. Chibnall, M., 'Matilda [Matilda of England]', p. 7.
74. Couch, D., 'Robert, First Earl of Gloucester', p. 5.
75. Chibnall, M., *The Empress Matilda,* pp. 156–158.
76. Hanley, C., *Matilda: Empress, Queen, Warrior*, pp. 223–224.
77. Chibnall, M., 'Matilda [Matilda of England]', p. 10.
78. Beem, C., 'The Virtuous Virago', pp. 95–96.
79. Chibnall, M., *The Empress Matilda,* p. 194.
80. Whitton, M., 'Motherhood and Power in Medieval Europe, West and East: The Strange Case of the Empress Eirene', in Leyser, C. and Smith, L. (eds.), *Motherhood, Religion and Society in Medieval Europe, 400–1400: Essays Presented to Henrietta Leyser,* (Routledge, New Haven and London, 2016), p. 86.

Chapter 4: Eleanor of Aquitaine

1. Turner, R.V., *Eleanor of Aquitaine, Queen of France, Queen of England,* (Yale University Press, New Haven and London, 2009), p. 15.
2. Owen, D.D.R., *Eleanor of Aquitaine, Queen and Legend,* (Blackwell Publishing, Oxford, 2000), p. 8.
3. Ibid., pp. 12–13.
4. Howell, M., 'Eleanor [Eleanor of Aquitaine], *suo jure* Duchess of Aquitaine', Oxford *Dictionary of National Biography,* (2004), p. 1.
5. Herdam, A. and Smallwood, D.J., 'The Queen from the South: Eleanor of Aquitaine as a Political Strategist and Lawmaker', in Gilleir, A. and Defurne, A. (eds.), *Strategic Imaginations: Women and the Gender of Sovereignty in European Culture,* (Leuven University Press, Leuven, 2020), p. 161.
6. Turner, R.V., 'Eleanor of Aquitaine, Twelfth-Century English Chroniclers and her "Black Legend"', *Nottingham Medieval Studies,* Vol. 52, (2008), p. 27.
7. Owen, D.D.R., *Eleanor of Aquitaine,* p. 14.
8. Evans, M.R., 'The Missing Queen? Eleanor of Aquitaine in the Early Reign of Louis VII', in Bardot, M.L., and Marvin, L.W. (eds.), *Louis VII and His World,* (Brill, Leiden, 2018), p. 106.

9. Turner, R.V., *Eleanor of Aquitaine, Queen of France*, p. 61.
10. Ibid., pp. 63–64.
11. Turner, R.V., *Eleanor of Aquitaine, Queen of France*, pp. 64–65.
12. Owen, D.D.R., *Eleanor of Aquitaine*, p. 20.
13. Chambers, F.M., 'Some Legends Concerning Eleanor of Aquitaine', *Speculum*, Vol. 16, No. 4, (1941), p. 459.
14. Turner, R.V., "Black Legend", p. 28.
15. Turner, R.V., *Eleanor of Aquitaine, Queen of France*, p. 73.
16. Ibid., p. 73.
17. Chambers, F.M., 'Some Legends Concerning Eleanor of Aquitaine', p. 459.
18. Turner, R.V., *Eleanor of Aquitaine, Queen of France*, p. 77.
19. *O City of Byzantium: Annals of Niketas Choniatēs*, Magoulias, H.J. (trans.), (Wayne State University Press, Detroit, 1984), p. 35.
20. Evans, M., 'Penthesilea on the Second Crusade: Is Eleanor of Aquitaine the Amazon Queen of Niketas *Choniatēs*?', *Crusades*, Vol. 8, No. 1, (2009), pp. 23–30.
21. Walker, C.H., 'Eleanor of Aquitaine and the Disaster at Cadmus Mount on the Second Crusade', *The American Historical Review*, Vol. 55, No. 4, (1950), pp. 857–861.
22. *William of Tyre, A History of Deeds Done Beyond the Sea, Vol II*, Babcock, E.A. and Krey, A.C. (eds. and trans.), (Columbia University Press, New York, 1943), p. 80.
23. Owen, D.D.R., *Eleanor of Aquitaine*, p. 25.
24. *William of Tyre, Vol. II*, pp. 180–181.
25. Turner, R.V., *Eleanor of Aquitaine, Queen of France*, pp. 88–89.
26. Castor, H., *She-Wolves*, p. 153.
27. Ibid., p. 154.
28. *William of Tyre, Vol. II*, p. 194.
29. Turner, R.V., *Eleanor of Aquitaine, Queen of France*, pp. 96–97.
30. Ibid., p. 97.
31. Ibid., p. 301.
32. Ibid., p. 107.
33. Castor, H., *She-Wolves*, pp. 158–159.
34. Turner, R.V., *Eleanor of Aquitaine, Queen of France*, p. 107.
35. Brown, E.A., 'Eleanor of Aquitaine: Parent, Queen, and Duchess', in Kibler, W. (ed.), *Eleanor of Aquitaine: Patron and Politician*, (University of Texas Press, New York, 1976), pp. 15–16.
36. Turner, R.V., *Eleanor of Aquitaine, Queen of France*, p. 103.
37. Warren, W.L., *Henry II*, (University of California Press, Berkeley, 1973), p. 207.
38. Turner, R.V., *Eleanor of Aquitaine, Queen of France*, p. 103.
39. Gillingham, J. *The Angevin Empire*, (Oxford University Press, New York, 2001), pp. 18–19.
40. Howell, M., 'Eleanor [Eleanor of Aquitaine]', p. 6.
41. Brown, E.A., 'Eleanor of Aquitaine: Parent, Queen, and Duchess', p. 16.
42. Aurell, M., 'Eleanor of Aquitaine: The Art of Governing', in Norrie, A., Harris, C., Messer, D.A., Woodacre, E., and Laynesmith, J.L., (eds.) *Norman to Early*

Plantagenet Consorts. Power, Influence, and Dynasty, (Palgrave Macmillan, Switzerland, 2023), p. 128.

43. Turner, R.V., 'Eleanor of Aquitaine and her Children: An Inquiry into Medieval Family Attachment', *Journal of Medieval History,* Vol. 14, No. 4, (1988), p. 324.

44. Warren, W.L., *Henry II,* pp. 108–111.

45. Brown, E.A., 'Eleanor of Aquitaine: Parent, Queen, and Duchess', p. 17.

46. Castor, H., *She-Wolves,* p. 170.

47. Gillingham, J., *Richard I,* (Yale University Press, New Haven and London, 1999), p. 40.

48. Turner, R.V., *Eleanor of Aquitaine, Queen of France,* pp. 311–313.

49. Evans, M.R., *Inventing Eleanor: The Medieval and Post-Medieval Image of Eleanor of Aquitaine,* (Bloomsbury Publishing, London, 2016), p. 72.

50. Strickland, M., *Henry the Young King, 1155–1183,* (Yale University Press, New Haven and London, 2016), p. 122.

51. Weiler, B., 'Kings and Sons: Princely Rebellions and the Structures of Revolt in Western Europe, c.1170–c.1280', *Historical Research,* Vol. 82, No. 215, (2008), p. 20.

52. Gillingham, J., *The Angevin Empire,* p. 34.

53. Turner, R.V., "Black Legend", p. 33.

54. Gillingham, J., *Richard I,* p. 47.

55. Strickland, M., *Henry the Young King,* p. 130.

56. Ibid., p. 131.

57. Gillingham, J., *Richard I,* p. 43.

58. Castor, H., *She-Wolves,* p. 183.

59. Turner, R.V., "Black Legend", p. 34 .

60. Strickland, M., *Henry the Young King,* p. 211.

61. Turner, R.V., *Eleanor of Aquitaine, Queen of France,* pp. 236–239.

62. Strickland, M., *Henry the Young King,* p. 306.

63. Castor, H., *She-Wolves,* pp. 187–189.

64. Gillingham, J., *Richard I,* p. 77.

65. Ibid., pp. 79–80.

66. Castor, H., *She-Wolves,* pp. 194–195.

67. Turner, R.V., *Eleanor of Aquitaine, Queen of France,* p. 258.

68. Ibid., p. 258.

69. Howell, M., 'Eleanor [Eleanor of Aquitaine]', p. 9.

70. Brown, E.A., 'Eleanor of Aquitaine: Parent, Queen, and Duchess', pp. 20–21.

71. Castor, H., *She-Wolves,* pp. 198–199.

72. Brown, E.A., 'Eleanor of Aquitaine: Parent, Queen, and Duchess', p. 21; Turner, R.V., *Eleanor of Aquitaine, Queen of France,* pp. 268.

73. Saul, N., *The Three Richards: Richard I, Richard II and Richard III,* (Hambledon Continuum, London, 2006), p. 44.

74. Aurell, M., 'Eleanor of Aquitaine: The Art of Governing', in Norrie, A., Harris, C., Messer, D.A., Woodacre, E. and Laynesmith, J.L. (eds.), *Norman to Early Plantagenet Consorts: Power, Influence, and Dynasty,* (Palgrave Macmillan, Cham, 2023), p. 132.

75. Gillingham, J., *Richard I*, p. 252.

76. Gillingham, J., *Richard I*, p. 324.

77. Turner, R.V., "Black Legend", p. 39.

78. Owen, D.D.R., *Eleanor of Aquitaine*, p. 95..

79. Howell, M., 'Eleanor [Eleanor of Aquitaine]', p. 10.

80. Herdam, A. and Smallwood, D.J., 'The Queen from the South', p. 175.

Chapter 5: Isabella of France

1. Thomas Gray, 'The Bard', in Rolfe, W.J. (ed.), *Select Poems of Thomas Gray*, (Harper and Brothers, New York, 1883), p. 28.

2. Warner, K., *Isabella of France, The Rebel Queen: The Story of the Queen who Deposed her Husband Edward II*, (Amberley, Stroud, 2016), p. 34.

3. The Chronicles of Froissart, Bourcher, J. (trans.), (Macmillan, London, 1895), p. 3.

4. Menache, S., 'Isabella of France, Queen of England: A Postscript', *Revue Belge de Philologie et d'Histoire*, Vol. 90, No. 2, (2012), p. 494.

5. Warner, K., *Isabella of France*, p. 42.

6. Evans, M.R., 'Isabella of France: She-Wolf and Rebel Queen?', in Harris, C., Woodacre, E., Norrie, A., Messer, D.R., and Laynesmith, J.L. (eds.), *Later Plantagenet and the Wars of the Roses Consorts*, (Palgrave Macmillan, Cham, 2023), p. 32.

7. John, L.B.S., *Three Medieval Queens: Queenship and the Crown in Fourteenth-Century England*, (Palgrave Macmillan, Basingstoke, 2012), p. 38.

8. Warner, K., *Isabella of France*, p. 78.

9. Ibid., pp. 78–79.

10. John, L.B.S., *Three Medieval Queens*, pp. 135–136.

11. Carmi Parson, J., 'Isabella [Isabella of France]', *Oxford Dictionary of National Biography*, (2018), p. 2.

12. Johnstone, H., 'The Eccentricities of Edward II', *The English Historical Review*, Vol. 48, (1933), p. 265.

13. Haines, R.M., *King Edward II: Edward of Caernarfon, His Life, His Reign, and Its Aftermath, 1284–1330*, (McGill-Queen's University Press, Montreal and Kingston, 2003), p. 36.

14. Johnstone, H., 'Isabella, The She-Wolf of France', *History*, Vol. 21, (1936), p. 213.

15. Haines, R.M., *King Edward II*, p. 47.

16. Ibid., p. 52.

17. Covert, A., 'Sine Communi Favore: The Intersection of Power, Perception, and Sexual Morality in the Careers of Piers Gaveston and the "Royal Favourites" of Fourteenth-Century England', in Storey, G. and Rohr, Z.E. (eds.), *Premodern Ruling Sexualities: Representation, Identity, and Power*, (Manchester University Press, Manchester, 2024), p. 235.

18. Evans, M.R., 'Isabella of France: She-Wolf and Rebel Queen?', p. 28.

19. Carmi Parson, J., 'Isabella [Isabella of France]', *Oxford Dictionary of National Biography*, (2018), p. 1.

20. Brown, A.R., 'The Political Repercussions of Family Ties in the Early Fourteenth Century: The Marriage of Edward II of England and Isabelle of France', *Speculum*, Vol. 63, No. 3 (1988), p. 583.

21. Tebbit, A., 'Household Knights and Military Service under the Direction of Edward II', in Dodd, G. and Musson, A. (eds.), *The Reign of Edward II: New Perspectives,* (Boydell & Brewer, Woodbridge, 2006), p. 85.

22. *The Anonimalle Chronicle 1307 to 1334 From Brotherton Collection MS 29,* Childs, W.R. and Taylor, J. (eds. and trans.), (University of Leeds, Leeds, 1991), pp. 80–83.

23. Doherty, P., *Isabella and the Strange Death of Edward II,* (Constable & Robinson, London, 2013), p. 49.

24. Ibid.

25. Warner, K., *Isabella of France,* p. 63.

26. Childs, W.R., 'Chronicles and Politics in the Reign of Edward II', in Burton, J., Marx, W. and O'Mara, V. (eds.), *Leeds Studies in English New Series XLI,* (School of English, University of Leeds, 2010), p. 50.

27. Evans, M.R., 'Isabella of France: She-Wolf and Rebel Queen?', p. 29.

28. Covert, A., 'Sine Communi Favore', p. 237.

29. Ibid.

30. Warner, K., *Isabella of France,* p. 61.

31. Ibid., p. 92.

32. *The Anonimalle Chronicle,* pp. 86–87.

33. John, L.B.S., 'In the Best Interest of the Queen: Isabella of France, Edward II and the Image of a Functional Relationship', in Hamilton, J.S., *Fourteenth Century England VIII,* (Boydell & Brewer, Woodbridge, 2014), p. 30; *Vita Edwardi Secundi,* Childs, W.R. (ed. and trans.), (Oxford University Press, Oxford, 2005), pp. 152–153.

34. Phillips, S., *Edward II,* (Yale University Press, New Haven and London, 2012), pp. 366–369.

35. John, L.B.S., 'In the Best Interest of the Queen', p. 30; *Vita Edwardi Secundi,* p. 35.

36. Earenfight, T., *Queenship,* p. 149.

37. Evans, M.R., 'Isabella of France: She-Wolf and Rebel Queen?', p. 34.

38. Ibid., p. 37.

39. Doherty, P., *Isabella and the Strange Death of Edward II,* pp. 96–97.

40. Phillips, S., *Edward II,* pp. 430–431.

41. Ibid.

42. John, L.B.S., 'In the Best Interest of the Queen', p. 37.

43. Warner, K., *Isabella of France,* p. 160.

44. Castor, H., *She-Wolves,* p. 287.

45. Menache, S., 'Isabella of France', p. 500.

46. Ibid.

47. Castor, H., *She-Wolves,* p. 289.

48. Evans, M.R., 'Isabella of France: She-Wolf and Rebel Queen?', p. 38.

49. Mortimer, I., 'Sermons of Sodomy: A Reconsideration of Edward II's Sodomitical Reputation', in Dodd, G. and Musson, A. (eds.), *The Reign of Edward II: New Perspectives*, (Boydell & Brewer, Woodbridge, 2006), p. 2.

50. Evans, M.R., 'Isabella of France and Roger Mortimer: Lovers or Allies?', in Storey, G. and Rohr, Z.E., (eds.), *Premodern Ruling Sexualities: Representation, Identity, and Power*, (Manchester University Press, Manchester, 2024), pp. 89–91.

51. *The Chronicle of Geoffrey Le Baker of Swinbrook*, Preest, D. and Barber, R. (eds. and trans.), (Boydell & Brewer, Woodbridge, 2012), p. 20.

52. Evans, M.R., 'Isabella of France: She-Wolf and Rebel Queen?', pp. 38–39.

53. *The Chronicle of Geoffrey Le Baker of Swinbrook*, p. 45.

54. Doherty, P., *Isabella and the Strange Death of Edward II*, p. 104.

55. *Vita Edwardi Secundi*, pp. 242–243.

56. Slater, L., 'Defining Queenship at Greyfriars London, *c.*1300–58', *Gender & History*, Vol. 27, No.1, (2015), p. 262.

57. Slater, L., 'Defining Queenship', p. 262.

58. Mortimer, I., 'Sermons of Sodomy', p. 51.

59. Slater, L., 'Defining Queenship', p. 263.

60. *Calendar of the Close Rolls, Edward II, 1323–1327*, (Public Record Office, London, 1898), p. 543.

61. Ibid., p. 579.

62. Earenfight, T., *Queenship*, p. 149..

63. Dean, S.E., 'The Treason Against Edward II: Favourites and Feuds', *Medieval Warfare*, Vol. 5, No. 1, (2015), p. 34.

64. Mortimer, I., *The Greatest Traitor: The Life of Sir Roger Mortimer, 1st Earl of March*, (Random House, London, 2010), p. 151.

65. Dean, S.E., 'The Treason Against Edward II', p. 34.

66. Castor, H., *She-Wolves*, pp. 299–300.

67. Ibid., pp. 301.

68. Westerhof, D., 'Deconstructing Identities on the Scaffold: The Execution of Hugh Despenser the Younger, 1326', *Journal of Medieval History*, Vol. 33, (2007), p. 93.

69. Valente, C., 'The Deposition and Abdication of Edward II', *The English Historical Review*, Vol. 113, No. 453, (1998), pp. 852–881.

70. Ibid., p. 852.

71. Castor, H., *She-Wolves*, pp. 307.

72. Mortimer, I., 'Sermons of Sodomy', pp. 55–56.

73. Doherty, P., *Isabella and the Strange Death of Edward II*, p. 255.

74. Carmi Parson, J., 'Isabella [Isabella of France]', *Oxford Dictionary of National Biography*, (2018), p. 4.

75. Earenfight, T., *Queenship*, p. 149.

76. Carmi Parson, J., 'Isabella [Isabella of France]', p. 4

77. Ormrod, W.M., *Edward III*, (Yale University Press, New Haven and London, 2012), pp. 86–87.

78. Evans, M.R., 'Isabella of France and Roger Mortimer', p. 91.

79. Ormrod, W.M., *Edward III*, pp. 92–93.

80. Ibid., p. 124.
81. Johnstone, H., 'Isabella, The She-Wolf of France', *History,* Vol. 21, (1936), p. 213.
82. Warner, K., *Isabella of France,* p. 265.
83. Ibid., p. 266
84. Evans, M.R., 'Isabella of France: She-Wolf and Rebel Queen?', p. 36.
85. Johnstone, H., 'Isabella, The She-Wolf of France', *History,* Vol. 21, (1936), p. 212.

Chapter 6: Sikelgaita

1. *Alexiad,* p. 54.
2. Van Houts, E., *The Normans in Europe,* p. 224.
3. Loud, G.A., *The Age of Robert Guiscard: Southern Italy and the Northern Conquest,* (Routledge, New Haven and London, 2013), p. 19.
4. Van Houts, E., *The Normans in Europe,* p. 237.
5. Skinner, P., '"Halt! Be Men!": Sikelgaita of Salerno, Gender and the Norman Conquest of Southern Italy', *Gender and History,* Vol. 12, No. 3, (2000), p. 626.
6. Ibid., pp. 624–625.
7. Eads, V., 'Sichelgaita of Salerno: Amazon or Trophy Wife?', in Devries, K. and Rogers, C.J. (eds.), *Journal of Medieval Military History,* (Boydell & Brewer, Woodbridge, 2005), p. 81.
8. Donald, M., *The Norman Kingdom of Sicily,* (Cambridge University Press, Cambridge, 1992), p. 11.
9. Loud, G.A., *The Age of Robert Guiscard,* p. 160.
10. Drell, J.H., *Kinship and Conquest: Family Strategies in the Principality of Salerno During the Norman Period, 1077–1194,* (Cornell University Press, Ithaca, 2002), p. 1.
11. Van Houts, E., *The Normans in Europe,* p. 237.
12. Balfour, D., '"A Formidable Sight": Sichelgaita of Salerno at Dyrrhachium', *Medieval Warfare,* Vol. 4, No. 2, (2014), p. 14.
13. Skinner, P., 'Halt! Be Men!', p. 627.
14. Eads, V., 'Sichelgaita of Salerno', p. 83.
15. Balfour, D., 'A Formidable Sight', p. 14
16. Brown, P., 'The *Gesta Roberti Wiscardi:* A "Byzantine" History?', *Journal of Medieval History,* Vol. 37, No. 2, (2011), p. 164.
17. Skinner, P., 'Halt! Be Men!', p. 629.
18. Ibid., pp. 629–630.
19. Loud, G.A., *The Age of Robert Guiscard,* pp. 290–291.
20. Eads, V., 'Sichelgaita of Salerno', p. 76.
21. Ibid.
22. *Alexiad,* p. 376. For a discussion of Irene accompanying Alexius on military campaign, see Anna Comnena.
23. *Alexiad,* p. 377.
24. Eads, V., 'Sichelgaita of Salerno', p. 74.
25. *Alexiad,* p. 59.

26. Eads, V., 'Sichelgaita of Salerno', p. 75.
27. Balfour, D., 'A Formidable Sight', p. 15.
28. *Alexiad*, p. 69.
29. *Alexiad*, p. 66.
30. Eads, V., 'Sichelgaita of Salerno', p. 81.
31. Balfour, D., 'A Formidable Sight', p. 17.
32. *Alexiad*, p. 147.
33. Eads, V., 'Sichelgaita of Salerno', p. 86.
34. Ibid, p. 76.
35. Skinner, P., 'Halt! Be Men!', p. 623.
36. Eads, V., 'Sichelgaita of Salerno', p. 75.
37. *Alexiad*, p. 191.
38. *The Deeds of Robert Guiscard by William of Apulia,* Loud, G.A. (trans.), (Institute for Medieval Studies, University of Leeds, Unpublished Translation) https://eprints.whiterose.ac.uk/id/eprint/211662/ [26 April 2025].
39. Drell, J.H., *Kinship and Conquest,* p. 135.
40. Orderic Vitalis, *The Ecclesiastical History, Vol. 4,* Chibnall, M. (ed.), (Oxford University Press, Oxford, 1973), pp. 30–31.
41. Skinner, P., 'Halt! Be Men!', p. 631.
42. Ibid.
43. Cowdrey, H.E., *The Age of Abbot Desiderius* (Oxford University Press, Oxford, 1983), p. 180.

Chapter 7: Matilda of Tuscany

1. For a discussion of the problem of the *Vita Mathildis* as a historical source, see Eads, V., 'The Last Italian Expedition of Henry IV: Re-reading the Vita Mathildis of Donizone of Canossa', in Rogers, C.J., Devries, K. and France, J. (eds.), *Journal of Medieval Military History,* (Boydell & Brewer, Woodbridge, 2010), pp. 23–68.
2. Spike, M., *Tuscan Countess: The Life and Extraordinary Times of Matilda of Canossa,* (Vendome Press, New York, 2004), p. 17.
3. Gillis, F.M., 'Matilda, Countess of Tuscany', *The Catholic Historical Review,* Vol. 10, No. 2, (1924), p. 236.
4. Ibid., pp. 235–236.
5. Nash, P., *Empress Adelheid and Countess Matilda: Medieval Female Rulership and the Foundations of European Society,* (Palgrave Macmillan, New York, 2017), p. 38.
6. Ibid, p. 4.
7. Robinson, I.S., *Henry IV of Germany 1056–1106,* (Cambridge University Press, Cambridge, 2003), p. 43.
8. Nash, P., *Empress Adelheid and Countess Matilda,* p. 58.
9. Ibid., pp. 57–58.
10. Cowdrey, H.E.J., *Pope Gregory VII, 1073–1085,* (Oxford University Press, Oxford, 1998), pp. 137–138.

11. Nash, P., *Empress Adelheid and Countess Matilda,* p. 5.

12. Cassagnes-Brouquet, S. and Greer, M., 'In the Service of the Just War: Matilda of Tuscany (Eleventh-Twelfth Centuries)', *Clio (English Edition),* No. 39, (2014), p. 40.

13. Robinson, I.S., *Henry IV of Germany,* pp. 159–160.

14. Creber, A., 'Women at Canossa: The Role of Royal and Aristocratic Women in the Reconciliation Between Pope Gregory VII and Henry IV of Germany', *Storicamente,* (2005), p. 8.

15. Eads, V., 'Means, Motive, Opportunity: Medieval Women and the Recourse to Arms', *Paper Presented at The Twentieth Barnard Medieval & Renaissance Conference 'War and Peace in the Middle Ages & Renaissance',* (2 December 2006). Found at: http://www.deremilitari.org/wp-content/uploads/2012/09/Eads-MeansMotivesOpp.pdf [Accessed 13 June 2024].

16. Creber, A., 'Women at Canossa', pp. 18–19.

17. Ibid., p. 9.

18. Cowdrey, H.E.J., *Pope Gregory VII,* p. 156.

19. Blumenthal, U.R., *The Investiture Controversy: Church and Monarchy from the Ninth to the Twelfth Century,* (University of Pennsylvania Press, Philadelphia, 1988), p. 123.

20. Bryce, J., 'The Papacy Master of the Field', in Morrison, K.F. (ed.), *The Investiture Controversy: Issues, Ideals, and Results,* (Holt, Rinehart and Winston, New York, 1971), pp. 87–88.

21. Robinson, I.S., *Henry IV of Germany,* pp. 168–169.

22. Nash, P., *Empress Adelheid and Countess Matilda,* p. 5..

23. Cassagnes-Brouquet, S. and Greer, M., 'In the Service of the Just War', pp. 40–41.

24. Robinson, I.S., *Henry IV of Germany,* pp. 229–230.

25. Blumenthal, U.R., *The Investiture Controversy,* p. 126.

26. Eads, V., 'The Last Italian Expedition of Henry IV', p. 29 .

27. Nash, P., *Empress Adelheid and Countess Matilda,* p. 5.

28. Eads, V., 'The Last Italian Expedition of Henry IV', p. 30.

29. Gillis, F.M., 'Matilda, Countess of Tuscany', p. 241.

30. Nash, P., *Empress Adelheid and Countess Matilda,* p. 158.

31. Raffensperger, C., 'The Missing Russian Women: The Case of Evpraksia Vsevolodovna', in Goldy, C.N. and Livingstone, A. (eds.), *Writing Medieval Women's Lives,* (Palgrave Macmillan, Basingstoke, 2012), pp. 76–77.

32. Nash, P., *Empress Adelheid and Countess Matilda,* p. 51.

33. Cassagnes-Brouquet, S. and Greer, M., 'In the Service of the Just War', p. 41.

34. Nash, P., *Empress Adelheid and Countess Matilda,* p. 179.

35. Creber, A., 'The Princely Woman and the Emperor: Imagery of Female Rule in Benzo of Alba's Ad Heinricum IV', *Royal Studies Journal, Vol.* 5, No. 2, (2018), pp. 23–24.

36. Cassagnes-Brouquet, S. and Greer, M., 'In the Service of the Just War', p. 42.

37. Moore, I., *The First European Revolution, c. 970–1215,* (Blackwell Publishing, Oxford, 2000), p. 97.

38. Guerri, F., 'Nihil Terrenum, Nihilque Carnale in Ea: Matilda of Tuscany and Anselm of Lucca during the Investiture Controversy', *Storicamente*, Vol. 31, (2017), p. 29.

39. Cassagnes-Brouquet, S. and Greer, M., 'In the Service of the Just War', pp. 43–44.

40. Apgar, B., 'Authority and Resistance in the Vita Mathildis (Vat. Lat. 4922)', *Religions,* Vol. 16, No. 3, (2025), p. 6.

41. Cassagnes-Brouquet, S. and Greer, M., 'In the Service of the Just War', p. 43.

42. Nicholson, H.J., *Women and the Crusades,* (Oxford University Press, Oxford, 2023), p. 36.

43. *William of Tyre, Vol. I,* p. 386.

44. Nash, P., *Empress Adelheid and Countess Matilda,* p. 226.

45. Gillis, F.M., 'Matilda, Countess of Tuscany', p. 243.

46. Holman, B.L., '*Exemplum* and *Imitatio*: Countess Matilda and Lucrezia Pico della Mirandola at Polirone', *The Art Bulletin*, Vol. 81, No. 4, (1999), p. 640.

47. Apgar, B., 'Authority and Resistance in the Vita Mathildis', p. 9.

48. Nash, P., *Empress Adelheid and Countess Matilda,* pp. 66–67.

49. Holman, B.L., '*Exemplum* and *Imitatio*', p. 640.

Chapter 8: Joan of Arc

1. Sumption, J., *The Hundred Years War, Vol. 5: Triumph and Illusion,* (Faber & Faber, London, 2023), p. 273.

2. Taylor, L.J., *The Virgin Warrior: The Life and Death of Joan of Arc,* (Yale University Press, New Haven and London, 2019), p. 6.

3. Ibid., p. 7.

4. *Trial*, p. 53.

5. Sumption, J., *The Hundred Years War,* p. 273.

6. Taylor, L.J., *The Virgin Warrior,* p. 1.

7. *Trial*, pp. 53 and 65–66.

8. Ibid., p. 92.

9. Ibid., p. 54.

10. Taylor, L.J., *The Virgin Warrior,* pp. 22–23.

11. *Trial*, p. 93.

12. Ibid.

13. Orgelfinger, G., *Joan of Arc in the English Imagination, 1429–1829,* (Pennsylvania State University Press, Pennsylvania, 2019), p. 20.

14. 'Deposition of Durand Laxart (31 January 1456)', in Taylor, C., *Joan of Arc: La Pucelle,* (Manchester University Press, Manchester, 2006), p. 273.

15. *Trial*, p. 54.

16. Taylor, L.J., *The Virgin Warrior,* p. 34.

17. Ibid., p. 35.

18. Ibid.

19. 'Deposition of Catherine, wife of Henri Le Royer (31 January 1456)', in Taylor, C., *Joan of Arc: La Pucelle,* p. 275.

20. Ibid., p. 275.

21. *Trial*, p. 129.

22. Hinde Stewart, J., 'The Maid and the Milkmaid: Joan of Arc and Marie Antoinette', *The French Review,* Vol. 93, No. 4, (May 2020), pp. 18–19.

23. Taylor, L.J., *The Virgin Warrior,* pp. 59–60.

24. *Trial*, p. 55.

25. 'Deposition of Simon Charles (7 May 1456)', in Taylor, C., *Joan of Arc: La Pucelle,* p. 318.

26. Taylor, C., *Joan of Arc: La Pucelle,* pp. 12–13.

27. Warner, M., *Joan of Arc: The Image of Female Heroism,* (Oxford University Press, Oxford, 2013), p. 48.

28. Taylor, L.J., *The Virgin Warrior,* p. 42.

29. 'The Chronicle of Charles VII by Jean Chartier (c.1445–1450)', in Taylor, C., *Joan of Arc: La Pucelle,* p. 250.

30. Taylor, L.J., *The Virgin Warrior,* p. 84.

31. Taylor, L.J., 'Joan of Arc, the Church, and the Papacy, 1429–1920', *The Catholic Historical Review*, Vol. 98, No. 2, (2012), pp. 218–219.

32. Taylor, L.J., *The Virgin Warrior,* p. 43.

33. 'Deposition at Lyon of Jean d'Aulon (28 May 1456)' in Taylor, C., *Joan of Arc: La Pucelle,* p. 340.

34. Taylor, L.J., *The Virgin Warrior,* p. 52.

35. *Trial*, pp. 67–68.

36. DeVries, K., *Joan of Arc: A Military Leader,* (Sutton Publishing, Stroud, 1999), p. 50.

37. Ibid., p. 53.

38. 'Joan of Arc's letter to the English (22 March 1429)', in Taylor, C., *Joan of Arc: La Pucelle,* p. 74.

39. Taylor, L.J., *The Virgin Warrior,* p. 61.

40. Ibid., p. 63.

41. Castor, H., *Joan of Arc: A History,* (Faber & Faber, London, 2014), p. 105.

42. Warner, M., *Joan of Arc,* p. 95.

43. Sumption, J., *The Hundred Years War,* p. 303.

44. Wood, C. T., *Joan of Arc and Richard III: Sex, Saints, and Government in the Middle Ages*, (Oxford University Press, Oxford, 1991), p. 140.

45. Sumption, J., *The Hundred Years War,* p. 305.

46. Castor, H., *Joan of Arc,* p. 115.

47. Warner, M., *Joan of Arc,* p. 58.

48. Ibid., p. 61.

49. Taylor, L.J., *The Virgin Warrior,* pp. 98–100.

50. Gies, F., *Joan of Arc: The Legend and the Reality,* (Harper & Row, New York, 1981), p. 143.

51. 'Letter from Henry VI to Pierre Cauchon (3 January 1431)', in Taylor, C., *Joan of Arc: La Pucelle*, p. 136.

52. Sullivan, K., *The Interrogation of Joan of Arc,* (University of Minnesota Press, Minnesota, 1999), pp. 89–90.

53. *Trial*, p. 4.
54. Cook, C. H., *Hearing Spiritual Voices: Medieval Mystics, Meaning and Psychiatry*, (Bloomsbury Publishing, London, 2023), p. 72.
55. *Trial*, p. 74.
56. Ibid., p. 49.
57. Ibid., p. 62.
58. Ibid., p. 63.
59. Ibid., p. 33.
60. Naylor, P.C., 'Joan of Arc's Mystery, History, and Intelligibility', in Tallon, M.E., *Joan of Arc at the University*, (Marquette University Press, Milwaukee, 1997), p. 38.
61. Sullivan, K., *The Interrogation of Joan of Arc*, p. 30.
62. Taylor, L.J., *The Virgin Warrior*, p. 26.
63. Sullivan, K., *The Interrogation of Joan of Arc*, p. 31.
64. Taylor, L.J., *The Virgin Warrior*, p. 25.
65. 'Fourth public examination (Tuesday 27 February 1431)', Taylor, C., *Joan of Arc: La Pucelle*, p. 153.
66. Cook, C. H., *Hearing Spiritual Voices*, p. 81.
67. Barstow, A.L., *Joan of Arc: Heretic, Mystic, Shaman*, (Edwin Mellen Press, New York, 1986), p. 91.
68. Ibid, pp. 91–92.
69. Hinde Stewart, J., 'The Maid and the Milkmaid', p. 21.
70. Taylor, L.J., *The Virgin Warrior*, p. 160.
71. Ibid., pp. 160–161.
72. *Trial*, p. 197.
73. Ibid., p. 198.
74. Taylor, L.J., *The Virgin Warrior*, pp. 165–166.
75. 'The Sentence of Nullification (7 July 1456)', in Taylor, C., *Joan of Arc: La Pucelle*, p. 348.
76. Sullivan, K., *The Interrogation of Joan of Arc*, p. 162.
77. Taylor, L.J., *The Virgin Warrior*, p. 183.
78. Warner, M., *Joan of Arc*, p. 55.
79. Taylor, L.J., *The Virgin Warrior*, p. 88.
80. Ibid., pp. 76–77.
81. Zupko, R.E., 'The Many Faces of Joan', in Tallon, M.E. (ed.) *Joan of Arc at the University*, (Marquette University Press, Milwaukee, 1997), p. 10.
82. Taylor, L.J., *The Virgin Warrior*, p. 85.

Chapter 9: Anna Comnena

1. *Alexiad*, p. 17.
2. Ibid., p. 196.
3. Garland, L. and Rapp, S., '"Mary of Alania": Woman and Empress Between Two Worlds', in Garland, L. (ed.), *Byzantine Women: Varieties of Experience 800–1200*, (Ashgate, Aldershot, 2006), pp. 91–124.

4. Smythe, D., 'Middle Byzantine Family Values and Anna Komnene's *Alexiad*', in Garland, L. (ed.), *Byzantine Women: Varieties of Experience 800–1200*, (Ashgate, Aldershot, 2006), p. 126.

5. *Alexiad*, p. 198.

6. Cooper, G.M., 'Byzantium between East and West: Competing Hellenisms in the *Alexiad* of Anna Komnene and her Contemporaries', in Classen, A. (ed.), *East Meets West in the Middle Ages and Early Modern Times: Transcultural Experiences in the Premodern World*, (De Gruyter, Inc., Berlin, 2013), p. 271.

7. *Alexiad*, p. 17.

8. Browning, R., 'An Unpublished Funeral Oration on Anna Comnena', *Proceedings of the Cambridge Philological Society*, Vol. 188, No. 8, (1962), p. 5.

9. Laiou, A.E., 'Introduction: Why Anna Komnene?', in Gouma-Peterson, T. (ed.), *Anna Komnene and Her Times*, (Garland Publishing, New York, 2000), p. 5.

10. Hodgson, N.R., *Women, Crusading and the Holy Land*, p. 65.

11. Böhm, M., 'Nikephoros Bryennios the Younger – the First One Not to Become a Blind Man? Political and Military History of the Bryennios Family in the 11th and Early 12th Century', *Studia Ceranea*, Vol. 10, (2020), p. 39.

12. Buckler, G., *Anna Comnena: A Study*, (Oxford University Press, Oxford, 2000), p. 116.

13. *Alexiad*, p. 220.

14. Ibid., pp. 319–323.

15. Böhm, M., 'Nikephoros Bryennios the Younger', p. 38.

16. Browning, R., 'An Unpublished Funeral Oration on Anna Comnena', p. 5.

17. *Alexiad*, p. 448 and f.n. 15.

18. Cooper, G.M., 'Byzantium between East and West', p. 272.

19. Ibid., p. 273.

20. Garland, L., *Byzantine Empresses: Women and Power in Byzantium, AD 527–1204*, (Routledge, New Haven and London, 1999), p. 197.

21. *Alexiad*, pp. 510–513.

22. *O City of Byzantium*, p. 6.

23. Herrin, J., *Unrivalled Influence: Women and Empire in Byzantium*, (Princeton University Press, Princeton, 2013), pp. 231–232.

24. Garland, L., *Byzantine Empresses*, pp. 197–198.

25. Böhm, M., 'Nikephoros Bryennios the Younger', p. 40.

26. Smythe, D., 'Middle Byzantine Family Values', p. 124.

27. Garland, L., *Byzantine Empresses*, p. 198.

28. Cooper, G.M., 'Byzantium between East and West, p. 274.

29. Browning, R., 'An Unpublished Funeral Oration on Anna Comnena', p. 5.

30. *Alexiad*, p. 514.

31. Browning, R., 'An Unpublished Funeral Oration on Anna Comnena', p. 5.

32. Howard-Johnston, J., 'Anna Komnene and the Alexiad', in Mullett, M. and Smythe, D. (eds.), *Alexios I Komnenos: Papers on the Second Belfast Byzantine International Colloquium, 14–16 April 1989*, (Belfast Byzantine Enterprises, Belfast, 1996), p. 297.

33. *Alexiad*, pp. 19–20.
34. Ibid., pp. 375–6. For a further discussion of Irene's accompaniment of Alexius on military campaign, see chapter on *Sikelgaita*.
35. Smythe, D., 'Middle Byzantine Family Values', p. 128.
36. For a discussion of Anna's account of the First Crusade, see Frankopan, P., 'Perception and Projection of Prejudice: Anna Comnena, the *Alexiad* and the First Crusade', in Edgington, S.B. and Lambert, S. (eds.), *Gendering the Crusades*, (Columbia University Press, New York, 2002), pp. 59–76.

Chapter 10: Christine de Pizan

1. Cooper-Davis, C., *Christine de Pizan: Life, Work, Legacy*, (Reaktion Books, London, 2021), p. 8.
2. Willard, C.C., *The Writings of Christine de Pizan*, (Persea Books, New York, 1994), p. 18.
3. Ibid., pp. 17–20.
4. Willard, C.C., *The Writings of Christine de Pizan*, p. 22.
5. Cruse, M., 'The Louvre of Charles V: Legitimacy, Renewal, and Royal Presence in Fourteenth-Century Paris', *L'Esprit Créateur,* Vol. 54, No. 2, (2014), p. 19.
6. Ibid., p. 23.
7. 'The Book of Fortune's Transformation', in Blumenfeld-Kosinski, R. and Brownlee, K. (eds. and trans.), *The Selected Writings of Christine de Pizan*, (W.W. Norton & Company, New York, 1997), p. 94.
8. Blumenfeld-Kosinski, R. and Brownlee, K. (eds. and trans.), *The Selected Writings of Christine de Pizan*, p. xii.
9. Cooper-Davis, C., *Christine de Pizan*, p. 8.
10. 'Christine's Vision', in Willard, C.C., *The Writings of Christine de Pizan*, p. 8.
11. 'The Path of Long Study' in Blumenfeld-Kosinski, R. and Brownlee, K. (eds. and trans.), *The Selected Writings of Christine de Pizan*, (W.W. Norton & Company, New York, 1997), p. 62.
12. Cooper-Davis, C., *Christine de Pizan*, p. 10 .
13. 'Ballad 26' in Willard, C.C., *The Writings of Christine de Pizan*, p. 51.
14. Willard, C.C., *The Writings of Christine de Pizan*, pp. 42–43.
15. Cooper-Davis, C., *Christine de Pizan*, p. 10.
16. Ibid., p. 11.
17. 'The Book of the Three Virtues' Blumenfeld-Kosinski, R. and Brownlee, K. (eds. and trans.), *The Selected Writings of Christine de Pizan*, pp. 169–170.
18. 'The Book of Fortune's Transformation', in Blumenfeld-Kosinski, R. and Brownlee, K. (eds. and trans.), *The Selected Writings of Christine de Pizan*, p. 106.
19. Ibid., p. 107.
20. Blumenfeld-Kosinski, R. and Brownlee, K. (eds. and trans.), *The Selected Writings of Christine de Pizan*, p. xii.
21. Villalon, A., and Kagay, D., *The Hundred Years War: A Wider Focus,* (Brill, Leiden, 2005), pp. xxxvi– xxxvii.

22. Gibbons, R., 'Isabeau of Bavaria, Queen of France (1385–1422): The Creation of an Historical Villainess', *Transactions of the Royal Historical Society*, Vol. 6, (1996), p. 55.

23. Hicks-Bartlett, A., 'War, Tears, and Corporeal Response in Christine de Pizan', in Davies, D. and Perry, R.D. (eds.), *Literatures of the Hundred Years War,* (Manchester University Press, Manchester, 2024), pp. 246–247.

24. Adams, T., *The Life and Afterlife of Isabeau of Bavaria,* (Johns Hopkins University Press, Baltimore, 2010), pp. 184–186.

25. Gibbons, R., 'Isabeau of Bavaria', p. 75.

26. Broad, J., and Green, K., *A History of Women's Political Thought in Europe, 1400–1700.* (Cambridge University Press, Cambridge, 2009), p. 29.

27. Brown-Grant, R., *Christine de Pizan and the Moral Defence of Women: Reading Beyond Gender*, (Cambridge University Press, Cambridge, 2001), p. 175.

28. Adams, T. and Rechtschaffen, G., 'Isabeau of Bavaria, Anne of France, and the History of Female Regency in France', *Early Modern Women*, Vol. 8, (2013), p. 135.

29. Brown-Grant, R., *Christine de Pizan and the Moral Defence of Women: Reading Beyond Gender*, (Cambridge University Press, Cambridge, 2001), pp. 134–135.

30. Paakkinen, I., 'The Metaphysics of Gender in Christine de Pizan's Thought', in Muravyeva, M. and Toivo, M.R. (eds.), *Gender in Late Medieval and Early Modern Europe,* (Routledge, New Haven and London, 2013), p. 47.

31. 'The Book of the Three Virtues' in Blumenfeld-Kosinski, R. and Brownlee, K. (eds. and trans.), *The Selected Writings of Christine de Pizan*, p. 157.

32. Hult, D.F. (ed. and trans.), *Debate of the Romance of the Rose*, (University of Chicago Press, Chicago, 2010), p. 12.

33. Rubin, M., 'The Languages of Late-Medieval Feminism', in Akkerman, T. and Stuurman, S. (eds.), *Perspectives on Feminist Political Thought in European History: From the Middle Ages to the Present,* (Routledge, New Haven and London, 1998), p. 43.

34. 'The God of Love's Letter', in Blumenfeld-Kosinski, R. and Brownlee, K. (eds. and trans.), *The Selected Writings of Christine de Pizan*, p. 16.

35. Ibid., pp. 22–23.

36. 'Moral Teachings', in Hult, D.F. (ed. and trans.), *Debate of the Romance of the Rose*, p. 43

37. 'Christine de Pizan to Jean de Montreuil (June to July 1401)', in Hult, D.F. (ed. and trans.), *Debate of the Romance of the Rose*, p. 62 .

38. Ibid., p. 62 .

39. Ibid., p. 63.

40. Rubin, M., 'The Languages of Late-Medieval Feminism', p. 44.

41. Margolis, N., 'Royal Biography as Reliquary: Christine de Pizan's *Livre des Fais et bonnes meurs du sage roy Charles V*', in Bradbury, N. and Adams, J. (eds.), *Medieval Women and Their Objects*, (University of Michigan Press, Michigan, 2020), p. 128.

42. McGrady, D., *The Writer's Gift or the Patron's Pleasure?: The Literary Economy in Late Medieval France*, (University of Toronto Press, Toronto, 2019), pp. 210–211.

43. Margolis, N., 'Royal Biography as Reliquary', p. 123.

44. Brauer, M., 'Politics or Leisure? A Day in the Life of King Charles V of France (1364–80)', *The Medieval History Journal*, (2015, 18 Vol. 1), p. 48.

45. Margolis, N., 'Royal Biography as Reliquary', p. 128.

46. Taylor, C., *Chivalry and the Ideals of Knighthood in France During the Hundred Years War*, (Cambridge University Press, Cambridge, 2013), p. 10.

47. Adams, T., *Christine de Pizan and the Fight for France*, (Pennsylvania State University Press, Pennsylvania, 2018), pp. 160–162.

48. Taylor, C., *Chivalry and the Ideals of Knighthood*, p. 171.

49. Ibid., p. 154.

50. Ibid., p. 199.

51. Adams, T., *Christine de Pizan and the Fight for France*, p. 169.

52. Taylor, C., *Chivalry and the Ideals of Knighthood*, p. 15.

53. Adams, T., *Christine de Pizan and the Fight for France*, p. 173.

54. Langdon Forhan, K., 'Reflecting Heroes. Christine de Pizan and the Mirror Tradition' in Margarete Zimmermann, M. and De Rentiis, D. (eds.), *The City of Scholars: New Approaches to Christine de Pizan*, (Walter de Gruyter, Berlin, 1994), p. 193.

55. McWebb, C., 'Joan of Arc and Christine de Pizan: The Symbiosis of Two Warriors in the Ditié de Jehanne d'Arc', in Wheeler, B. and Wood, C.T. (eds.), *Fresh Verdicts on Joan of Arc*, (Garland, New York, 1996), pp. 133–136 .

56. Cooper-Davis, C., *Christine de Pizan*, p. 7.

57. Adams, T., 'Christine de Pizan', *French Studies: A Quarterly Review*, Vol. 71, No. 3, (2017), p. 390.

58. Chance, J., 'Christine de Pizan as Literary Mother: Women's Authority and Subjectivity in "The Floure and the Leafe" and "The Assembly of Ladies"', in Zimmermann, M. and De Rentiis, D. (eds.), *The City of Scholars: New Approaches to Christine de Pizan*, (Walter de Gruyter, Berlin, 1994), p. 252.

59. Gottileb, B., 'The Problem of Feminism in the Fifteenth Century' in Blumenfeld-Kosinski, R. and Brownlee, K. (eds. and trans.), *The Selected Writings of Christine de Pizan*, pp. 274–275.

60. De Beauvoir, S., *The Second Sex*, (Vintage Books, London, 2014), p. 71.

61. Gottlieb, B., 'The Problem of Feminism in the Fifteenth Century', in Blumenfeld-Kosinski, R. and Brownlee, K. (eds. and trans.), *The Selected Writings of Christine De Pizan*, (W.W. Norton & Company, New York, 1997), pp. 274–275.

62. Delany, S., '"Mothers to Think Back Through", Who Are They? The Ambiguous Example of Christine de Pizan', in Blumenfeld-Kosinski, R. and Brownlee, K. (eds. and trans.), *The Selected Writings of Christine De Pizan*, (W.W. Norton & Company, New York, 1997), pp. 312–329.

Chapter 11: Margery Kempe

1. Winstead, K. A., *Fifteenth-Century Lives: Writing Sainthood in England*, (University of Notre Dame Press, Notre Dame, 2020), p. 2.
2. Fitzpatrick, J., 'Reimagining This Creature: Hospitality and Autohagiography in the Visions of Margery Kempe', *History*, Vol. 106, (2021), p. 562.
3. Bowers, T.N., 'Margery Kempe as Traveler', *Studies in Philology*, Vol. 97, No. 1 (2000), p. 11
4. Ibid.
5. *BMK*, p. 33.
6. *The Book of Margery Kempe*, Bale A. (trans.) (Oxford University Press, Oxford, 2015), p. x
7. Goodman, A.E., *Margery Kempe and Her World*, (Routledge, New Haven and London, 2002), pp. 49–51.
8. *BMK*, p. 10.
9. Phillips, K.M., 'Margery Kempe and the Ages of Woman', in Arnold, J.H. and Lewis, K.J. (eds.), *A Companion to the Book of Margery Kempe*, (Boydell & Brewer, Woodbridge, 2004), p. 24.
10. Delany, S., 'Sexual Economics, Chaucer's Wife of Bath and *The Book of Margery Kempe*', in Evans, R. and Johnson, L. (eds.), *Feminist Readings in Middle English Literature: The Wife of Bath and All Her Sect*, (Routledge, New Haven and London, 1994), p. 76.
11. *BMK*, p. 44.
12. Maddock, S., 'Margery Kempe's Home Town and Worthy Kin', in Kalas, L. and Varnam, L. (eds.), *Encountering the Book of Margery Kempe*, (Manchester University Press, Manchester, 2021), p. 171.
13. *BMK*, p. 221.
14. Ibid., p. 41.
15. Ibid., pp. 41 42.
16. Ibid., p. 42.
17. Ibid., pp. 49–50.
18. Ibid., pp. 58–60.
19. Delany, S., 'Sexual Economics', pp. 82–83.
20. *BMK*, p. 123.
21. Yoshikawa, N.K., 'The Jerusalem Pilgrimage: The Centre of the Structure of the Book of Margery Kempe', *English Studies*, Vol. 86, (2005), p. 198.
22. Atkinson, C.W., *Mystic and Pilgrim: The Book and the World of Margery Kempe*, (Cornell University Press, Ithaca, 1983), p. 194.
23. Jenkins, J., 'Reading and the Book of Margery Kempe', in Arnold, J.H. and Lewis, K.J. (eds.), *A Companion to the Book of Margery Kempe*, (Boydell & Brewer, Woodbridge, 2004), p. 124.
24. *BMK*, p. 132.
25. Bale, A. and Giousé, D., 'A Women's Network in Fifteenth-Century Rome: Margery Kempe Encounters "Margaret Florentyne"', in Kalas, L. and Varnam, L.

(eds.), *Encountering the Book of Margery Kempe*, (Manchester University Press, Manchester, 2021), p. 191.

26. *BMK*, p. 54.
27. Ibid., pp. 54 and 87.
28. Ibid., p. 162.
29. Salih, S., *Versions of Virginity in Late Medieval England,* (Boydell & Brewer, Woodbridge, 2001), p. 220.
30. Erler, M.C., 'Margery Kempe's White Clothes', *Medium Aevum,* Vol. 62, (1993), p.79.
31. Lochrie, K., *Margery Kempe and the Translations of the Flesh,* (University of Pennsylvania Press, Philadelphia, 1994), p. 159.
32. Salih, S., *Versions of Virginity,* p. 217.
33. Yoshikawa, N.K., 'The Jerusalem Pilgrimage', p. 193.
34. *BMK*, p. 97.
35. Ibid., p. 98 .
36. Park, H., 'Mealtime Sanctity: The Devotional and Social Significance of Mealtimes in *The Book of Margery Kempe'*, *Parergon*, Vol. 36, (2019), p. 63.
37. Ibid., p. 73.
38. Staley, L., *Margery Kempe's Dissenting Fictions*, (Pennsylvania State University Press, Philadelphia, 1994), p. 190.
39. *BMK*, p. 120.
40. Ibid., pp. 272–275.
41. Bowers, T.N., 'Margery Kempe as Traveler', p. 3.
42. *BMK*, pp. 63–64.
43. Ibid., p. 64.
44. Atkinson, C.W., *Mystic and Pilgrim',* p. 103.
45. Yoshikawa, N.K., 'The Making of The Book of Margery Kempe: The Issue of *Discretio Spirituum* Reconsidered', *English Studies*, Vol. 92, (2011), p. 129.
46. *BMK*, p. 155.
47. Ibid., p. 153.
48. Bowers, T.N., 'Margery Kempe as Traveler', p. 13.
49. *BMK*. p. 162.
50. Ibid., p. 164.
51. Ibid., p. 163.
52. Ibid.
53. Arnold, J.H., 'Margery's Trials: Heresy, Lollardy and Dissent', in Arnold, J.H. and Lewis, K.J. (eds.), *A Companion to the Book of Margery Kempe*, (Boydell & Brewer, Woodbridge, 2004), p. 78.
54. Frick, D., *Authority and Authorship in Medieval and Seventeenth-Century Women's Visionary Writings,* (Transcript Verlag, Bielefeld, 2021), p. 76.
55. *BMK*, p. 168.
56. Bowers, T.N., 'Margery Kempe as Traveler', pp. 12–13.
57. Long, J., 'Mysticism and Hysteria: The Histories of Margery Kempe and Anna O', in Evans, R. and Johnson, L. (eds.), *Feminist Readings in Middle English*

Literature: The Wife of Bath and All Her Sect*, (Routledge, New Haven and London, 1994), p. 101.
58. Bowers, T.N., 'Margery Kempe as Traveler', p. 13.
59. Ibid., p. 11.
60. Arnold, J.H., 'Margery's Trials', p. 81.

Chapter 12: Margaret of Anjou

1. Shakespeare, *Henry VI Part 3*, 1.4.111.
2. Maurer, H., 'Delegitimizing Lancaster: The Yorkist Use of Gendered Propaganda During the Wars of the Roses', in Biggs, D., Michalove, S. and Reeves, C. (eds.), *Reputation and Representation in Fifteenth-Century Europe*, (Brill, Leiden, 2004), pp. 169–186.
3. Dunn, D.E.S., 'Margaret [Margaret of Anjou]', *Oxford Dictionary of National Biography,* (2004), p. 2.
4. Laynesmith, J.L., *The Last Medieval Queens*, (Oxford University Press, Oxford, 2006), p. 75.
5. Levin, C., 'Margaret of Anjou: Passionate Mother', in Harris, C., et.al. (eds.), *Later Plantagenet and the Wars of the Roses Consorts*, (Palgrave Macmillan, Cham, 2023), p. 196.
6. Gristwood, S., *Blood Sisters: The Women Behind the Wars of the Roses,* (Basic Books, New York, 2013), pp. 5–6.
7. Strickland, A. and Strickland, E., *Lives of the Queens of England from the Norman Conquest*, (Cambridge University Press, Cambridge, 2010), p. 183.
8. Loades, D., *The Tudor Queens of England,* (Bloomsbury Publishing, New York, 2010), p. 26.
9. Ibid., p. 27.
10. Lee, P.A., 'Reflections of Power: Margaret of Anjou and the Dark Side of Queenship', *Renaissance Quarterly,* Vol. 39, No. 2, (1986), p. 185.
11. Dunn, D.E.S., 'Margaret [Margaret of Anjou]', p. 3.
12. Strickland, A. and Strickland, E., *Lives of the Queens of England,* p. 109.
13. Cook, D.R., *Lancastrians and Yorkists: The Wars of the Roses*, (Routledge, New Haven and London, 1984), p. 17.
14. Dunn, D., '"The Principal Place of Honour about the Person of the Queen". Margaret of Anjou and Alice Chaucer, Duchess of Suffolk: The Making of a Friendship', in Clark, L., *et al.* (eds.), *The Fifteenth Century XX: Essays presented to Rowena E. Archer.* (Boydell & Brewer, Woodbridge, 2024), pp. 61–62.
15. Lee, P.A., 'Reflections of Power', p. 191.
16. Lewis, K.J., *Kingship and Masculinity,* pp. 180–181.
17. Maurer, H.E., *Margaret of Anjou: Queenship and Power in Late Medieval England,* (Boydell & Brewer, Woodbridge, 2005), pp. 67–74.
18. Laynesmith, J.L., *The Last Medieval Queens*, pp. 162–163.
19. Cook, D.R., *Lancastrians and Yorkists,* pp. 20–21.
20. Maurer, H.E., *Margaret of Anjou,* p. 40.

21. Ibid., p. 41.
22. For analysis of the couple's initial childlessness and its ramifications, see Lewis, K.J., *Kingship and Masculinity,* pp. 198–208.
23. Lewis, K.J., *Kingship and Masculinity* p. 219.
24. Ibid., pp. 221–222.
25. Laynesmith, J.L., *The Last Medieval Queens*, p. 161.
26. Lewis, K.J., *Kingship and Masculinity,* p. 221.
27. Levin, C., 'Margaret of Anjou: Passionate Mother', p. 200.
28. Ibid., p. 200.
29. Loades, D., *The Tudor Queens of England,* p. 33.
30. Griffiths, R.A., *The Reign of King Henry VI: The Exercise of Royal Authority, 1422–1461,* (University of California Press, Berkeley, 1981), pp. 743–745.
31. Dunn, D.E.S., 'Margaret [Margaret of Anjou]', p. 6.
32. Laynesmith, J.L., *The Last Medieval Queens*, p. 164.
33. Ibid.
34. Lewis, K.J., *Kingship and Masculinity,* p. 229.
35. Maurer, H.E., *Margaret of Anjou,* p. 157.
36. Geaman, K., 'A Bastard and a Changeling? England's Edward of Westminster and Delayed Childbirth', in Schutte, V. (ed.), *Unexpected Heirs in Early Modern Europe: Potential Kings and Queens*, (Palgrave Macmillan, New York, 2017), p. 15.
37. Maurer, H.E., *Margaret of Anjou,* p. 178.
38. Ibid.
39. Maurer, H., 'Delegitimizing Lancaster', p. 178.
40. Maurer, H.E., *Margaret of Anjou,* p. 47; Maurer, H., 'Delegitimizing Lancaster', p. 179.
41. Cook, D.R., *Lancastrians and Yorkists,* p. 26.
42. Sadler, J., *The Red Rose and the White: The Wars of the Roses, 1453–1487,* (Routledge, New Haven and London, 2009), pp. 110–112.
43. Loades, D., *The Tudor Queens of England,* pp. 35–36.
44. Ibid., p. 36.
45. Lee, P.A., 'Reflections of Power', pp. 216–217.
46. Levin, C., 'Margaret of Anjou: Passionate Mother', p. 205.
47. Maurer, H.E., *Margaret of Anjou,* p. 62.
48. Dunn, D., 'The Queen at War: The Role of Margaret of Anjou in the Wars of the Roses', in Dunn, D. (ed.), *War and Society in Medieval and Early Modern Britain,* (Liverpool University Press, Liverpool, 2000), p. 153.
49. Ibid., p. 154.
50. Loades, D., *The Tudor Queens of England,* p. 38.
51. Levin, C., 'Margaret of Anjou: Passionate Mother', p. 208.
52. Griffiths, R.A., 'Henry VI', *Oxford Dictionary of National Biography,* (2015), p. 21.
53. Dunn, D.E.S., 'Margaret [Margaret of Anjou]', p. 11.
54. Dunn, D., 'The Queen at War', p. 155.

55. Maurer, H.E., *Margaret of Anjou,* p. 208.

56. Dunn, D., '"The Principal Place of Honour about the Person of the Queen"', p. 65

57. Crawford, A., *Letters of the Queens of England 1100–1547,* (Sutton Publishing, Stroud, 1997), p. 124.

58. Dunn, D., 'The Queen at War', p. 156.

Chapter 13: Elizabeth Woodville

1. Carpenter, C. (ed.), *Kingsford's Stonor Letters and Papers, 1290–1483,* (Cambridge University Press, Cambridge, 1996), p. 123; Laynesmith, J.L., 'Elizabeth Woodville: The Knight's Widow', in Harris, C., *et al.* (eds.), *Later Plantagenet and the Wars of the Roses Consorts,* (Palgrave Macmillan, Cham, 2023), p. 217.

2. Laynesmith, J.L., 'Elizabeth Woodville: The Knight's Widow', p. 271.

3. Griffiths, R.A., *The Reign of King Henry VI,* p. 486.

4. Licence, A., *Red Roses: Blanche of Gaunt to Margaret Beaufort,* (The History Press, London, 2016), pp. 173–174.

5. Laynesmith, J.L., 'Elizabeth Woodville: The Knight's Widow', p. 217.

6. Laynesmith, J.L., *The Last Medieval Queens,* pp. 55–56.

7. Laynesmith, J.L., 'Elizabeth Woodville: The Knight's Widow', p. 218.

8. Sadler, J., *The Red Rose and the White,* p. 160.

9. Crawford, A., *The Yorkists: The History of a Dynasty,* (Bloomsbury Publishing, London, 2007), p. 68.

10. Ross, C., *Edward IV,* (Eyre Methuen, London, 1974), p. 92.

11. Laynesmith, J.L., 'Elizabeth Woodville: The Knight's Widow', p. 219.

12. Laynesmith, J.L., *The Last Medieval Queens,* p. 57.

13. Crawford, A., *The Yorkists,* p. 68.

14. Hicks, M., 'Elizabeth [née Elizabeth Woodville]', *Oxford Dictionary of National Biography,* (2011), p. 4.

15. Laynesmith, J.L., *Cecily, Duchess of York,* (Bloomsbury Publishing, London, 2017), pp. 115–116.

16. Ibid, p. 116.

17. Visser-Fuchs, L., 'English Events in Caspar Weinreich's Danzig Chronicle, 1461–1495', *The Ricardian,* Vol. 7, No. 95, (1986), p. 313.

18. Chamberlayne, J.L., 'Crowns and Virgins: Queen Making During the Wars of the Roses', in Lewis, K.J., Menuge, N.J. and Phillips, K.M. (eds.), *Young Medieval Women,* (St. Martin's Press, New York, 1999), p. 48.

19. Laynesmith, J.L., 'Elizabeth Woodville: The Knight's Widow', p. 222.

20. Ibid., pp. 221–222.

21. Laynesmith, J.L., *The Last Medieval Queens,* p. 109.

22. *Calendar of State Papers and Manuscripts Existing in the Archives and Collections of Milan. Vol. I. 1385–1618,* Hinds, A.B. (ed.), (HMSO, London, 1912), p. 131.

23. Laynesmith, J.L., 'Elizabeth Woodville: The Knight's Widow', p. 223.

24. Morrical, M., *Usurpers, A New Look at Medieval Kings,* (Pen & Sword Books, Barnsley, 2021), p. 155.

25. Laynesmith, J.L., *Cecily, Duchess of York*, p. 119.
26. Scofield, C.L., *The Life and Reign of Edward the Fourth, King of England and of France and Lord of Ireland, Vol. I*, (Longmans, Green and Co., London, 1923), pp. 395–396.
27. Ibid., p. 396; Laynesmith, J.L., *The Last Medieval Queens*, p. 118.
28. *Calendar of State Papers and Manuscripts Existing in the Archives and Collections of Milan. Vol. I. 1385–1618*, p. 129.
29. Crawford, A., *The Yorkists*, pp. 78–79.
30. Horrox, R., 'Edward IV', *Oxford Dictionary of National Biography*, (2011), p. 6.
31. Tucker, P., 'The Lincolnshire Rebellion of 1470 Revisited', *The English Historical Review*, Vol. 136, (2021), p. 1.
32. Ibid., pp. 1–25.
33. Laynesmith, J.L., 'Elizabeth Woodville: The Knight's Widow', p. 230.
34. Ibid.
35. Loades, D., *The Tudor Queens of England*, pp. 53–54.
36. Okerlund, A., *Elizabeth: England's Slandered Queen*, (Tempus, Stroud, 2006), p. 132.
37. Ross, C., *Edward IV*, p. 415.
38. Crawford, A., *The Yorkists*, p. 123.
39. Hicks, M., *Richard III: The Self-Made King*, (Yale University Press, New Haven and London, 2019), p. 237.
40. Crawford, A., *The Yorkists*, p. 125.
41. Hicks, M., *Richard III*, p. 248.
42. Hicks, M., *The Wars of the Roses, 1455–1485*, (Yale University Press, New Haven and London, 2012), p. 218.
43. Laynesmith, J.L., *Cecily, Duchess of York*, p. 154.
44. Laynesmith, J.L., 'Elizabeth Woodville: The Knight's Widow', p. 232.
45. Ibid., p. 233.
46. *Yorkshire Archaeological Society Record Series Vol. 98: York Civic Records, Vol. I (Transcripts of House Books) 1475–1487*, Raine, A. (ed.), (Yorkshire Archaeological & Historical Society, York, 1939), pp. 73–74.
47. Pollard, A.J., 'Elizabeth Woodville and Her Historians', in Biggs, D. (ed.), *Traditions and Transformations in Late Medieval England*, (Brill, Leiden, 2002), p. 155.
48. Laynesmith, J.L., 'Elizabeth Woodville: The Knight's Widow', p. 233.
49. Leland, J., 'Witchcraft and the Woodvilles: A Standard Medieval Smear?', in Biggs, D., Michalove, S. and Reeves, C. (eds.), *Reputation and Representation in Fifteenth-Century Europe*, (Brill, Leiden, 2004), p. 272.
50. Ibid., pp. 276.
51. Pollard, A.J., 'Elizabeth Woodville and Her Historians', p. 155.
52. Leland, J., 'Witchcraft and the Woodvilles', pp. 275–276.
53. Ashdown-Hill, J., 'Edward IV's Uncrowned Queen: The Lady Eleanor Talbot, Lady Butler', *The Ricardian*, Vol. 11, (1997), p. 166.
54. Okerlund, A., *Elizabeth: England's Slandered Queen*, pp. 233–234.

55. Laynesmith, J.L., 'Elizabeth Woodville: The Knight's Widow', p. 235.
56. Loades, D., *The Tudor Queens of England,* p. 62.
57. Wood, C.T., 'The First Two Queens Elizabeth, 1464–1503', in Fradenburg, L.O.A. (ed.), *Women and Sovereignty* (Edinburgh University Press, Edinburgh, 1992), p. 128.
58. Okerlund, A., *Elizabeth: England's Slandered Queen,* p. 257.

Chapter 14: Margaret Beaufort

1. Jones, M.K. and Underwood, M.G., 'Beaufort, Margaret [known as Lady Margaret Beaufort], Countess of Richmond and Derby', *Oxford Dictionary of National Biography,* (2014), pp. 1–2.
2. *Croyland,* p. 399.
3. Talis, N., *Uncrowned Queen: The Fateful Life of Margaret Beaufort, Tudor Matriarch,* (Michael O'Mara Books, London, 2019), p. 45.
4. Jones, M.K., *The King's Mother: Lady Margaret Beaufort, Countess of Richmond and Derby,* (Cambridge University Press, Cambridge, 1992), p. 35.
5. Ibid., pp. 32–33.
6. Norton, E., *Margaret Beaufort: Mother of the Tudor Dynasty,* (Amberley, Stroud, 2010), p. 27.
7. Mayor, J.E.B. (ed.), *The English Works of John Fisher,* (Trübner, London, 1876), pp. 292–293.
8. Jones, M.K., *The King's Mother,* p. 38.
9. Ibid., p. 95.
10. Gristwood, S., *Blood Sisters,* p. 49.
11. Ibid., p. 49.
12. Jones, M.K., *The King's Mother,* p. 40.
13. Wilson, R.S.K., *Tudor Feminists: Ten Renaissance Women Ahead of Their Time,* (Pen & Sword Books, Barnsley, 2024), pp. 34–35.
14. Jones, M.K., *The King's Mother,* p. 40.
15. Ibid., p. 24.
16. Scofield, C.L., *The Life and Reign of Edward the Fourth,* p. 203.
17. Jones, M.K. and Underwood, M.G., 'Beaufort, Margaret [known as Lady Margaret Beaufort]', p. 3.
18. Jones, M.K., *The King's Mother,* pp. 51–52.
19. Hicks, M., *The Wars of the Roses,* p. 12.
20. Wilson, R.S.K., *Tudor Feminists,* p. 39.
21. Chrimes, S.B., *Henry VII,* (Yale University Press, New Haven and London, 1999), p. 18.
22. Gristwood, S., *Blood Sisters,* p. 126.
23. Jones, M.K., *The King's Mother,* pp. 59–61.
24. Wilson, R.S.K., *Tudor Feminists,* p. 41 .
25. Hicks, M., *Richard III: The Self-Made King,* (Yale University Press, New Haven and London, 2019), pp. 282–283.

26. Simon, L., *Of Virtue Rare: Margaret Beaufort, Matriarch of the House of Tudor*, (Houghton Mifflin, Boston, 1982), pp. 70–71.

27. Gill, L., *Richard III and Buckingham's Rebellion*, (Sutton Publishing, Stroud, 1999), p. 70.

28. Ibid., p. 13.

29. Simon, L., *Of Virtue Rare*, p. 70.

30. Jones, M.K., *The King's Mother*, pp. 63–64.

31. Gill, L., *Richard III and Buckingham's Rebellion*, p. 64.

32. Jones, M.K., *The King's Mother*, p, 64.

33. Hicks, M., *Richard III*, p. 295.

34. Jones, M.K., *The King's Mother*, p. 62.

35. Chrimes, S.B., *Henry VII*, p. 28.

36. Jones, M.K., *The King's Mother*, p. 64.

37. Browne, L.R., 'Elizabeth of York: Tudor Trophy Wife', in Norrie, A., *et al.* (eds.), *Tudor and Stuart Consorts: Power, Influence, and Dynasty*, (Palgrave Macmillan, Cham, 2022), pp. 22–23.

38. Warnicke, R.N., 'Margaret Tudor, Countess of Richmond, and Elizabeth of York: Dynastic Competitors or Allies', in Schutte, V. (ed.), *Unexpected Heirs in Early Modern Europe: Potential Kings and Queens*, (Palgrave Macmillan, New York, 2017), p. 36.

39. Gristwood, S., *Blood Sisters*, p. 223.

40. *Croyland*, p. 501.

41. Wilson, R.S.K., *Tudor Feminists*, pp. 44–45.

42. Jones, M.K., *The King's Mother*, p. 66.

43. Talis, N., *Uncrowned Queen*, p. 15.

44. Okerlund, A., *Elizabeth of York*, (Palgrave Macmillan, Basingstoke, 2009), pp. 94–95.

45. Jones, M.K., *The King's Mother*, p. 67.

46. Mayor, J.E.B. (ed.), *The English Works of John Fisher*, p. xiv.

47. McIntosh, M.K., 'The Benefits and Drawbacks of Femme Sole Status in England, 1300–1630', *Journal of British Studies*, Vol. 44 (2005), p. 410.

48. Jones, M.K., *The King's Mother*, pp. 169–170.

49. Delman, R.M., 'The Vowesses, the Anchoresses and the Aldermen's Wives: Lady Margaret Beaufort and the Devout Society of Late Medieval Stamford', *Urban History*, Vol. 49, (2022), p. 255.

50. Olson, R., 'Margaret Beaufort, Royal Tapestries, and Confinement at the Tudor Court', *Textile History*, Vol. 48, No. 2, (2017), p. 238.

51. Jones, M.K. and Underwood, M.G., 'Beaufort, Margaret [known as Lady Margaret Beaufort]', p. 5.

52. Jones, M.K., *The King's Mother*, p. 87.

53. Licence, A., *Red Roses*, p. 228.

54. Harris, B.J., 'Women and Politics in Early Tudor England', *The Historical Journal*, Vol. 33, No. 2, (1990), p. 264.

55. Fisher, S., '"Margaret R": Lady Margaret Beaufort's Self-fashioning and Female Ambition', in Fleiner, C. and Woodacre, E. (eds.), *Virtuous or Villainess? The Image of the Royal Mother*, (Palgrave Macmillan, New York, 2016), p. 152.

56. Wilson, R.S.K., *Tudor Feminists*, pp. 45–46.
57. Jones, M.K., *The King's Mother*, p. 73.
58. Browne, L.R., 'Elizabeth of York', p. 31.
59. Gristwood, S., *Blood Sisters*, pp. 259–260.
60. *Records of the Borough of Nottingham: Being a Series of Extracts from the Archives of the Corporation of Nottingham, Vol. III*, (Quaritch, London, 1882), p. 301.
61. Okerlund, A., *Elizabeth of York*, p. 97.
62. Bergenroth, G.A. (ed. and trans.), *Calendar of Letters, Despatches, and State Papers, Relating to the Negotiations between England and Spain, Preserved in the Archives at Simancas and Elsewhere*, (Longmans, Green, London, 1862), p. 164.
63. Warnicke, R.N., 'Margaret Tudor', pp. 43–44.
64. See chapter on *Elizabeth of York*.
65. Gristwood, S., *Blood Sisters*, p. 259.
66. Okerlund, A., *Elizabeth of York*, p. 97.
67. Simon, L., *Of Virtue Rare*, pp. 105–106.
68. Ibid., pp. 113–114.
69. Jones, M.K., *The King's Mother*, pp. 157–158.
70. Ibid., pp. 91–92.
71. Ibid., p. 92.
72. Mayor, J.E.B. (ed.), *The English Works of John Fisher*, p. 306.

Chapter 15: Elizabeth of York

1. Okerlund, A., *Elizabeth of York*, p. 2.
2. Loades, D., *The Tudor Queens of England*, p. 73.
3. Okerlund, A., *Elizabeth of York*, pp. 3–4.
4. Okerlund, A., *Elizabeth: England's Slandered Queen*, p. 119.
5. Browne, L.R., 'Elizabeth of York: Tudor Trophy Wife', p. 20.
6. Loades, D., *The Tudor Queens of England*, p. 72.
7. Okerlund, A., *Elizabeth of York*, p. 14.
8. Ibid., p. 72.
9. Adams, B., *Elizabeth of York and the Birth of the Tudor Dynasty: Uniting the Roses*, (Pen & Sword Books, Barnsley, 2025), p. 56.
10. Okerlund, A., *Elizabeth of York*, p. 8.
11. Ibid., pp 9–10.
12. Ibid., pp. 11–12.
13. Harvey, N.L., *Elizabeth of York, Tudor Queen*, (Arthur Barker, London, 1973), pp. 8–9.
14. Warnicke, R.N., 'Margaret Tudor, Countess of Richmond, and Elizabeth of York', p. 48.
15. Crawford, A., *The Yorkists*, p. 8.
16. Okerlund, A., *Elizabeth of York*, pp. 15–16.
17. Langley, P., *The Princes in the Tower: How History's Greatest Cold Case Was Solved*, (The History Press, London, 2023), pp. 61–62.

18. Harvey, N.L., *Elizabeth of York*, p. 92.
19. Loades, D., *The Tudor Queens of England*, pp. 73–74.
20. Wood, C.T., 'The First Two Queens Elizabeth', p. 129.
21. Ibid., p. 129.
22. Bennett, M., 'Henry IV, the Royal Succession and the Crisis of 1406', in Biggs, D., and Dodd, G. (eds.), *The Reign of Henry IV: Rebellion and Survival, 1403–1413*, (Boydell & Brewer, Woodbridge, 2008), p. 9.
23. Wood, C.T., 'The First Two Queens Elizabeth', p. 125.
24. Okerlund, A., *Elizabeth of York*, p. 34.
25. *Croyland*, p. 499.
26. Ibid., pp. 498–499.
27. Horrox, R., 'Elizabeth [Elizabeth of York] (1466–1503), Queen of England, Consort of Henry VII', *Oxford Dictionary of National Biography*, (2020), p. 3.
28. *The History of King Richard the Third (1619) by Sir George Buck*, Kincaid, A.N. (ed.), (Alan Sutton, Stroud, 1982), p. 191 .
29. Hanham, A., 'Sir George Buck and Princess Elizabeth's Letter: A Problem in Detection', *The Ricardian*, Vol. 7, No. 97, (1987), p. 400.
30. Okerlund, A., *Elizabeth of York*, pp. 37–38.
31. Hanham, A., 'Sir George Buck and Princess Elizabeth's Letter', p. 399.
32. *Croyland*, p. 499.
33. Kelly, H.A., 'Canonical Implications of Richard III's Plan to Marry His Niece', *Traditio*, Vol. 23, (1967), p. 307.
34. Wood, C. T., *Joan of Arc and Richard III*, p. 202.
35. *Croyland*, p. 500.
36. Wood, C. T., *Joan of Arc and Richard III*, p. 202.
37. Lockyer, R. and Thrush, A., *Henry VII*, (Routledge, New Haven and London, 1997), p. 7.
38. Ibid., p. 7.
39. Okerlund, A., *Elizabeth of York*, p. 27.
40. Loades, D., *The Tudor Queens of England*, p. 74.
41. Okerlund, A., *Elizabeth of York*, p. 29.
42. Earenfight, T., *Queenship*, p. 218.
43. Okerlund, A., *Elizabeth of York*, p. 40–41.
44. Earenfight, T., *Queenship*, p. 218 .
45. *Croyland*, p. 512.
46. Harvey, N.L., *Elizabeth of York*, pp. 121–122.
47. Okerlund, A., *Elizabeth of York*, p. 48.
48. Laynesmith, J.L., *The Last Medieval Queens*, p. 59.
49. Warnicke, R.N., 'Margaret Tudor, Countess of Richmond, and Elizabeth of York', p. 38.
50. Okerlund, A., *Elizabeth of York*, pp. 47–48.
51. Gristwood, S., *Blood Sisters*, p. 242.
52. Laynesmith, J.L., *The Last Medieval Queens*, p. 81.
53. Lindfield, P.N., *The Marriage Bed of Henry VII and Elizabeth of York: A Masterpiece of Tudor Craftsmanship*, (Oxbow Books, Oxford, 2023), p. 75.

54. Okerlund, A., *Elizabeth of York,* p. 53.
55. Loades, D., *The Tudor Queens of England,* p. 77.
56. Ibid., p. 79.
57. Laynesmith, J.L., *The Last Medieval Queens,* p. 155.
58. Elton, G.R., *England under the Tudors,* (Routledge, New Haven and London, 2018), p. 24.
59. Strickland, A. and Strickland, E., *Lives of the Queens of England,* pp. 429–430.
60. For a recent examination of the possibility that Perkin Warbeck was, in fact, Richard of York, see Langley, P., *The Princes in the Tower.* For a challenge to Langley's hypothesis, see Hicks, M., 'Historic Doubts about the Survival of the Princes in the Tower after 1485', *Historical Research,* Vol. 97, (2024), pp. 437–442.
61. Okerlund, A., *Elizabeth of York,* p. 75.
62. Ibid.
63. Ibid., p. 79.
64. Hammond, P.W., 'The Coronation of Elizabeth of York', *The Ricardian,* Vol 6, No. 83, (1983), pp. 270–272, p. 271.
65. Crawford, A., *The Yorkists,* p. 153.
66. Ibid., p. 154.
67. Okerlund, A., *Elizabeth of York,* pp. 193–193.
68. Ibid., p. 137.
69. Ibid., p. 144.
70. Wood, C.T., 'The First Two Queens Elizabeth', p. 126.
71. Bergenroth, G.A. (ed. and trans.), *Calendar of Letters,* p. 178.
72. Horrox, R., 'Elizabeth [Elizabeth of York] (1466–1503), Queen of England, Consort of Henry VII', *Oxford Dictionary of National Biography,* (2020), pp. 4–5.
73. Bergenroth, G.A. (ed. and trans.), *Calendar of Letters,* p. 178.
74. Okerlund, A., *Elizabeth of York,* p. 57.
75. Loades, D., *The Tudor Queens of England,* p. 78.
76. Crawford, A., *Letters of the Queens of England,* p. 157.
77. Bergenroth, G.A. (ed. and trans.), *Calendar of Letters,* p. 156.
78. Okerlund, A., *Elizabeth of York,* p. 185.
79. Ibid., p. 186.
80. Crawford, A., *The Yorkists,* p. 167.
81. Okerlund, A., *Elizabeth of York,* p. 209 .

Bibliography

Primary Sources

The Alexiad of Anna Comnena, Sewter, E.R.A. (trans.), (Penguin Books, Baltimore, 1969).

Alfred the Great: Asser's Life of King Alfred and Other Contemporary Sources, Keynes, S. and Lapidge, M. (ed. and trans.), (Penguin Books, Harmondsworth, 1983).

The Anglo-Saxon Chronicle, Garmonsway, G.N. (ed. and trans.), (J.M. Dent & Sons, London, 1972).

Annals of Ireland, Three Fragments, Copied from Ancient Sources by Dubhaltach MacFirbisigh; and Edited, with a Translation and Notes, from a Manuscript Preserved in the Burgundian Library at Brussels, (Dublin Irish Archaeological and Celtic Society, Dublin, 1860).

The Anonimalle Chronicle 1307 to 1334 From Brotherton Collection MS 29, Childs, W.R. and Taylor, J. (eds. and trans.), (University of Leeds, Leeds, 1991).

The Book of the City of Ladies, (Christine de Pizan), Richards, E.J. (trans.), (Persea Books, New York, 1982).

The Book of Margery Kempe, Windeatt, B.A. (trans.), (Penguin Classics, London, 2004).

The Book of Margery Kempe, Bale A. (trans.) (Oxford University Press, Oxford, 2015).

Calendar of Letters, Despatches, and State Papers, Relating to the Negotiations between England and Spain, Preserved in the Archives at Simancas and Elsewhere, Bergenroth, G.A. (ed. and trans.), (Longmans, Green, London, 1862).

Calendar of State Papers and Manuscripts Existing in the Archives and Collections of Milan. Vol. I. 1385–1618, Hinds, A.B. (ed.), (HMSO, London, 1912).

Calendar of the Close Rolls, Edward II, 1323–1327, (Public Record Office, London, 1898).

The Chronicle of Geoffrey Le Baker of Swinbrook, Preest, D. and Barber, R. (eds. and trans.), (Boydell & Brewer, Woodbridge, 2012).

The Chronicle of Henry of Huntingdon, Forester, T. (ed. and trans.), (Henry G. Bohn, London, 1853).

The Chronicles of Froissart, Bourcher, J. (trans.), (Macmillan, London, 1895).

The Deeds of Robert Guiscard by William of Apulia, Loud, G.A. (trans.), (Institute for Medieval Studies, University of Leeds, Unpublished Translation) https://eprints.whiterose.ac.uk/id/eprint/211662/ [26 April 2025].

The Ecclesiastical History, Vol. 4, (Orderic Vitalis), Chibnall, M. (ed.), (Oxford University Press, Oxford, 1973).

Encomium Emmae Reginae, Campbell, A. (ed. and trans.), (Cambridge University Press, Cambridge, 1998).

The English Works of John Fisher, Mayor, J.E.B. (ed.), (Trübner, London, 1876).

Gesta Stephani, Potter, K.R. and Davis, R.H.C. (eds. and trans.), (Clarendon Press, Oxford, 1976).

Historia Anglorum: The History of the English People, (Henry, Archdeacon of Huntingdon), Greenway, D. (ed. and trans.), (Oxford: Clarendon Press, 1996).

The History of King Richard the Third (1619) by Sir George Buck, Kincaid, A.N. (ed.), (Alan Sutton, Stroud, 1982).

Ingulph's Chronicle of the Abbey of Croyland, Riley, H.T. (trans.), (H. G. Bohn, London, 1854).

O City of Byzantium: Annals of Niketas Choniatēs, Magoulias, H.J. (trans.), (Wayne State University Press, Detroit, 1984).

Records of the Borough of Nottingham: Being a Series of Extracts from the Archives of the Corporation of Nottingham, Vol. III, (Quaritch, London, 1882).

The Selected Writings of Christine de Pizan, Blumenfeld-Kosinski, R. and Brownlee, K. (eds. and trans.), (W.W. Norton & Company, New York, 1997).

The Trial of Joan of Arc, Hobbins, D. (ed. and trans.), (Harvard University Press, London, 2005).

Vita Edwardi Secundi, Childs, W.R. (ed. and trans.), (Oxford University Press, Oxford, 2005).

William of Tyre, A History of Deeds Done Beyond the Sea, 2 Vols. Babcock, E.A. and Krey, A.C. (eds. and trans.), (Columbia University Press, New York, 1943).

Secondary Sources

Adams, B., *Elizabeth of York and the Birth of the Tudor Dynasty: Uniting the Roses,* (Pen & Sword Books, Barnsley, 2025).

Adams, T., 'Christine de Pizan', *French Studies: A Quarterly Review*, Vol. 71, No. 3, (2017), pp. 388–400.

Adams, T., *Christine de Pizan and the Fight for France,* (Pennsylvania State University Press, Pennsylvania, 2018).

Adams, T., *The Life and Afterlife of Isabeau of Bavaria,* (Johns Hopkins University Press, Baltimore, 2010).

Adams, T. and Rechtschaffen, G., 'Isabeau of Bavaria, Anne of France, and the History of Female Regency in France', *Early Modern Women*, Vol. 8, (2013), pp. 119–147.

Anlezark, D., *Alfred the Great*, (Arc Humanities Press, Kalamazoo, 2017).

Apgar, B., 'Authority and Resistance in the Vita Mathildis (Vat. Lat. 4922)', *Religions*, Vol. 16, No. 3, (2025), pp. 1–23.

Arman, J., *The Warrior Queen: The Life and Legend of Æthelflæd, Daughter of Alfred the Great,* (Amberley, Stroud, 2017).

Arnold, J.H., 'Margery's Trials: Heresy, Lollardy and Dissent', in Arnold, J.H. and Lewis, K.J. (eds.), *A Companion to the Book of Margery Kempe,* (Boydell & Brewer, Woodbridge, 2004), pp. 75–94.

Ashdown-Hill, J., 'Edward IV's Uncrowned Queen: The Lady Eleanor Talbot, Lady Butler', *The Ricardian*, Vol. 11, (1997), pp. 166–190.

Atkinson, C.W., *Mystic and Pilgrim: The Book and the World of Margery Kempe,* (Cornell University Press, Ithaca, 1983).

Aurell, M., 'Eleanor of Aquitaine: The Art of Governing', in Norrie, A., Harris, C., Messer, D.A., Woodacre, E. and Laynesmith, J.L. (eds.), *Norman to Early Plantagenet Consorts: Power, Influence, and Dynasty*, (Palgrave Macmillan, Cham, 2023), pp. 119–137.

Bailey, M., 'Ælfwynn, Second Lady of the Mercians', in Higham, N.J. and Hill, D.H. (eds.), *Edward the Elder: 899–924,* (Routledge, New Haven and London, 2001), pp. 112–127.

Bale, A. and Giousé, D., 'A Women's Network in Fifteenth-Century Rome: Margery Kempe Encounters "Margaret Florentyne"', in Kalas, L. and Varnam, L. (eds.), *Encountering the Book of Margery Kempe*, (Manchester University Press, Manchester, 2021), pp. 185–204.

Balfour, D., '"A Formidable Sight": Sichelgaita of Salerno at Dyrrhachium', *Medieval Warfare*, Vol. 4, No. 2, (2014), pp. 13–18 .

Banham, D., 'Did the Lady of the Mercians Make Her Own Bread? Gender, Status, and Food Production in Early Medieval England', in Hardie, R. (ed.), *Æthelflæd, Lady of the Mercians, and Women in Tenth-Century England,* (Medieval Institute Publications, Boston, 2023), pp. 165–186 .

Barstow, A.L., *Joan of Arc: Heretic, Mystic, Shaman,* (Edwin Mellen Press, New York, 1986).

Beem, C., '"Greater by Marriage": The Matrimonial Career of the Empress Matilda', in Levin, C. and Bucholz, R. (eds.), *Queens and Power in Medieval and Early Modern England,* (University of Nebraska Press, Nebraska, 2009), pp. 1–15.

Beem, C., 'The Virtuous Virago: The Empress Matilda and the Politics of Womanhood in Twelfth-Century England', in Levin, C. and Stewart-Nuz, C. (eds.), *Scholars and Poets Talk about Queens,* (Palgrave Macmillan, Basingstoke, 2015), pp. 85–98.

Bennett, M., 'Henry IV, the Royal Succession and the Crisis of 1406', in Biggs, D., and Dodd, G. (eds.), *The Reign of Henry IV: Rebellion and Survival, 1403–1413,* (Boydell & Brewer, Woodbridge, 2008), pp. 9–27.

Blake, M. and Sargent, A., '"For the Protection of All the People": Æthelflæd and Her Burhs in Northwest Mercia', *Midland History,* Vol. 43, No. 2, (2018), pp. 120–154.

Blumenthal, U.R., *The Investiture Controversy: Church and Monarchy from the Ninth to the Twelfth Century,* (University of Pennsylvania Press, Philadelphia, 1988).

Böhm, M., 'Nikephoros Bryennios the Younger – the First One Not to Become a Blind Man? Political and Military History of the Bryennios Family in the 11th and Early 12th Century', *Studia Ceranea,* Vol. 10, (2020), pp. 31–45 .

Bolton, T., 'Ælfgifu of Northampton: Cnut the Great's "Other Woman"', *Nottingham Medieval Studies*, Vol. 51, No. 1, (2007), p. 247–268 .

Bowers, T.N., 'Margery Kempe as Traveler', *Studies in Philology*, Vol. 97, No. 1 (2000), pp. 1–28.

Bradbury, J., *Stephen and Matilda: The Civil War of 1139–53*, (Alan Sutton Publishing, Stroud, 1996).

Brauer, M., 'Politics or Leisure? A Day in the Life of King Charles V of France (1364–80)', *The Medieval History Journal*, (2015, 18 Vol. 1), pp. 46–63.

Broad, J., and Green, K., *A History of Women's Political Thought in Europe, 1400–1700*. (Cambridge University Press, Cambridge, 2009).

Brown, A.R., 'The Political Repercussions of Family Ties in the Early Fourteenth Century: The Marriage of Edward II of England and Isabelle of France', *Speculum*, Vol. 63, No. 3 (1988), pp. 573–595.

Brown, E.A., 'Eleanor of Aquitaine: Parent, Queen, and Duchess', in Kibler, W. (ed.), *Eleanor of Aquitaine: Patron and Politician*, (University of Texas Press, New York, 1976), pp. 9–34.

Brown, P., 'The *Gesta Roberti Wiscardi:* A "Byzantine" History?', *Journal of Medieval History*, Vol. 37, No. 2, (2011), pp. 162–179.

Brown-Grant, R., *Christine de Pizan and the Moral Defence of Women: Reading Beyond Gender*, (Cambridge University Press, Cambridge, 2001).

Browne, L.R., 'Elizabeth of York: Tudor Trophy Wife', in Norrie, A., Harris, C., Laynesmith, J. L., Messer, D. R. and Woodacre, E. (eds.), *Tudor and Stuart Consorts: Power, Influence, and Dynasty*, (Palgrave Macmillan, Cham, 2022), pp. 19–40.

Browning, R., 'An Unpublished Funeral Oration on Anna Comnena', *Proceedings of the Cambridge Philological Society,* Vol. 188, No. 8, (1962), pp. 1–12.

Bryce, J., 'The Papacy Master of the Field', in Morrison, K.F. (ed.), *The Investiture Controversy: Issues, Ideals, and Results,* (Holt, Rinehart and Winston, New York, 1971).

Buckler, G., *Anna Comnena: A Study*, (Oxford University Press, Oxford, 2000).

Butler, E., 'Authority and Language in the Encomium Emmae Reginae', *English Studies*, Vol. 101, No. 1, (2020), pp. 6–22.

Carmi Parson, J., 'Isabella [Isabella of France]', *Oxford Dictionary of National Biography,* (2018).

Carpenter, C. (ed.), *Kingsford's Stonor Letters and Papers, 1290–1483,* (Cambridge University Press, Cambridge, 1996).

Carpenter, D.A., *The Struggle for Mastery: Britain, 1066–1284,* (Oxford University Press, Oxford, 2003).

Carver, M., 'Living in a Material World: Æthelflæd's Archaeology', in Hardie, R. (ed.), *Æthelflæd, Lady of the Mercians, and Women in Tenth-Century England,* (Medieval Institute Publications, Boston, 2023), pp. 31–57.

Cassagnes-Brouquet, S. and Greer, M., 'In the Service of the Just War: Matilda of Tuscany (Eleventh-Twelfth Centuries)', *Clio (English Edition)*, No. 39, (2014), pp. 35–52.

Castor, H., *Joan of Arc: A History,* (Faber & Faber, London, 2014).

Castor, H., *She-Wolves: The Women Who Ruled England Before Elizabeth,* (HarperCollins, New York, 2012).

Cavendish, R., 'The St Brice's Day Massacre', *History Today*, Vol. 52, (2002), pp. 62–63.

Chamberlayne, J.L., 'Crowns and Virgins: Queen Making During the Wars of the Roses', in Lewis, K.J., Menuge, N.J. and Phillips, K.M. (eds.), *Young Medieval Women*, (St. Martin's Press, New York, 1999), pp. 47–68.

Chambers, F.M., 'Some Legends Concerning Eleanor of Aquitaine', *Speculum*, Vol. 16, No. 4, (1941), pp. 459–468.

Chance, J., 'Christine de Pizan as Literary Mother: Women's Authority and Subjectivity in "The Floure and the Leafe" and "The Assembly of Ladies"', in Zimmermann, M. and De Rentiis, D. (eds.), *The City of Scholars: New Approaches to Christine de Pizan*, (Walter de Gruyter, Berlin, 1994), pp. 246–259.

Chibnall, M., 'Matilda [Matilda of England]', *Oxford Dictionary of National Biography*, (2004).

Chibnall, M., *The Empress Matilda, Queen Consort, Queen Mother and Lady of the English*, (Blackwell Publishing, Oxford, 1992).

Childs, W.R., 'Chronicles and Politics in the Reign of Edward II', in Burton, J., Marx, W. and O'Mara, V. (eds.), *Leeds Studies in English New Series XLI*, (School of English, University of Leeds, 2010), pp. 45–55.

Chrimes, S.B., *Henry VII*, (Yale University Press, New Haven and London, 1999).

Cook, C. H., *Hearing Spiritual Voices: Medieval Mystics, Meaning and Psychiatry*, (Bloomsbury Publishing, London, 2023).

Cook, D.R., *Lancastrians and Yorkists: The Wars of the Roses*, (Routledge, New Haven and London, 1984).

Cooper, G.M., 'Byzantium between East and West: Competing Hellenisms in the *Alexiad* of Anna Komnene and her Contemporaries', in Classen, A. (ed.), *East Meets West in the Middle Ages and Early Modern Times: Transcultural Experiences in the Premodern World*, (De Gruyter, Inc., Berlin, 2013), pp. 263–290.

Cooper-Davis, C., *Christine de Pizan: Life, Work, Legacy*, (Reaktion Books, London, 2021).

Costambeys, M., 'Æthelflæd', *Oxford Dictionary of National Biography*, (2018).

Couch, D., 'Robert, First Earl of Gloucester', *Oxford Dictionary of National Biography*, (2006).

Covert, A., 'Sine Communi Favore: The Intersection of Power, Perception, and Sexual Morality in the Careers of Piers Gaveston and the "Royal Favourites" of Fourteenth-Century England', in Storey, G. and Rohr, Z.E. (eds.), *Premodern Ruling Sexualities: Representation, Identity, and Power*, (Manchester University Press, Manchester, 2024), pp. 232–251.

Cowdrey, H.E.J., *Pope Gregory VII, 1073–1085*, (Oxford University Press, Oxford, 1998).

Cowdrey, H.E.J., *The Age of Abbot Desiderius*, (Oxford University Press, Oxford, 1983).

Crawford, A., *Letters of the Queens of England 1100–1547*, (Sutton Publishing, Stroud, 1997).

Crawford, A., *The Yorkists: The History of a Dynasty*, (Bloomsbury Publishing, London, 2007).

Creber, A., 'The Princely Woman and the Emperor: Imagery of Female Rule in Benzo of Alba's Ad Heinricum IV', *Royal Studies Journal, Vol.* 5, No. 2, (2018), pp. 7–26.

Creber, A., 'Women at Canossa: The Role of Royal and Aristocratic Women in the Reconciliation Between Pope Gregory VII and Henry IV of Germany', *Storicamente,* (2005), pp. 1–44.

Cruse, M., 'The Louvre of Charles V: Legitimacy, Renewal, and Royal Presence in Fourteenth-Century Paris', *L'Esprit Créateur,* Vol. 54, No. 2, (2014), pp.19–32.

De Beauvoir, S., *The Second Sex,* (Vintage Books, London, 2014).

Dean, S.E., 'The Treason Against Edward II: Favourites and Feuds', *Medieval Warfare,* Vol. 5, No. 1, (2015), pp. 28–35.

Delany, S., '"Mothers to Think Back Through", Who Are They? The Ambiguous Example of Christine de Pizan', in Blumenfeld-Kosinski, R. and Brownlee, K. (eds. and trans.), *The Selected Writings of Christine De Pizan,* (W.W. Norton & Company, New York, 1997), pp. 312–329.

Delany, S., 'Sexual Economics, Chaucer's Wife of Bath and *The Book of Margery Kempe',* in Evans, R. and Johnson, L. (eds.), *Feminist Readings in Middle English Literature: The Wife of Bath and All Her Sect,* (Routledge, New Haven and London, 1994), pp. 72–87.

Delman, R.M., 'The Vowesses, the Anchoresses and the Aldermen's Wives: Lady Margaret Beaufort and the Devout Society of Late Medieval Stamford', *Urban History,* Vol. 49, (2022), pp. 248–264.

DeVries, K., *Joan of Arc: A Military Leader,* (Sutton Publishing, Stroud, 1999).

Doherty, P., *Isabella and the Strange Death of Edward II,* (Constable & Robinson, London, 2013).

Donald, M., *The Norman Kingdom of Sicily,* (Cambridge University Press, Cambridge, 1992).

Drell, J.H., *Kinship and Conquest: Family Strategies in the Principality of Salerno During the Norman Period, 1077–1194,* (Cornell University Press, Ithaca, 2002).

Dunn, D., 'Margaret [Margaret of Anjou]', *Oxford Dictionary of National Biography,* (2004).

Dunn, D., '"The Principal Place of Honour about the Person of the Queen". Margaret of Anjou and Alice Chaucer, Duchess of Suffolk: The Making of a Friendship', in Clark, L., Condon, M., Cunningham, S., Dunn, D., Flannigan, L., Griffiths, R., Gross, A., Lane, S., Payling, S., Powell, E., Rawcliffe, C., Ross, J. and Vale, M. (eds.), *The Fifteenth Century XX: Essays presented to Rowena E. Archer.* (Boydell & Brewer, Woodbridge, 2024), pp. 46–66.

Dunn, D., 'The Queen at War: The Role of Margaret of Anjou in the Wars of the Roses', in Dunn, D. (ed.), *War and Society in Medieval and Early Modern Britain,* (Liverpool University Press, Liverpool, 2000), pp. 141–161.

Eads, V., 'Means, Motive, Opportunity: Medieval Women and the Recourse to Arms', *Paper Presented at The Twentieth Barnard Medieval & Renaissance Conference 'War and Peace in the Middle Ages & Renaissance',* (2 December 2006). Found at: http://www.deremilitari.org/wp-content/uploads/2012/09/Eads-MeansMotivesOpp.pdf [Accessed 13 June 2024].

Eads, V., 'Sichelgaita of Salerno: Amazon or Trophy Wife?', in Devries, K. and Rogers, C.J. (eds.), *Journal of Medieval Military History*, (Boydell & Brewer, Woodbridge, 2005), pp. 72–87.

Eads, V., 'The Last Italian Expedition of Henry IV: Re-reading the Vita Mathildis of Donizone of Canossa', in Rogers, C.J., Devries, K. and France, J. (eds.), *Journal of Medieval Military History,* (Boydell & Brewer, Woodbridge, 2010), pp. 23–68.

Earenfight, T., *Queenship in Medieval Europe*, (Palgrave Macmillan, Basingstoke, 2013).

Elton, G.R., *England under the Tudors,* (Routledge, New Haven and London, 2018).

Erler, M.C., 'Margery Kempe's White Clothes', *Medium Aevum,* Vol. 62, (1993), pp. 78–83.

Evans, M., 'Penthesilea on the Second Crusade: Is Eleanor of Aquitaine the Amazon Queen of Niketas Choniatēs?', *Crusades*, Vol. 8, No. 1, (2009), pp. 23–30.

Evans, M.R., *Inventing Eleanor: The Medieval and Post-Medieval Image of Eleanor of Aquitaine,* (Bloomsbury Publishing, London, 2016).

Evans, M.R., 'Isabella of France and Roger Mortimer: Lovers or Allies?', in Storey, G. and Rohr, Z.E., (eds.), *Premodern Ruling Sexualities: Representation, Identity, and Power,* (Manchester University Press, Manchester, 2024), pp. 89–104.

Evans, M.R., 'Isabella of France: She-Wolf and Rebel Queen?', in Harris, C., Woodacre, E., Norrie, A., Messer, D.R., and Laynesmith, J.L. (eds.), *Later Plantagenet and the Wars of the Roses Consorts*, (Palgrave Macmillan, Cham, 2023), pp. 27–47.

Evans, M.R., 'The Missing Queen? Eleanor of Aquitaine in the Early Reign of Louis VII', in Bardot, M.L., and Marvin, L.W. (eds.), *Louis VII and His World*, (Brill, Leiden, 2018), pp. 105–113.

Firth, A.S., *The Creation of the Jerusalemite Dynasty in the Twelfth Century: Kingship, Military Masculinity and Fatherhood in William of Tyre's Historia,* (Unpublished Ph.D. Dissertation, University of Huddersfield, 2016).

Firth, M., *Early English Queens, 850–1000: Potestas Reginae,* (Routledge, New Haven and London, 2013).

Firth, M., 'On the Dating of the Norse Siege of Chester' *Notes and Queries,* Vol. 69 No. 1, (2022), pp. 1–4 .

Fisher, S., '"Margaret R": Lady Margaret Beaufort's Self-fashioning and Female Ambition', in Fleiner, C. and Woodacre, E. (eds.), *Virtuous or Villainess? The Image of the Royal Mother,* (Palgrave Macmillan, New York, 2016), pp. 151–172.

Fitzpatrick, J., 'Reimagining This Creature: Hospitality and Autohagiography in the Visions of Margery Kempe', *History*, Vol. 106, (2021), pp. 561–577.

Foot, S., 'Æthelstan', *Oxford Dictionary of National Biography,* (2011).

Foot, S., *Æthelstan: The First King of England,* (Yale University Press, New Haven and London, 2011).

Frankopan, P., 'Perception and Projection of Prejudice: Anna Comnena, the *Alexiad* and the First Crusade', in Edgington, S.B. and Lambert, S. (eds.), *Gendering the Crusades*, (Columbia University Press, New York, 2002), pp. 59–76.

Frick, D., *Authority and Authorship in Medieval and Seventeenth-Century Women's Visionary Writings,* (Transcript Verlag, Bielefeld, 2021).

Garland, L., *Byzantine Empresses: Women and Power in Byzantium, AD 527–1204*, (Routledge, New Haven and London, 1999).

Garland, L. and Rapp, S., '"Mary of Alania": Woman and Empress Between Two Worlds', in Garland, L. (ed.), *Byzantine Women: Varieties of Experience 800–1200*, (Ashgate, Aldershot, 2006), pp. 91–124.

Geaman, K., 'A Bastard and a Changeling? England's Edward of Westminster and Delayed Childbirth', in Schutte, V. (ed.), *Unexpected Heirs in Early Modern Europe: Potential Kings and Queens*, (Palgrave Macmillan, New York, 2017), pp. 11–34.

Gibbons, R., 'Isabeau of Bavaria, Queen of France (1385–1422): The Creation of an Historical Villainess', *Transactions of the Royal Historical Society*, Vol. 6, (1996), pp. 51–73.

Gies, F., *Joan of Arc: The Legend and the Reality*, (Harper & Row, New York, 1981).

Gill, L., *Richard III and Buckingham's Rebellion*, (Sutton Publishing, Stroud, 1999).

Gillingham, J., *Richard I*, (Yale University Press, New Haven and London, 1999).

Gillingham, J., *The Angevin Empire*, (Oxford University Press, New York, 2001).

Gillis, F.M., 'Matilda, Countess of Tuscany', *The Catholic Historical Review*, Vol. 10, No. 2, (1924), pp. 234–245.

Goodman, A.E., *Margery Kempe and Her World*, (Routledge, New Haven and London, 2002).

Gottlieb, B., 'The Problem of Feminism in the Fifteenth Century', in Blumenfeld-Kosinski, R. and Brownlee, K. (eds. and trans.), *The Selected Writings of Christine De Pizan*, (W.W. Norton & Company, New York, 1997), pp. 274–296.

Griffiths, R.A., 'Henry VI', *Oxford Dictionary of National Biography*, (2015).

Griffiths, R.A., *The Making of the Tudor Dynasty*, (Sutton Publishing, Stroud, 1987).

Griffiths, R.A., *The Reign of King Henry VI: The Exercise of Royal Authority, 1422–1461*, (University of California Press, Berkeley, 1981).

Gristwood, S., *Blood Sisters: The Women Behind the Wars of the Roses*, (Basic Books, New York, 2013).

Guerri, F., 'Nihil Terrenum, Nihilque Carnale in Ea: Matilda of Tuscany and Anselm of Lucca during the Investiture Controversy', *Storicamente*, Vol. 31, (2017), pp. 1–37.

Gunn, S., *Henry VII's New Men and the Making of Tudor England*, (Oxford University Press, Oxford, 2016).

Haines, R.M., *King Edward II: Edward of Caernarfon, His Life, His Reign, and Its Aftermath, 1284–1330*, (McGill-Queen's University Press, Montreal and Kingston, 2003).

Hammond, P.W., 'The Coronation of Elizabeth of York', *The Ricardian*, Vol 6, No. 83, (1983), pp. 270–272.

Hanham, A., 'Sir George Buck and Princess Elizabeth's Letter: A Problem in Detection', *The Ricardian*, Vol. 7, No. 97, (1987), pp. 398–400.

Hanley, C., *Matilda: Empress, Queen, Warrior*, (Yale University Press, New Haven and London, 2019).

Hardie, R., 'Æthelflæd Then and Now: Introduction', in Hardie, R. (ed.), *Æthelflæd, Lady of the Mercians, and Women in Tenth-Century England*, (Medieval Institute Publications, Boston, 2023), pp. 1–27.

Harris, B.J., 'Women and Politics in Early Tudor England', *The Historical Journal*, Vol. 33, No. 2, (1990), pp. 259–281.

Harvey, N.L., *Elizabeth of York, Tudor Queen,* (Arthur Barker, London, 1973).

Herdam, A. and Smallwood, D.J., 'The Queen from the South: Eleanor of Aquitaine as a Political Strategist and Lawmaker', in Gilleir, A. and Defurne, A. (eds.), *Strategic Imaginations: Women and the Gender of Sovereignty in European Culture,* (Leuven University Press, Leuven, 2020), pp. 159–180.

Herrin, J., *Unrivalled Influence: Women and Empire in Byzantium,* (Princeton University Press, Princeton, 2013).

Heyam, K., *The Reputation of Edward II, 1305–1697: A Literary Transformation of History*, (Amsterdam University Press, Leiden, 2020).

Hicklin, A., 'Æthelflaed and Female Power in Tenth-Century Europe', in Hardie, R. (ed.), *Æthelflæd, Lady of the Mercians, and Women in Tenth-Century England,* (Medieval Institute Publications, Boston, 2023), pp. 89–112.

Hicks, M., 'Elizabeth [née Elizabeth Woodville]', *Oxford Dictionary of National Biography*, (2011).

Hicks, M., 'Historic Doubts about the Survival of the Princes in the Tower after 1485', *Historical Research*, Vol. 97, (2024), pp. 437–442.

Hicks, M., *Richard III: The Self-Made King*, (Yale University Press, New Haven and London, 2019).

Hicks, M., *The Wars of the Roses, 1455–1485*, (Yale University Press, New Haven and London, 2012).

Hicks-Bartlett, A., 'War, Tears, and Corporeal Response in Christine de Pizan', in Davies, D. and Perry, R.D. (eds.), *Literatures of the Hundred Years War,* (Manchester University Press, Manchester, 2024), pp. 241–268.

Hill, B., 'Actions Speak Louder than Words: Anna Komnene's Attempted Usurpation', in Gouma-Peterson, T. (ed.), *Anna Komnene and Her Times*, (Garland Publishing, New York, 2000), pp. 45–62.

Hinde Stewart, J., 'The Maid and the Milkmaid: Joan of Arc and Marie Antoinette', *The French Review,* Vol. 93, No. 4, (May 2020), pp. 13–30.

Hindman, S.L., 'With Ink and Mortar: Christine de Pizan's *Cité des Dames*', *Feminist Studies*, Vol. 10, No. 3, (1984), pp. 457–83.

Hodgson, N.R., *Women, Crusading and the Holy Land in Historical Narrative,* (Boydell & Brewer, Woodbridge, 2007).

Hoffman, B., *They Never Reigned: Heirs to the British Throne Who Never Became the Monarch*, (Austin Macauley Publishers, London, 2023).

Hollister, W.C. and Keefe, T.K., 'The Making of the Angevin Empire', *Journal of British Studies,* Vol. 12, No. 2, (1973), pp 1–25.

Holman, B.L., '*Exemplum* and *Imitatio*: Countess Matilda and Lucrezia Pico della Mirandola at Polirone', *The Art Bulletin*, Vol. 81, No. 4, (1999), pp. 637–664.

Horrox, R., 'Edward IV', *Oxford Dictionary of National Biography*, (2011).

Horrox, R., 'Elizabeth [Elizabeth of York] (1466–1503), Queen of England, Consort of Henry VII', *Oxford Dictionary of National Biography,* (2020).

Howard, I., *Harthacnut: The Last Danish King of England*, (The History Press, Cheltenham, 2008).

Howard-Johnston, J., 'Anna Komnene and the Alexiad', in Mullett, M. and Smythe, D. (eds.), *Alexios I Komnenos: Papers on the Second Belfast Byzantine International Colloquium, 14–16 April 1989*, (Belfast Byzantine Enterprises, Belfast, 1996), pp. 260–302.

Howell, M., 'Eleanor [Eleanor of Aquitaine], *suo jure* Duchess of Aquitaine', Oxford *Dictionary of National Biography*, (2004).

Hult, D.F. (ed. and trans.), *Debate of the Romance of the Rose*, (University of Chicago Press, Chicago, 2010).

Huneycutt, L.L., 'Female Succession and the Language of Power in the Writings of twelfth-century Churchmen', in Parsons, J.C. (ed.), *Medieval Queenship*, (Alan Sutton Publishing, Stroud, 1994), pp. 189–201.

Huneycutt, L.L., 'Intercession and the High-Medieval Queen: The Esther Topos', in Carpenter, J. and MacLean, S.B. (eds.), *Power of the Weak: Studies on Medieval Women*, (University of Illinois Press, Urbana and Chicago, 1995), pp. 126–146.

Huneycutt, L.L., *Matilda of Scotland: A Study in Medieval Queenship*, (Boydell & Brewer, Woodbridge, 2003).

Insley, C., 'Collapse, Reconfiguration or Renegotiation? The Strange End of the Mercian Kingdom, 850–924', *Reti Medievali Rivista*, Vol. 17, No. 2, (2016), pp. 231–249.

Jenkins, J., 'Reading and the Book of Margery Kempe', in Arnold, J.H. and Lewis, K.J. (eds.), *A Companion to the Book of Margery Kempe*, (Boydell & Brewer, Woodbridge, 2004), pp. 113–128.

John, L.B.S., 'In the Best Interest of the Queen: Isabella of France, Edward II and the Image of a Functional Relationship', in Hamilton, J.S., *Fourteenth Century England VIII*, (Boydell & Brewer, Woodbridge, 2014), pp. 21–42.

John, L.B.S., *Three Medieval Queens: Queenship and the Crown in Fourteenth-Century England*, (Palgrave Macmillan, Basingstoke, 2012).

Johnstone, H., 'Isabella, The She-Wolf of France', *History*, Vol. 21, (1936), pp. 208–218.

Johnstone, H., 'The Eccentricities of Edward II', *The English Historical Review*, Vol. 48, (1933), pp. 264–267.

Jones, M.K., *The King's Mother: Lady Margaret Beaufort, Countess of Richmond and Derby*, (Cambridge University Press, Cambridge, 1992).

Jones, M.K. and Underwood, M.G., 'Beaufort, Margaret [known as Lady Margaret Beaufort], Countess of Richmond and Derby', *Oxford Dictionary of National Biography*, (2014).

Kelly, H.A., 'Canonical Implications of Richard III's Plan to Marry His Niece', *Traditio*, Vol. 23, (1967), pp. 269–311.

Keynes, S., 'A Tale of Two Kings: Alfred the Great and Æthelred the Unready', *Transactions of the Royal Historical Society*, Vol. 36, No. 12, (1986), pp. 195–217.

Keynes, S., 'Emma [Ælfgifu]', *Oxford Dictionary of National Biography*, (2014).

Kibbee, D.A., *For to Speke Frenche Trewely: The French Language in England, 1000–1600. Its Status, Description and Instruction*, (John Benjamins Publishing Company, Philadelphia, 1991).

King, E., *King Stephen*, (Yale University Press, New Haven and London, 2011).

Klimek, K., 'Æthelflæd: History and Legend', *Quidditas,* 34, (2013), pp. 11–28.

Laiou, A.E., 'Introduction: Why Anna Komnene?', in Gouma-Peterson, T. (ed.), *Anna Komnene and Her Times*, (Garland Publishing, New York, 2000), pp. 1–14.

Langdon Forhan, K., 'Reflecting Heroes. Christine de Pizan and the Mirror Tradition' in Margarete Zimmermann, M. and De Rentiis, D. (eds.), *The City of Scholars: New Approaches to Christine de Pizan*, (Walter de Gruyter, Berlin, 1994), pp. 189–196.

Langley, P., *The Princes in the Tower: How History's Greatest Cold Case Was Solved*, (The History Press, London, 2023).

Lawrence, M., 'Rise of a Royal Favourite: The Early Career of Hugh Despenser the Elder', in Dodd, G. and Musson, A. (eds.), *The Reign of Edward II: New Perspectives*, (Boydell & Brewer, Woodbridge, 2006), pp. 205–219.

Laynesmith, J.L., *Cecily, Duchess of York*, (Bloomsbury Publishing, London, 2017).

Laynesmith, J.L., 'Elizabeth Woodville: The Knight's Widow', in Harris, C., Woodacre, E., Norrie, A., Messer, D.R., and Laynesmith, J.L. (eds.), *Later Plantagenet and the Wars of the Roses Consorts,* (Palgrave Macmillan, Cham, 2023), pp. 215–236.

Laynesmith, J.L., *The Last Medieval Queens*, (Oxford University Press, Oxford, 2006).

Lee, P.A., 'Reflections of Power: Margaret of Anjou and the Dark Side of Queenship', *Renaissance Quarterly,* Vol. 39, No. 2, (1986), pp. 183–217.

Leland, J., 'Witchcraft and the Woodvilles: A Standard Medieval Smear?', in Biggs, D., Michalove, S. and Reeves, C. (eds.), *Reputation and Representation in Fifteenth-Century Europe,* (Brill, Leiden, 2004), pp. 267–288.

Levin, C., 'Margaret of Anjou: Passionate Mother', in Harris, C., Woodacre, E., Norrie, A., Messer, D.R., and Laynesmith, J.L. (eds.), *Later Plantagenet and the Wars of the Roses Consorts*, (Palgrave Macmillan, Cham, 2023), pp. 195–213.

Lewis, K.J., *Kingship and Masculinity in Late Medieval England*, (Routledge, New Haven and London, 2013).

Lewis, M., *Stephen and Matilda's Civil War,* (Pen & Sword Books, Barnsley, 2020).

Licence, A., *Red Roses: Blanche of Gaunt to Margaret Beaufort*, (The History Press, London, 2016).

Lindfield, P.N., *The Marriage Bed of Henry VII and Elizabeth of York: A Masterpiece of Tudor Craftsmanship,* (Oxbow Books, Oxford, 2023).

Loades, D., *The Tudor Queens of England,* (Bloomsbury Publishing, New York, 2010).

Lochrie, K., *Margery Kempe and the Translations of the Flesh,* (University of Pennsylvania Press, Philadelphia, 1994).

Lockyer, R. and Thrush, A., *Henry VII*, (Routledge, New Haven and London, 1997).

Long, J., 'Mysticism and Hysteria: The Histories of Margery Kempe and Anna O', in Evans, R. and Johnson, L. (eds.), *Feminist Readings in Middle English Literature: The Wife of Bath and All Her Sect*, (Routledge, New Haven and London, 1994), pp. 88–111.

Loud, G.A., *The Age of Robert Guiscard: Southern Italy and the Northern Conquest,* (Routledge, New Haven and London, 2013).

Maddock, S., 'Margery Kempe's Home Town and Worthy Kin', in Kalas, L. and Varnam, L. (eds.), *Encountering the Book of Margery Kempe*, (Manchester University Press, Manchester, 2021), pp. 163–184.

Marafioti, N., *The King's Body: Burial and Succession in Late Anglo-Saxon England*, (University of Toronto Press, Toronto, 2014).

Margolis, N., 'Royal Biography as Reliquary: Christine de Pizan's *Livre des Fais et bonnes meurs du sage roy Charles V*', in Bradbury, N. and Adams, J. (eds.), *Medieval Women and Their Objects*, (University of Michigan Press, Michigan, 2020), pp. 123–143.

Maurer, H., 'Delegitimizing Lancaster: The Yorkist Use of Gendered Propaganda During the Wars of the Roses', in Biggs, D., Michalove, S. and Reeves, C. (eds.), *Reputation and Representation in Fifteenth-Century Europe*, (Brill, Leiden, 2004), pp. 169–186.

Maurer, H.E., *Margaret of Anjou: Queenship and Power in Late Medieval England*, (Boydell & Brewer, Woodbridge, 2005).

McGrady, D., *The Writer's Gift or the Patron's Pleasure?: The Literary Economy in Late Medieval France*, (University of Toronto Press, Toronto, 2019).

McIntosh, M.K., 'The Benefits and Drawbacks of Femme Sole Status in England, 1300–1630', *Journal of British Studies*, Vol. 44 (2005), pp. 410–438.

McNamara, J.A., 'Canossa and the Ungendering of the Public Man', in Berman, C.H. (ed.), *Medieval Religion: New Approaches. (Rewriting Histories)*, (Routledge, New Haven and London, 2005), pp. 102–122.

McWebb, C., 'Joan of Arc and Christine de Pizan: The Symbiosis of Two Warriors in the Ditié de Jehanne d'Arc', in Wheeler, B. and Wood, C.T. (eds.), *Fresh Verdicts on Joan of Arc*, (Garland, New York, 1996), pp. 133–144.

Menache, S., 'Isabella of France, Queen of England: A Postscript', *Revue Belge de Philologie et d'Histoire*, Vol. 90, No. 2, (2012), pp. 493–512.

Moore, I., *The First European Revolution, c.970–1215*, (Blackwell Publishing, Oxford, 2000).

Morrical, M., *Usurpers, A New Look at Medieval Kings*, (Pen & Sword Books, Barnsley, 2021).

Mortimer, I., 'Sermons of Sodomy: A Reconsideration of Edward II's Sodomitical Reputation', in Dodd, G. and Musson, A. (eds.), *The Reign of Edward II: New Perspectives*, (Boydell & Brewer, Woodbridge, 2006), pp. 48–60.

Mortimer, I., 'The Death of Edward II in Berkeley Castle', *English Historical Review*, Vol. 120, No. 489, (2005), pp. 1175–1214.

Mortimer, I., *The Greatest Traitor: The Life of Sir Roger Mortimer, 1st Earl of March*, (Random House, London, 2010).

Nash, P., *Empress Adelheid and Countess Matilda: Medieval Female Rulership and the Foundations of European Society*, (Palgrave Macmillan, New York, 2017).

Naylor, P.C., 'Joan of Arc's Mystery, History, and Intelligibility', in Tallon, M.E., *Joan of Arc at the University*, (Marquette University Press, Milwaukee, 1997), pp. 35–41.

Nicholson, H.J., *Women and the Crusades*, (Oxford University Press, Oxford, 2023).

Norton, E., *Margaret Beaufort: Mother of the Tudor Dynasty*, (Amberley, Stroud, 2010).

Okerlund, A., *Elizabeth: England's Slandered Queen*, (Tempus, Stroud, 2006).

Okerlund, A., *Elizabeth of York*, (Palgrave Macmillan, Basingstoke, 2009).

Olson, R., 'Margaret Beaufort, Royal Tapestries, and Confinement at the Tudor Court', *Textile History*, Vol. 48, No. 2, (2017), pp. 233–247.

Orchard, A., 'The Literary Background to the "Encomium Emmae Reginae"', *The Journal of Medieval Latin*, Vol. 11, (2001), pp. 156–183.

Orgelfinger, G., *Joan of Arc in the English Imagination, 1429–1829,* (Pennsylvania State University Press, Pennsylvania, 2019).

Ormrod, W.M., *Edward III*, (Yale University Press, New Haven and London, 2012).

Owen, D.D.R., *Eleanor of Aquitaine, Queen and Legend*, (Blackwell Publishing, Oxford, 2000).

Paakkinen, I., 'The Metaphysics of Gender in Christine de Pizan's Thought', in Muravyeva, M. and Toivo, M.R. (eds.), *Gender in Late Medieval and Early Modern Europe*, (Routledge, New Haven and London, 2013), pp. 37–52.

Park, H., 'Mealtime Sanctity: The Devotional and Social Significance of Mealtimes in *The Book of Margery Kempe', Parergon*, Vol. 36, (2019), pp. 61–80.

Phillips, K.M., 'Margery Kempe and the Ages of Woman', in Arnold, J.H. and Lewis, K.J. (eds.), *A Companion to the Book of Margery Kempe,* (Boydell & Brewer, Woodbridge, 2004), pp. 17–34.

Phillips, S., *Edward II*, (Yale University Press, New Haven and London, 2012).

Pollard, A.J., 'Elizabeth Woodville and Her Historians', in Biggs, D. (ed.), *Traditions and Transformations in Late Medieval England,* (Brill, Leiden, 2002), pp. 145–158.

Poulet, A., 'Capetian Women and the Regency: The Genesis of a Vocation', in Parsons, J.C. (ed.), *Medieval Queenship,* (Alan Sutton Publishing, Stroud, 1994), pp. 93–116.

Rabin, A., 'The Charters of Æthelflæd', in Hardie, R. (ed.), *Æthelflæd, Lady of the Mercians, and Women in Tenth-Century England,* (Medieval Institute Publications, Boston, 2023), pp. 113–136.

Raffensperger, C., 'The Missing Russian Women: The Case of Evpraksia Vsevolodovna', in Goldy, C.N. and Livingstone, A. (eds.), *Writing Medieval Women's Lives,* (Palgrave Macmillan, Basingstoke, 2012), pp. 70–84.

Raine, A. (ed.), *Yorkshire Archaeological Society Record Series Vol. 98: York Civic Records, Vol. I (Transcripts of House Books) 1475–1487,* (Yorkshire Archaeological & Historical Society, York, 1939).

Richards, E.J. 'Introduction', in Richards, E.J. (ed. and trans.), *The Book of the City of Ladies: Christine de Pizan,* (Persea Books, New York, 1982).

Roach, L., *Æthelred: The Unready,* (Yale University Press, New Haven and London, 2016).

Robinson, I.S., *Henry IV of Germany 1056–1106,* (Cambridge University Press, Cambridge, 2003).

Ross, C., *Edward IV,* (Eyre Methuen, London, 1974).

Rubin, M., 'The Languages of Late-Medieval Feminism', in Akkerman, T. and Stuurman, S. (eds.), *Perspectives on Feminist Political Thought in European History: From the Middle Ages to the Present,* (Routledge, New Haven and London, 1998), pp. 34–49.

Ryan, M.J., 'Conquest, Reform and the Making of England', in Higham, N. and Ryan, M.J. (eds.), *The Anglo-Saxon World,* (Yale University Press, New Haven and London, 2013), pp. 284–334.

Sadler, J., *The Red Rose and the White: The Wars of the Roses, 1453–1487*, (Routledge, New Haven and London, 2009).

Salih, S., *Versions of Virginity in Late Medieval England,* (Boydell & Brewer, Woodbridge, 2001).

Saul, N., 'The Despensers and the Downfall of Edward II', *The English Historical Review*, Vol. 99, No. 390, (1984), pp. 1–33.

Saul, N., *The Three Richards: Richard I, Richard II and Richard III,* (Hambledon Continuum, London, 2006).

Scofield, C.L., *The Life and Reign of Edward the Fourth, King of England and of France and Lord of Ireland, Vol. I,* (Longmans, Green and Co., London, 1923).

Simon, L., *Of Virtue Rare: Margaret Beaufort, Matriarch of the House of Tudor,* (Houghton Mifflin, Boston, 1982).

Skinner, P., '"Halt! Be Men!": Sikelgaita of Salerno, Gender and the Norman Conquest of Southern Italy', *Gender and History,* Vol. 12, No. 3, (2000), pp. 622–641.

Slater, L., 'Defining Queenship at Greyfriars London, *c.*1300–58', *Gender & History*, Vol. 27, No.1, (2015), pp. 53–76.

Slater, L., 'Rumour and Reputation Management in Fourteenth-Century England: Isabella of France in Text and Image', *Journal of Medieval History*, Vol. 47, No. 2, (2021), pp. 257–292.

Smythe, D., 'Middle Byzantine Family Values and Anna Komnene's *Alexiad*', in Garland, L. (ed.), *Byzantine Women: Varieties of Experience 800–1200,* (Ashgate, Aldershot, 2006), pp. 125–139.

Snook, B., 'Women in the Anglo-Saxon Chronicle Before AD 800', in Dresvina, J., and Sparks, N. (eds.), *Authority and Gender in Medieval and Renaissance Chronicles,* (Cambridge Scholars Publishing, Newcastle-upon-Tyne, 2012), pp. 32–60.

Spike, M., *Tuscan Countess: The Life and Extraordinary Times of Matilda of Canossa,* (Vendome Press, New York, 2004).

Stafford, P., 'Emma: The Powers of the Queen in the Eleventh Century', in Duggan, A. (ed.), *Queens and Queenship in Medieval Europe,* (Boydell & Brewer, Woodbridge, 1997), pp. 3–26.

Stafford, P., 'Political Women in Mercia, Eighth to Early Tenth Centuries', in Brown, M.P., Farr, C.A. (eds.), *Mercia: An Anglo-Saxon Kingdom in Europe,* (Bloomsbury Publishing, London, 2005), pp. 35–49.

Stafford, P., *Queen Emma and Queen Edith, Queenship and Power in Eleventh-Century England,* (Blackwell Publishing, Oxford, 1997).

Stafford, P., 'Sons and Mothers: Family Politics in the Early Middle Ages', in Baker, D. (ed.) *Medieval Women,* (The Ecclesiastical History Society, Oxford, 1978), pp. 79–100.

Stafford, P., 'The King's Wife in Wessex 800–1066', *Past & Present*, No. 91, (1981), pp. 3–27.

Staley, L., *Margery Kempe's Dissenting Fictions*, (Pennsylvania State University Press, Philadelphia, 1994).

Stenton, F.M., *Anglo-Saxon England,* (The Clarendon Press, Oxford, 1975).

Strickland, A. and Strickland, E., *Lives of the Queens of England from the Norman Conquest,* (Cambridge University Press, Cambridge, 2010).

Strickland, M., *Henry the Young King, 1155–1183*, (Yale University Press, New Haven and London, 2016).

Sullivan, K., *The Interrogation of Joan of Arc*, (University of Minnesota Press, Minnesota, 1999).

Sumption, J., *The Hundred Years War, Vol. 5: Triumph and Illusion*, (Faber & Faber, London, 2023).

Talis, N., *Uncrowned Queen: The Fateful Life of Margaret Beaufort, Tudor Matriarch*, (Michael O'Mara Books, London, 2019).

Taylor, C., *Chivalry and the Ideals of Knighthood in France During the Hundred Years War*, (Cambridge University Press, Cambridge, 2013).

Taylor, C., *Joan of Arc: La Pucelle*, (Manchester University Press, Manchester, 2006).

Taylor, L.J., 'Joan of Arc, the Church, and the Papacy, 1429–1920', *The Catholic Historical Review*, Vol. 98, No. 2, (2012), pp. 217–240.

Taylor, L.J., *The Virgin Warrior: The Life and Death of Joan of Arc*, (Yale University Press, New Haven and London, 2019).

Tebbit, A., 'Household Knights and Military Service under the Direction of Edward II', in Dodd, G. and Musson, A. (eds.), *The Reign of Edward II: New Perspectives*, (Boydell & Brewer, Woodbridge, 2006), pp. 76–96.

Thompson, K., 'Affairs of State: The Illegitimate Children of Henry I', *Journal of Medieval History*, Vol. 29, No. 2, (2003), pp. 129–151.

Thompson Smith, S., 'Remembering the Lady of Mercia', in Norris, R., Stephenson, R. and Trilling, R.R. (eds.), *Feminist Approaches to Early Medieval English Studies*, (Amsterdam University Press, Amsterdam, 2023), pp. 83–113.

Tolhurst, F., *Geoffrey of Monmouth and the Translation of Female Kingship*, (Palgrave Macmillan, Basingstoke, 2013).

Traves, A., 'Genealogy and Royal Women in Asser's *Life of King Alfred*: Politics, Prestige, and Maternal Kinship in Early Medieval England', *Early Medieval Europe*, Vol. 30, No. 1, (2022), pp.101–124.

Tucker, P., 'The Lincolnshire Rebellion of 1470 Revisited', *The English Historical Review*, Vol. 136, (2021), pp. 1–25.

Turner, R.V., 'Eleanor of Aquitaine and Her Children: An Inquiry into Medieval Family Attachment', *Journal of Medieval History*, Vol. 14, No. 4, (1988), pp. 321–335.

Turner, R.V., *Eleanor of Aquitaine, Queen of France, Queen of England*, (Yale University Press, New Haven and London, 2009).

Turner, R.V., 'Eleanor of Aquitaine, Twelfth-Century English Chroniclers and her "Black Legend"', *Nottingham Medieval Studies*, Vol. 52, (2008), pp. 17–42.

Tyler, E.M., 'Talking about History in Eleventh-Century England: the *Encomium Emmae Reginae* and the Court of Harthacnut', *Early Medieval Europe*, Vol. 13, No. 4, (2005), pp. 359–383.

Valente, C., 'The Deposition and Abdication of Edward II', *The English Historical Review*, Vol. 113, No. 453, (1998), pp. 852–881.

Van Houts, E., 'Queens in the Anglo-Norman/Angevin realm 1066–1216', in Zey, C. (ed.), *Mächtige Frauen? Königinnen und Fürstinnen im Europäischen Mittelalter*, (Verlagsgruppe Patmos, Düsseldorf, 2015), pp. 199–224.

Van Houts, E., *The Normans in Europe*, (Manchester University Press, Manchester, 2013).

Villalon, A., and Kagay, D., *The Hundred Years War: A Wider Focus,* (Brill, Leiden, 2005).

Visser-Fuchs, L., 'English Events in Caspar Weinreich's Danzig Chronicle, 1461–1495', *The Ricardian*, Vol. 7, No. 95, (1986), pp. 310–320.

Walker, C.H., 'Eleanor of Aquitaine and the Disaster at Cadmus Mount on the Second Crusade', *The American Historical Review,* Vol. 55, No. 4, (1950), pp. 857–861.

Warner, K., *Isabella of France, The Rebel Queen: The Story of the Queen who Deposed her Husband Edward II,* (Amberley, Stroud, 2016).

Warner, M., *Joan of Arc: The Image of Female Heroism*, (Oxford University Press, Oxford, 2013).

Warnicke, R.N., 'Margaret Tudor, Countess of Richmond, and Elizabeth of York: Dynastic Competitors or Allies', in Schutte, V. (ed.), *Unexpected Heirs in Early Modern Europe: Potential Kings and Queens*, (Palgrave Macmillan, New York, 2017), pp. 35–59.

Warren, W.L., *Henry II,* (University of California Press, Berkeley, 1973).

Weiler, B., 'Kings and Sons: Princely Rebellions and the Structures of Revolt in Western Europe, *c.*1170–*c.*1280', *Historical Research,* Vol. 82, No. 215, (2008), pp. 17–40.

Westerhof, D., 'Deconstructing Identities on the Scaffold: The Execution of Hugh Despenser the Younger, 1326', *Journal of Medieval History*, Vol. 33, (2007), pp. 87–106.

Whitton, M., 'Motherhood and Power in Medieval Europe, West and East: The Strange Case of the Empress Eirene', in Leyser, C. and Smith, L. (eds.), *Motherhood, Religion and Society in Medieval Europe, 400–1400: Essays Presented to Henrietta Leyser,* (Routledge, New Haven and London, 2016), pp. 84–120.

Willard, C.C., *The Writings of Christine de Pizan*, (Persea Books, New York, 1994).

Wilson, R.S.K., *Tudor Feminists: Ten Renaissance Women Ahead of Their Time*, (Pen & Sword Books, Barnsley, 2024).

Winstead, K. A., *Fifteenth-Century Lives: Writing Sainthood in England*, (University of Notre Dame Press, Notre Dame, 2020).

Wood, C. T., *Joan of Arc and Richard III: Sex, Saints, and Government in the Middle Ages*, (Oxford University Press, Oxford, 1991).

Wood, C.T., 'The First Two Queens Elizabeth, 1464–1503', in Fradenburg, L.O.A. (ed.), *Women and Sovereignty* (Edinburgh University Press, Edinburgh, 1992), pp. 121–131.

Wood, M., 'The Annals of Æthelflæd: Notes towards an Attempted Reconstruction', in Hardie, R. (ed.), *Æthelflæd, Lady of the Mercians, and Women in Tenth-Century England*, (Medieval Institute Publications, Boston, 2023), pp. 59–88.

Yoshikawa, N.K., 'The Jerusalem Pilgrimage: The Centre of the Structure of the Book of Margery Kempe', *English Studies*, Vol. 86, (2005), pp.193–205.

Yoshikawa, N.K., 'The Making of The Book of Margery Kempe: The Issue of *Discretio Spirituum* Reconsidered', *English Studies*, Vol. 92, (2011), pp.119–137.

Zupko, R.E., 'The Many Faces of Joan', in Tallon, M.E. (ed.) *Joan of Arc at the University*, (Marquette University Press, Milwaukee, 1997), pp. 21–54

Index

Dear Reader,

We hope you have enjoyed this book, but why not share your views on social media? You can also follow our pages to see more about our other products: facebook.com/penandswordbooks or follow us on X @penswordbooks

You can also view our products at www.pen-and-sword.co.uk (UK and ROW) or www.penandswordbooks.com (North America).

To keep up to date with our latest releases and online catalogues, please sign up to our newsletter at: www.pen-and-sword.co.uk/newsletter

If you would like a printed catalogue with our latest books, then please email: enquiries@pen-and-sword.co.uk or telephone: 01226 734555 (UK and ROW) or email: uspen-and-sword@casematepublishers.com or telephone: (610) 853-9131 (North America).

We respect your privacy and we will only use personal information to send you information about our products.

Thank you!